# KARL MARX:
Economy, Class and Social Revolution

*the Making of Sociology series*
EDITOR: RONALD FLETCHER

The Making of Sociology
Vol. 1 *Beginnings and Foundations*
Vol. 2 *Developments*
Vol. 3 *Reassessments: Consolidation and Advance?*
RONALD FLETCHER

Karl Marx
Z. A. JORDAN

Herbert Spencer
STANISLAV ANDRESKI

Max Weber
J. E. T. ELDRIDGE

John Stuart Mill
RONALD FLETCHER

Sociology and Industrial Life
J. E. T. ELDRIDGE

Deviance and Society
LAURIE TAYLOR

# KARL MARX:
## ECONOMY, CLASS AND SOCIAL REVOLUTION

Edited and with an introductory essay by
## Z. A. JORDAN
CARLETON UNIVERSITY, OTTAWA

NELSON

THOMAS NELSON AND SONS LTD
36 Park Street London W1Y 4DE
PO Box 18123 Nairobi Kenya

Thomas Nelson (Australia) Ltd
597 Little Collins Street Melbourne 3000

Thomas Nelson and Sons (Canada) Ltd
81 Curlew Drive Don Mills Ontario

Thomas Nelson (Nigeria) Ltd
PO Box 336 Apapa Lagos

Thomas Nelson and Sons (South Africa) (Proprietary) Ltd
51 Commissioner Street Johannesburg

ISBN 0 17 712079 7

Printed in Great Britain by A. Wheaton and Co., Exeter

## ACKNOWLEDGEMENTS

I am grateful to the following for permission to reproduce extracts in works in which they hold the copyright: International Publishers, New York, for permission to quote from *On Malthus* by Marx and Engels; C. A. Watts & Co. Ltd., London, for permission to quote from *Karl Marx: Early Writings* by T. B. Bottomore; and Lawrence & Wishart, London, for permission to quote extensively from the following of their works by Marx and Engels —*On Religion*, *The Poverty of Philosophy*, *Capital* Volume III, *Selected Correspondence*, *The Holy Family*, *Selected Works*, *Theories of Surplus Value*, and *The German Ideology*.

# CONTENTS

# Introduction by Ronald Fletcher

Professor Jordan's volume on the work of Karl Marx is one of the first to appear in the new series of text books on 'The Making of Sociology'.

This 'order' of publication is no accident.

Since the time of the French Revolution, the making of sociology has been an inseparable part of the task of re-making their society with which men have been faced: of grappling with the dilemmas of the inhumanities and disruptions on the one hand, and the progressive improvements on the other, of the spread of industrial capitalism, in such a way as to create a more humane society. From Comte to Tönnies, Durkheim, and Weber, this preoccupation has been central: the need for a science of society on the basis of which men could first *understand*, and then *deliberately change and improve* the nature of their social order.

In this continuing effort, Karl Marx was one of the most powerful and influential thinkers. He remains so. It is therefore an essential task of any student of society to come to terms with his thought. Marx was incomplete, ambiguous, mistaken in many ways. His limitations were worsened by the narrow didactic statements of Engels, and by the subsequent dogmatic formulations of Lenin, Stalin, and other theorists. It is difficult to disentangle his thought from that of his followers and commentators, and from the vast tide of political doctrine and practice which has since flowed, and still flows, about him—whether in 'little red books' in China, or in 'closed books' of a more sombre colour in the Soviet Union and Czechoslovakia.

And yet Marx was not the unique and isolated figure he is often made to appear. The central importance of capital-accumulation for the entirety of social development; the significant position of the new industrial proletariat for the acceptance of the new scientific knowledge and technology, and the desire to move towards new collectivized modes of production; the insistence that the analysis of *economic* activity could only be satisfactory if it was seen within the entire institutional activity of society—political, legal, military, religious, ideological, etc. (a view which the Economics Editor of *The Times* is now teaching\*); all such ideas had already been clearly stated by earlier French theorists—and especially by Comte. The insistence that society was essentially a *historical* process, and that its institutional patterns of order and change could only be understood within a perspective of evolution and development, was an insistence commonly held among all nineteenth century theorists. Some of Engels's (and later Lenin's and Stalin's) statements of 'Dialectical Materialism' were indistinguishable from Herbert Spencer's statement of 'Evolution'—excepting that they were far less carefully and sufficiently thought out than his.

There was much in Marx, then, which was *common* to all the contributions which went into the making of sociology during the nineteenth century, as well as something *distinctive* in his own particular *emphases*.

All of which means that the work of Marx requires the most scrupulous study if the worth of his contribution to social science and to the contemporary political task of re-making society is *truly* to be assessed. For the task of making sociology and of re-making industrial society is still with us. Indeed, the problems grow as the complexity of societies and the global scale of their interdependencies grow. The understanding of the making of sociology is not by any means an 'academic' matter only: it lies still—as an essential basis—at the heart of our practical and political concerns, if our efforts are going to be reliably directed and effective.

*Satisfactory study—with a commitment to truth and accuracy—is a first essential*: and Dr Jordan's book offers a firm foundation for this. His introductory essay and his careful selection of Marx's writings—some of which he has specially translated, and some translations of which he has revised—give a broad and reliable picture of all the dimensions of Marx's thought. Dr Jordan's special interest lies in the philosophical aspects of social theory and the history of ideas in the social sciences, and he is the author of a notable study of 'The Evolution of Dialectical Materialism'. He is therefore well qualified to provide this new critical presentation of the many-sided work of Marx.

\* See: Peter Jay, Inflating Inflation. *The Times*, April 3, 1970.

# Sources and Abbreviations

The editions from which the selection in this book is made and their abbreviated titles are listed below.

The date which appears in parentheses after the title of a book or article by Marx is the date of its first publication. However, in the case of some of the works which were published posthumously, the date in parentheses indicates the year or years of their composition.

Some extracts in the present work have been translated by the Editor. In a few cases, the available translations have been revised. All revisions are indicated in the references.

The notes of Marx and those of his editors or translators are shown by figures. But many of them have been omitted because their content does not justify inclusion in a selection of limited length. The notes of the Editor of this book are initialed (Z.A.J.) and marked by asterisks. In some cases they draw upon explanatory comments in *MEW*. Since they are indicated by a different sign, they can easily be distinguished from the notes of Marx and his editors or translators.

Marx frequently underlined certain words, phrases or whole sentences. It is customary to show Marx's emphases by the use of italics. In this sense, the italics throughout the text are Marx's own.

*EW:*     K. Marx, *Early Writings*. Translated and edited by T. B. Bottomore. London, 1963.

*GKPÖ:*   K. Marx, *Grundrisse der Kritik der politischen Ökonomie (Rohentwurf)*, (1857–1858). Berlin, 1953.

*MEW:*    K. Marx–F. Engels, *Werke*. Berlin, 1958 ff.

*OR:*     K. Marx–F. Engels, *On Religion*. Moscow, 1957.

*SA:*     K. Marx–F. Engels, *Studienausgabe in 4 Bänden*.

For a complete bibliography see M. Rubel, *Bibliographie des Oeuvres de Karl Marx*. Paris, 1956, and *Supplément à la Bibliographie des Oeuvres de Karl Marx*. Paris, 1960.

|  | Herausgegeben von I. Fetscher. Frankfurt am M., 1966. |
|---|---|
| *SW:* | K. Marx–F. Engels, *Selected Works in Two Volumes.* Moscow, 1951. |
| *TM:* | K. Marx, *Theorien über den Mehrwert*, T. 1–3. Berlin, 1956–62. |
| *ACL:* | *Address of the Central Committee to the Communist League* (1850), *SW* I, *MEW* B. 7. |
| *BCR:* | *The Bourgeoisie and the Counter-Revolution*, Second Article, (1848), *SW* I, *MEW* B. 6. |
| *C* I, III: | *Capital*, vol. I (1867) and vol. III. Moscow, 1958–9, *MEW* Bde. 23, 25. |
| *C I-A:* | *Afterword to the Second German Edition of Capital* (1873), *C* I, *MEW* B. 23. |
| *C I-P:* | *Preface to the First German Edition of Capital* (1867), *C* I, *MEW* B. 23. |
| *CGP:* | *Critique of the Gotha Program* (1875), *SW* II, *SA* B. 3. |
| *CH:* | *The Chartists*, *NYDT* of 25 August 1852. |
| *CHPR:* | *Contribution to the Critique of Hegel's Philosophy of Right: Introduction* (1844), *EW*, *MEW* B. 1. |
| *CMN:* | *Critical Marginal Notes on the Article 'The King of Prussia and Social Reform. By a Prussian'* (1844), *MEW* B.1. |
| *CPE:* | *A Contribution to the Critique of Political Economy* (1859). Translated by N. I. Stoke. Calcutta, s.a., *MEW* B. 13. |
| *CPE-I:* | *Introduction to the Critique of Political Economy* (1857–8), *CPE*, *GKPÖ* and *MEW* B. 13. |
| *CPE-P:* | Preface to *A Contribution to the Critique of Political Economy* (1859), *SW* I, *MEW* B. 13. |
| *CRB:* | *The Communism of the Paper 'Rheinischer Boobachter'* (1847), *OR*, *MEW* B. 4. |
| *CSF:* | *The Class Struggles in France, 1848 to 1850* (1850), *SW* I, *MEW* B. 7. |
| *CWF:* | *The Civil War in France* (1871), *SW* I, *SA* B. 4. |
| *EBLB:* | *The Eighteenth Brumaire of Louis Bonaparte* (1852), *SW* I, *MEW* B. 8. |
| *EPM:* | *Economic and Philosophical Manuscripts of 1844* (1844), *EW*, *SA* B. 1 and B. 2. |

*FRBRI:*    *The Future Results of the British Rule in India,*
            *NYDT* of 8 August 1853 and *SW* I.
*GI:*       *The German Ideology* (1845–6). Moscow, 1964,
            *MEW* B. 3.
*HF:*       *The Holy Family* (1845). Moscow, 1956, *MEW* B. 2.
*IAWMIA:*   *Inaugural Address of the Working Men's International*
            *Association* (1864), *SW* I.
*KHS:*      *Kritik des Hegelschen Staatsrechts* (1843), *MEW* B. 1.
*LAKZ:*     *The Leading Article of No. 179 of Kölnische Zeitung*
            (1842), *OR, MEW* B. 1.
*MCCM:*     *Moralizing Critique and Criticizing Morality. A*
            *Contribution to the German Cultural History.*
            *Against Carl Heinzen* (1847), *MEW* B. 4.
*MCP:*      *Manifesto of the Communist Party* (1848), *SW* I,
            *MEW* B. 4.
*MCP-P:*    Preface to the German Edition of the *Manifesto of*
            *the Communist Party* (1872), *SW* I, *MEW* B. 4.
*NYDT:*     *New York Daily Tribune.*
*OM:*       *On Malthus. Selection from the Writings of Marx and*
            *Engels Dealing with the Theories of Thomas*
            *Robert Malthus.* Edited with an Introductory
            Essay and Notes by R. L. Meek. Translated by
            D. L. Meek and R. L. Meek. New York, 1954.
*PEF:*      *Pre-Capitalistic Economic Formations.* Translated by
            J. Cohen. Edited and with an Introduction by
            E. J. Hosbawm. London, 1964.
*PP:*       *The Poverty of Philosophy.* Translated from the
            French (1847). Moscow, s.a., *MEW* B. 4.
*SAPP:*     *Speech at the Anniversary of The People's Paper*
            (1856), *SW* I or *The People's Paper* of 19 April
            1856.
*SC:*       *Selected Correspondence.* Moscow, s.a.
*SHC:*      *Speech on the Hague Congress* (1872), *La Liberté* of
            15 September 1872, *MEW* B. 18.
*TF:*       *Theses on Feuerbach* (1845), *SW* II, *MEW* B. 3.
*TSV-I:*    *Theories of Surplus-Value*, Part I (1862–3). Moscow,
            s.a.
*WLC:*      *Wage Labour and Capital* (1849), *SW* I, *MEW* B. 6.
*WPP:*      *Wages, Price and Profit* (1865), *SW* I.

*Introductory Essay:*
*Karl Marx as a Philosopher and*
*a Sociologist*

# BASIC ASSUMPTIONS

Like Auguste Comte, Marx was both a philosopher and a sociologist. This is not meant merely to imply that Marx was concerned with the problems which today are assigned either to philosophy or sociology. Marx believed, as so many other thinkers did at that time, that sociology and philosophy were parts of a common whole and logically constituted a single field of enquiry. While philosophy provides a conceptual framework for the investigation of society, sociology helps to resolve some philosophical problems which otherwise are intractable or insoluble. For instance, such questions as 'What is man?', 'What is language?', 'What is society?', 'What is religion?' or 'What is history?' are incapable of solution as long as they are regarded as problems of speculative philosophy and are examined by the procedure that transcends experience and logical reasoning. These are in fact empirical questions which belong to a new discipline, for which Comte coined the term 'sociology' and for which Marx, in the *Economic and Philosophical Manuscripts of 1844*, used the Saint-Simonian phrase 'the science of man'. They are empirical questions because they cannot be answered by reflexive analysis nor by speculative deductions in the manner of Kant or Hegel, but by observing the activities of men in society and history. They are not independent of philosophy, however, because philosophy alone can discover the implications of the science of man for the totality of human knowledge and evaluate their significance. Although Marx attacked Hegel's speculative reason which, untainted and unimpeded by sense experience, pronounced all kinds of oracular truths about the universe, he remained a Kantian in the sense that he considered the world as we know it to be an interpretation of observable phenomena in terms of a conceptual framework which we impose upon the sense experience. This conceptual framework is not freely invented but biologically and socially conditioned. It is the work of 'all previous history' which humanizes man's senses and impresses man's distinctive nature, his human characteristics, upon the world.[1]

Contrary to common belief, Marx was not a materialist in the metaphysical sense of this term. He did not claim that matter is the ultimate constituent of the universe and that there is nothing else

9

in the world. Materialism—by which he meant the materialism of Hobbes, Lamettrie or Holbach—cannot account for the existence of the human mind and its achievements, of society and its evolution, of history and its progress; neither mind nor society nor history can be reduced to and explained in terms of the mechanical laws of inanimate objects. Materialism is incapable of dealing with a wide range of distinctively human activity and of accounting for man's moral, religious, artistic or intellectual experience. Consequently, Marx described mechanistic materialism, the only variety of materialism he knew, as implacable in its logic but hostile to humanity.[2]

Nature was for Marx a more comprehensive concept than matter. Man is as much a natural entity as any other physical object; he does not hold a privileged position in the universe. As a natural entity man is neither a mere body nor only a mind or soul, but an indissoluble unity of both body and mind. Marx was following in the footsteps of Feuerbach who argued, against Hegel, that neither matter nor nature could be explained as a result of intelligence; on the contrary, nature was the basis of intelligence, without itself having any basis. 'Spirit without Nature is an unreal abstraction; consciousness develops only out of Nature.'[3] Therefore, if man is a natural entity, and not an immortal spirit in a carnal tomb, confronting nature as its judge and arbiter, the knowledge of man must be acquired and validated in the same way as the knowledge of other natural objects, that is, be based on sense experience.

We understand by naturalism the view that mind is a part of nature;[4] that mind should be investigated by the same methods as those applied in the study of other natural objects, that is, empirically and not speculatively, by means of scientific method and not by metaphysical deductions; and that the categories of time, space, and causality are basic for the acquisition of knowledge of the physical and social world. Marx was a naturalistic philosopher in the described sense, and not a materialist. Still less was he a dialectical materialist. The .conceptual distinction between materialism and naturalism was not generally established in Marx's time and Marx himself made occasional use of the two terms synonymously. But when he used them in the same sense, he was making a contrast between his own views and the supernaturalism of Hegel and the Young Hegelians, that is, he denied the independent existence of a timeless and transcendental self or

mind, the supremacy of ideas and ideals over the natural sequence
of events, and the adequacy of the teleological order in history and
human affairs.

Marx's conception of man is philosophical in origin but his
science of man is a sociological and empirical, not a philosophical
and speculative, theory. If man is a natural entity, we come to
know human nature, human mind or spirit, by observing his
activity and the products of this activity. But man is never a
creature of nature pure and simple. The isolated hunter or fisherman of Adam Smith or David Ricardo was nothing more than a
figment of imagination according to Marx; the same could be said,
more generally, for the individuals of Hobbes, Rousseau, Locke or
Bentham who were supposed to have established society for the
protection of their self-interest or for the satisfaction of their social
inclinations. Man was never anything but a social being. As
Feuerbach suggested, a man existing alone would have no individuality and would be lost in the ocean of nature. Society is prior to
the individual for man becomes truly human and self-conscious
only through his fellow-men.[5] Many thinkers of the past had seen
clearly that he is born into society and that, not being made for
himself, he always desires to live together with others. To this
assumption of Aristotle, Montesquieu or Ferguson—to name
those studied by Marx—Marx was to give an interpretation of
his own.

Man has always been a social being because he must work in
order to live, and the production of the means of subsistence is
always a collective, social activity. Men produce only by co-operating and mutually exchanging their activities and products. In
order to produce, they enter into definite relations with one another
and only within these social relations does production take place.
Thus, the social world is created by interacting individuals. As
Marx himself put it, society is not an aggregate of individuals but
'the product of men's reciprocal action', and the science of man is
the study of the interactions among individuals in society.

In his theoretical assumptions Marx stood at the opposite pole to
the doctrine of psychological individualism which was being formulated concurrently by John Stuart Mill and supported essentially by Herbert Spencer.[6] Mill believed that society was an
aggregate of independent individuals and that social laws were
ultimately psychological laws, the study of society being therefore

reducible to psychology. Marx's implicit challenge to this view and his clear statement of an alternative position gave rise to a new conception of social phenomena which underlies much of the sociological thought of the last hundred years. Georg Simmel (1858–1918), Émile Durkheim (1855–1917), Max Weber (1864–1920) and Florian Znaniecki (1882–1958)—to mention only some prominent names—extended the range and depth of our understanding of society by using the Marxian assumptions in diverse, sometimes divergent, but always fruitful ways.

Marx's discovery that society is the name for individuals reciprocally connected by interaction did not belong to the main trend of the nineteenth century thought which was for the most part an unrelieved praise of individualism. Marx, however, was not alone in his opposition to it. Around the mid-century the view that society could be understood in terms of rational actions of isolated individuals, who intelligently pursue clearly recognized ends, was exposed to the impact of new philosophical and scientific ideas.[7] The Saint-Simonists spoke often of the social importance of association, which they considered as the exact contrary of individualism. Comte formulated his ideas about social reality and the relationship between society and individual before Marx did, and the similarity of their views on this particular matter is undeniable. Yet in spite of these historical connections and influences Marx's contribution stands out as an important landmark in the history of social thought.

Marx formulated his basic assumption with a greater clarity than anybody else at that time and went on to derive all kinds of important conclusions from it. He substituted a new conception for the long-established belief that society was an artificial creation, the outcome of human designs or social contract, to be described in terms of means and ends, values and norms. According to this new conception, society is brought about by natural causes which originate with men but are subject to laws in the same sense as are all other phenomena of nature, that is, regardless of what men intend or fail to do. The world of human affairs is governed as much as the natural world by invariable laws.[8]

To this basic sociological assumption concerning the relationship between the individual and society Marx added the hypothesis of social evolution. Since men produce only by co-operating and exchanging their activities, and this mutual dependence constantly increases through a progressive division of labour, the entire history of the world should be considered as a creation of man. Man's spiritual life, his social, cultural and intellectual advance stem from his social involvements. The naturalistic interpretation of man and society is incompatible with the belief that mind or spirit have an independent causal efficacity in the realization of anything else. But the naturalistic interpretation does not preclude the belief in the existence and action of spiritual factors in social life. In community with others men produce together what transcends the powers of each of them acting separately, thereby extending the range of their mental and social activities, and developing their personalities. By participating in social life, acting together and interacting with each other, men produce language, government, social organization, law, art, science, and religion, and thus acquire their distinctive human characteristics. While society is produced by men, society itself produced man as man.[9] Social life does not derive from individuals, but it is the latter which derive from the former. Individuals are a product of social life in the sense that they are determined by social groups, of which they are members, and by the relationships among these groups. To put it differently, types of personality are conditioned by the social structure. Social structure is a network of the relationships among basic social groups, and types of personality are conditioned by the basic social groups of which the individuals are members.

It was the establishment of the science of man that enabled Marx to resolve the issue between materialism and idealism. Since the science of man showed how the whole range of man's spiritual experience developed out of social interaction and evolved in the course of social life, idealism with its claim of the primacy of spirit to nature lost the most convincing argument in its support; idealism provided no longer the only adequate and fruitful assumptions for the examination of the higher functions of the human mind. On the other hand, Marx offered considerable prospects for the development of sociology through his extension of the scope of natural phenomena, his recognition of society as a natural entity with a structure of its own which was subject to laws, and his view of the nature of man as the changing product of social evolution in a spontaneous, self-generating and cumulative process.

Durkheim observed that 'social science in the strict sense' came into being only when various social phenomena were recognized as parts of a whole, that is, as interdependent and bound together by necessary connections. Durkheim suggested that Montesquieu, without saying or perhaps even knowing what he was doing, gave 'posterity a first sample of such a science'.[10] While Montesquieu may be one of the forerunners of sociology, Marx and Comte better deserve the title of founders. The conception of society as a network of interactions among individuals restored that continuity between society and the individual, which had been disrupted by Hobbes and Rousseau, whose ideas had been accepted without any essential change by the classical economists, Bentham, Mill and Spencer. Furthermore, it implied the proposition that social phenomena are natural phenomena, subject to natural laws. The concept of interaction and its more specific forms—differentiation, specialization and division of labour—made it possible to account for the emergence of relatively permanent groups within society such as the family, the tribe, the guild, the caste, social classes and so forth. Thus, social phenomena of various categories could be shown to be interrelated; they co-exist or follow each other in conformity with laws. These assumptions, together with their various consequences, established a secure groundwork for the expansion of knowledge about society and made the development of sociology possible.

## THE CONCEPT OF ALIENATION

Although today the concept of alienation is frequently used with reference to Marx, Marx neither introduced the concept nor coined the term. While Fichte seems to have been the first thinker to use the concept of alienation, it was Hegel and Feuerbach who launched it upon the world.[11] In his youth Marx adopted and adapted it to his own requirements and, in particular, translated it from the language of speculative philosophy into the language of sociology. It is the sociological Marxian concept of alienation that is today the real or alleged source of many debates among social scientists about alienation. In contrast, the Existentialist and Neo-Marxist writers in France and Germany take their inspiration from the metaphysical, Hegelian concept of alienation, although they prefer to acknowledge its origin in Marx rather than in Hegel.

Fichte started with Kant's epistemological premise that reality is a construction made by man, an interpretation of observable facts by means of the forms and categories of pure reason, or, as we would say today, in terms of our concepts and theories. According to Kant, this interpretation is imposed upon the world, which, however, exists independently of the observer as the totality of things in themselves.

Fichte felt that Kant's philosophy required completion and this he proceeded to do by rejecting some of Kant's important qualifications.[12] He discarded the doctrine of things in themselves and declared that reality is nothing but a construction of man, a product of the Ego's action (*Handlung*). It is only by reflection that the Ego becomes aware of its creation. Knowledge is self-knowledge of the subject reflecting on its own previous actions and on their objective correlates (*das nicht-Ich*, in Fichte's terminology). The universal Ego, that is, mankind as distinct from particular individuals, posits and produces the whole world of objects. Objects seem to be independent of the subject—the universal Ego—but this is an illusion. For they are created by the subject and only as its creation do they become alienated from it and assume an independent existence in which form they act reflexively to confront and shape the universal Ego in turn.

Hegel reformulated and developed Fichte's ideas about alienation in *The Phenomenology of Mind* and *The Philosophy of History*. While in a sense it is true that men live in a world of their own creation, they only create the world as instruments of the World Spirit (*Weltgeist*) which uses human actions for attaining its own goals. Hegel's Mind or Spirit is Fichte's universal Ego removed still further to the more rarified metaphysical regions. Hegel spoke of the Spirit as the only 'self-contained existence', that is, an existence independent of anything else. The self-contained existence of Spirit is Freedom and self-consciousness, for nothing is truly free and truly knows its own nature unless its existence depends exclusively on itself. The Mind or Spirit, which operates through Historical States (e.g., the Greek, the Roman and the German world) and World-Historical Individuals (e.g., Napoleon or Hegel himself), produces the whole world of nature and the human world with its social and political institutions. But while the Spirit unfolds itself into its exterior manifestations, the created world becomes alienated from the Spirit and stands opposed to it as an objective force. According to Hegel, the alienation is inherent in the nature of all spiritual creation. It is, therefore, inevitable that men who are creators of the world, also experience it as something beyond their control, a force dominating their will, frustrating their desires and confounding their expectations. 'Thus', as Hegel wrote, 'Spirit is at war with itself; it has to overcome itself as its most formidable obstacle.' The essential purpose of historical progress is to overcome the alienation—the alienated forms of existence and the self-alienation of human consciousness—in and through the process of knowledge. Although the goal of the Spirit is to realize its ideal being, this goal is achieved through the stages of creation, alienation and sublimation, or, if you wish, of externalization, estrangement and sublation (*Entaüsserung*, *Entfremdung* and *Aufhebung*), ever recurring in a progressive succession.[13]

Feuerbach initiated the process of demolishing the fantastic world of Fichte's and Hegel's philosophical imagination, whose siren-like power can still be felt in the contemporary German and French Existentialist and Neo-Marxist philosophies. Starting with the premise that all knowledge comes through the senses or is based on sense experience, Feuerbach exposed the Fichtean and Hegelian alienation either as the objectification of human needs, as this happens in religion, or as the reification of the imaginary correlates of human activity, both practical and theoretical. For instance, the Divine Being is nothing else than the human being, purified, made objective and distinct in order to be contemplated and revered. In the personality of God man worships his own attributes, the personified law of morality and the fulfilled moral nature of man. 'The true sense of Theology', Feuerbach wrote, 'is Anthropology', for religion is human nature reflected in itself and the personality of God is nothing else than a projection of a perfected human personality. To put it differently, Man is God for himself, but he makes God an external object, that is, alienates Him from himself.[14] Religious self-alienation—man's sense of moral inadequacy or unworthiness—originates in the duplication of the world into a religious world and a secular one, although the sacred reality is entirely illusory, for no real duality of being is to be found anywhere.[15] Taking Feuerbach's critique of religion as a paradigm, one can easily explain Hegel's Spirit or Mind as an alienated, that is, externalized and reified, form of human reason. Similarly, social and political institutions, such as the historical form of bourgeois property relations or the bourgeois State, do not constitute an independent realm. They owe their existence 'in the clouds'—this is Marx's expression and analysis—to the duplication of the social world into human activities and reified correlates of these activities, which again has no justification in reality. We can liberate ourselves from the alienation in the sense given to it by Feuerbach by liberating ourselves from the abstractions which haunt our minds or establish themselves in the form of various institutions with a life of their own, independent of, and superior to, individuals. We liberate ourselves from these obsessive abstractions by discovering how they arise in the course of social life and what social function they perform.[16]

Marx discussed the problem of alienation and self-alienation only in his youthful writings, in the *Economic and Philosophical Manuscripts of 1844* and *The German Ideology*. The two discussions have certain points in common, but they differ in style and content. On the other hand, they jointly help one to understand why, after *The German Ideology*, Marx abandoned both the term and concept of alienation.

In the *Economic and Philosophical Manuscripts of 1844* Marx distinguishes three different forms of alienation—alienation from the product of work, alienation in the process of production (or briefly, alienation of labour), and alienation from society (the species). Alienation from the product of work is the Hegelian alienation, i.e. the crystallization and externalization of labour in the form of the means of production, which, as Marx says, stand opposed to and dominate the worker as an alien autonomous power. Since the means of production are an externalized and objectified product of labour, it is inevitable, according to Marx, that the more the worker expends himself in work, the more certain is his subjection, the more his consumption decreases, and the more he himself becomes worthless, crude, barbarous, and deficient in intelligence.

The alienation of labour is the self-alienation which can be described as the result of the connection between the socio-economic structure of society and the personality structure of the individual. These phenomena have been frequently described both before and after Marx. The alienation of labour means that work provides no satisfaction and fulfilment but is only a source of physical exhaustion and mental debasement. Alienated labour is always performed under compulsion, for it does not satisfy any essentially human needs. It constitutes merely a means of livelihood, a means of earning the wage sufficient to keep the worker alive. Since man's self as a social being is expressed, according to Marx, in the creative activity of work,[17] carried on together with his fellow men, the alienation of labour degrades man to the level of the animal kingdom and turns wage-labour into a quasi-biological function.

Finally, alienation from society means that man is alienated from other men. The alienation between man and man implies the dissolution of human relationships and social bonds. Men make use of each other, that is, treat each other as things or means of satisfying selfish interests. The alienation from society transform society into an aggregate of individuals and thus reinforces the alienation of labour. For the relation of man to himself is first realized in the relationship between each man and other men.

We find a somewhat different account of alienation in *The German Ideology*. Here again Marx refers to alienation in the metaphysical, Hegelian sense, that is, to the presence in social life of an alien, objective power, which, having been brought into existence by man, is not controlled by him but enslaves him and thwarts all his hopes. There are two main manifestations of this objective social power—the coercive authority of the class-dominated State and the restrictive barriers of the division of labour which enforces on every man a particular, exclusive sphere of activity.[18]

It may appear that Marx's views on alienation and self-alienation combine certain elements of Hegel's speculative philosophy with observations on the social and psychological consequences of the industrial system in general and of the division of labour in particular. Such observations were made by some writers among Marx's predecessors and contemporaries—Ferguson and Adam Smith, Jean-Baptiste Say, de Tocqueville, Comte, Proudhon and J. S. Mill. It is important to realize that despite his use of the Hegelian terminology, Marx was much closer to these perceptive writers than to Hegel from whom he was separated by an important difference of approach. Hegel spoke of alienation as a metaphysical fact, but for Marx alienation was a sociological, not a metaphysical, phenomenon. Marx argued that if the source of all alienation is an 'alien, hostile, powerful and independent object', not the object but the owner of this object is the ultimate source of all forms of alienation, for only men can constitute this alien power over men. If our activity is unfree, it is unfree because we are in the service, under the domination and coercion, of another man. Although the phenomenon of alienation is expressed in Hegelian terms, it does not refer to the alienation of men from the world of their creation but to the estrangement (self-alienation) of the workers from the social and economic system of capitalism, that is, from the relations of private property and from the class-determined structure of society. To put it differently, in the writings of the young Marx the phenomenon of alienation is not a metaphysically inevitable process. It is a phenomenon which can be accounted for sociologically and eliminated or remedied by human action. Since alienation in Marx's sense is no longer metaphysically conceived, knowledge alone is not sufficient, as it was for Hegel, to overcome it. For Marx, we are unable to transcend alienation merely by understanding its source and cause. We can transcend it only if we succeed in changing the circumstances, the social and economic structure of society, in which it arises. This is the meaning of the famous final Thesis on Feuerbach, 'The philosophers have only interpreted the world in various ways; the point is to change it'.

The definition of alienation in sociological terms explains the fact that while in later years Marx continued to refer to the phenomenon of self-alienation—as he did implicitly or explicitly whenever he spoke of the social relations in the capitalist industrial system—he discarded the term and concept of alienation altogether. Since the phenomena of alienation are inherent in the socio-economic formation of capitalism, they are fully considered in his study of the class struggle, class domination and the capitalist mode of production. Moreover, towards the end of his life Marx became doubtful as to whether the phenomena of alienation are indeed inherent in capitalism alone and would thus disappear with the abolition of its property and class relations. As one of the closing chapters in the third volume of *Capital* seems to indicate, Marx came to believe that estrangement (self-alienation) is an unavoidable consequence of the necessity to work. Since there is no escape from this necessity, estrangement is bound to exist, to a lesser or greater degree, in every system of production.

The contemporary wide-spread use of the term 'alienation', for which, at least in the English speaking world, Erich Fromm and C. Wright Mills are mainly responsible, is inspired by Marx or the 'young Marx' but has little more in common with his thought than the term itself. 'Alienation' as used by Erich Fromm and C. Wright Mills is a collective term for every real, possible or imaginary evil to be found in an advanced industrial society or even in any society.[19] According to Lewis Feuer, alienation is omnipresent and multiform; it eludes a 'fixed set of dimensions because it is as multi-potential as the varieties of human experience'.[20] Alienation is equated by Robert A. Nisbet, among other things, with a perspective, a sociological temper, the antithesis of the idea of progress and of rationalist individualism, the tragic view of life, the suffering from the liberation that history has given the individual, and similar grandiose and high-sounding things.[21] Such an all-inclusive term denotes practically anything and connotes nothing and, consequently, outside the emotive or directive use of language, is entirely useless. However, it creates a conceptual chaos and encourages woolly thinking.

In the writings of Existentialist writers, of Jean-Paul Sartre in particular, a Hegelian and speculative rather than a Marxian and sociological concept of alienation is employed. Sartre's Marx is a 'Hegelized Marx' and alienation in Sartre's sense is as much a universal and inescapable existential trait of the human situation as alienation in Hegel's sense is an essential characteristic of all spiritual and intellectual creation.[22] Sartre maintains that he tries to rescue Marx from the misinterpretations of his followers and that to carry out this mission he has to go back to the original texts. But his discoveries of what Marx really said consist of highly abstract, abstruse, if not entirely incomprehensible statements, better suited for the concealment than the disclosure of truth.

The recent contributions concerning the concept of alienation, made by Marxist writers in East European countries, also follow the Hegelian rather than the Marxian path, for their approach is clearly speculative and not empirical; metaphysical and not sociological. Even when they have doubts as to whether a speculative philosophy of man or an existentialist anthropology can be reconciled with Marx's views, they wish to leave the empirical question 'What is man?' to scientific research and retain for themselves the investigation of the concept of man as a whole. They continue to search for a speculative formula which would explain the 'human situation', thus confirming inadvertently the Feuerbachian discovery that as long as man is ignorant of his empirical nature he needs all kinds of disguises and illusions.[23]

Finally, there is a considerable revival of interest in the problems of alienation among Catholic thinkers who tend to equate alienation and sin, man's abandonment of God within himself and in the world. As they see it, the concept of alienation may become a connecting link between Christians and non-Christians, provided that the discussion is kept within the limit of a theorizing philosophical anthropology. They maintain that the original alienation is the interior alienation of man 'from God, from himself and from his fellow men' and consequently cannot be cured by a positivistically oriented sociology.[24]

All these vicissitudes of the concept of alienation are of little interest to an empirical or theoretical sociologist. Although they may be enormously significant and important for the sociology of knowledge, social and cultural history or the history of ideas, they are sociologically irrelevant, for they do not locate the origin of alienation in society. For the same reason, their link with the Marxian concept of alienation is very tenuous. *Homo peccator*, the metaphysically homeless man of Martin Buber or Heidegger, Sartre's individual condemned to his solitude, and other speculative conceptions of man, cannot be accommodated within the bounds of Marx's naturalistic sociology.

# THE THEORY OF SOCIAL CLASS

The theory of social class is probably the most widely known part of Marx's sociology. In spite of being widely known, the knowledge of it leaves much to be desired, for Marx never defined the basic concepts of his theory nor presented systematically its main propositions. It has thus remained a highly controversial theory in the sense that much of it is a question of how to interpret consistently its various statements, which are not always easy to reconcile. In the space available it is possible only to review the main problems, to which Marx's theory of social class has given rise.

The basic assumption of the Marxian theory is the belief that social classes perform a decisive function in the evolution of human society. Every significant social change is related, in one way or

B

another, to the class struggle. The origin of all social processes should be sought in the constitution of social classes and in the relationships among them, in their relative strength, and the state of class consciousness. More importantly, it is the class struggle that decides the transition of society from one evolutionary stage to another. Since Marx's sociology is so dominated by class relations and class antagonism, it may be rightly described as a sociology of the class struggle.

Apart from the undeniable fact that Marx wished his theory to provide the 'law of motion of modern society', that is, what we call today a 'theory of social change', this description is also apt for another reason. Throughout the ages and in the present time some philosophers and social scientists have held that social cohesion, order and development are founded on a predominant consensus of belief and value commitment and on a harmony or equilibrium of interests among the important groups in society. There also have been those who believe with Heraclitus that 'War is the father of all and the king of all; and some he has made gods and some men, some bond and some free' (J. Burnet, fr. 44). According to these thinkers, social cohesion, order and development result from conflict and are based on force and domination. The consensus and conflict orientations are reflected both in theories of society and in views concerning social structure, political power, or economic organization. Plato, Rousseau, Adam Smith, Spencer, Comte or Durkheim would represent the first approach; Aristotle, Hobbes, Simmel, Gumplowicz or Max Weber the other, with Kant and Saint-Simonists having one foot in each camp.[25] Among the philosophers and social scientists of the second school Marx is one of the most influential figures and is sometimes identified with it.

If the Marxian theory of social class is a theory of social change, it is hardly possible to consider it also as part of a general theory of social stratification which tries to establish a universally valid scheme of rank or gradation and which comprises, apart from social classes, such major social groups as Estates, Castes, Status Strata, or Ethnic Communities. As a matter of fact, there is no trace of a theory of social stratification in Marx's work. In the *Manifesto of the Communist Party* he spoke of a 'complicated arrangement of society into various orders, a manifold gradation of social rank' as an incident of the past which had been replaced by a dichotomously divided society.[26] This view—which was meant to be a forecast rather than a statement of fact and which failed as such—was a regressive step with respect to the accepted social knowledge at the time. For instance, in his famous *Essay on the History of Civil Society*, published one hundred years before *Capital*, Ferguson distinguished three main grounds of 'subordination' among men: the difference of natural talents, the unequal division of property, and the distinctions of the rank to which, as we would say today, occupation or profession, education and style of life give rise.[27] There are logical reasons, however, why Marx should have concentrated on the differentiation of social classes and ignored the stratification based on income, education or occupation.

Whenever Marx used the term 'social class' to refer to the *modus operandi* of social change, he used the term 'class' in the collective sense, that is, he spoke either of the class as a whole or of a certain class property which only a class as a whole, and not each and every member of this class, may have. For instance, when Marx described the proletariat as a revolutionary class, he did not wish to say that each and every proletarian was a revolutionary, but that the proletariat as a whole had this characteristic. Similarly, when he said that the bourgeoisie had played a progressive part in history, he did not intend to assert that each and every bourgeois played such a role but that the bourgeoisie as a whole contributed significantly to the increased rate of economic growth. Now, it is clear on the other hand that when we deal with classes in the distributive sense, that is, when a property is predicated of members of a class taken individually, we can easily order them hierarchically, for we are ordering individuals along a continuum according to a characteristic capable of gradation (such as education, size of income or prestige). Classes in the collective sense, however, cannot be ordered that way for the simple reason that the class determining properties are classificatory and not comparative concepts, that is, they do not signify a property which an object may have to a lesser or greater degree but one that it either has or has not got at all.

When the term 'class' is used in the collective sense, it denotes a real entity, while in the distributive sense it only assumes the existence of class members. A class in the distributive sense is not an entity but a construct by means of which we can speak of each and every member of the class. On this account an empiricist prefers using the term 'class' in the distributive sense and avoids making statements which would entail the existence of a class as a whole. But only a class in the collective sense has the kind of cohesiveness which appears to be necessary if classes are to be factors responsible for the 'motion', change and evolution of society. Furthermore, only a class in the collective sense may have the power of coercion which, according to Marx, social classes exercise over their members by imposing some definite patterns of action and thought upon them. When Durkheim said that a fact is social if and only if it is external to the individual and has a coercive power over him, he referred to the same characteristic of holistically conceived social facts which Marx had in mind. The pressure, which is the differentiating property of social phenomena, is the pressure exerted by the 'totality on the individual'. The constraining nature of social facts results from the way in which a whole is constituted. The whole is said to be more than the sum of its parts and, as Durkheim put it, 'represents a specific reality which has its own characteristics'. The laws of a whole are not deducible from the laws to which its parts taken separately are subject, but, on the contrary, the laws of a whole determine the behaviour of its parts. For instance, 'the group thinks, feels, and acts quite differently from the way in which its members would, were they isolated'.[28]

There is yet another reason why the Marxian theory of social class constitutes no part of a universal theory of social stratification, which leads us straight to the question 'What is a social class?'. Marx did not wish to formulate a universal theory of social class, valid always and everywhere. His explicitly stated intention was to construct a theory applicable to a historical stage of social evolution and thus universal but only within a certain time-space or cultural region. Although this assertion may be disputed, for Marx was not consistent in this respect, it is the only one compatible with Marx's firmly held methodological belief that sociological laws are never strictly universal statements in Popper's sense.[29] They are not strictly universal, because they are not universal in respect to spatio-temporal scope, that is, they apply to all relevant objects but only within a limited spatio-temporal region, outside which they are at best vacuously true.[30]

It is often tacitly assumed that the definition of social class, which Lenin made widely known, comes from Marx. According to Lenin's definitional statement,

Social classes are large groups of people differing from each other by the place they occupy in a historically determined system of social production, by their relation (in most cases fixed and formulated in law) to the means of production, by their role in the social organization of labour, and, consequently, by the dimensions of the share of social wealth of which they dispose and the mode of acquiring it.[31]

This statement can be found nowhere in Marx.[32] Moreover, although it is frequently, if not commonly accepted as an adequate and faithful summary of Marx's views on the matter, there is not the slightest doubt that Lenin reduced several of the defining characteristics of social class in Marx's sense to a single one. This reduction is unjustifiable, for the simple reason that the relative place in the system of production or the share of social wealth constitutes, as Ossowski emphasized, a necessary but not a sufficient condition for being a distinct social class in the Marxian sense. It is clear that the class structure of society varies enormously according to whether the means of production and distribution can or cannot be privately owned. But it is equally clear that the abolition of private property in the means of production and distribution does not entail the disappearance of social classes.

There seems to be a considerable measure of agreement among the writers who dealt with this matter in detail that a social class in the Marxian sense is defined by at least three different characteristics.[33] They are (1) the place in the system of social production and/or the relation to the means of production; the possession of, or exclusion from, the proprietary rights to them; (2) the will to compete for political power and to use it for the protection of economic interest; (3) class consciousness, that is, the ideological awareness which at least some members of the class have of their relative position in society, as determined by their situation in the process of production, and a programme of collective action (ideology) to maintain and extend their share of social wealth and political power. I shall discuss briefly these three criteria.[34]

Since in the last chapter of the third volume of *Capital* Marx said,

The owners merely of labour power, owners of capital, and land-owners, whose respective sources of income are wages, profit and ground rent, in other words, wage labourers, capitalists and land-owners, constitute then three big classes of modern society based upon the capitalist mode of production,

some writers maintain that for Marx the social classes are distinguished by the source of income.[35] This is precisely the view which Marx had started refuting in the third volume of *Capital* when he laid his pen aside for the last time. Not rent, profit and wages but the ownership of land, capital and labour power determine, in his opinion, the three classes of modern society. Nor is the distribution of income, with its division of people into rich and poor, the basis of class formation. Wealth may have influence within a class and, as Marx pointed out, the difference in the size of the purse may set its members one against the other. Social classes, however, are distinguished by the stability in the distribution of social wealth, and the distribution remains stable if it is founded on proprietary rights. Therefore, the distribution of property, and not the distribution of income, is the true basis of the formation of classes.[36]

This proposition was not discovered by Marx. 'By unequal shares in the distribution of property', wrote Ferguson, 'the ground of a permanent and palpable subordination is laid'.[37] What Ferguson stated in 1767 remains true two hundred years later, although with a certain qualification. Contrary to Lenin's statement the place which the classes occupy in a system of social production is not determined exclusively by proprietary rights (or their absence) to the means of production. The situation might have been different at the time of Marx, but in an advanced industrial society the place of classes is determined by the relation to the means of production or by technical qualifications irrespective of whether they are associated with proprietary rights. In this formulation the first criterion, which is central to Marx's thought, still describes adequately the economic basis of modern social classes.

But equally central to Marx's thought is another thesis concerning the economic basis of social classes, namely, that in the final stages of capitalism only two classes would remain, the proletariat and the bourgeoisie, the former having only their labour power for sale and the latter in control over all means of production. This second thesis is hardly compatible with the revised version of the first. Furthermore, since the second thesis seems to be falsified by the development of events in advanced industrial countries, it is also the most vulnerable part of Marx's theory of social class. It is widely felt that there must be something wrong with a theory of social class which overlooks entirely the phenomenon of social mobility and its effects;[38] predicts the disappearance of all inter-mediate and transitional classes, their polarization and reduction to two principal classes; and thus seems to be disconfirmed by the fact that new classes appear, the gulf between the principal classes does not widen and no polarization occurs.

Riches are power, wrote Hobbes, reaffirming a truth as old as the hills, because riches are a means of acquiring power and submit others to one's will.[39] Commenting on Hobbes's dictum, Adam Smith agreed that a great fortune may, but need not necessarily, secure power. 'The power which that possession immediately and directly conveys . . . is . . . a certain command over all the labour, or over all the produce of labour which is then in the market.'[40] Marx's concept of economic power is that of Hobbes and not of Adam Smith. He believed that the division into a propertied and propertyless class is co-extensive with the division into a ruling and a subject group. The class which 'has the means of material production at its disposal' is the ruling class; it conquers for itself exclusive political sway, that is, in modern times, the machinery of the State, through which it dominates society. In the case of the intermediate classes, Marx tended to endow them with political influence in proportion to their economic importance. There can only be dispute about a more specific question 'Does Marx's theory of social class assume a complete identification of economic and political power?'. Some writers answer it with an emphatic and unqualified 'yes'.[41] This view does not stand up to a closer scrutiny, but must be left for a more detailed discussion until later.

There remains the third and final criterion for the existence of social classes, the ideological consciousness of the group which thereby becomes a fully fledged social class. This is not only the consciousness of kind, a feeling of unity within and of separation from those on the wrong side of the boundary line, but also of hostility towards other social classes which involves a struggle for one's own interests and against the interests of others. 'The separate individuals form a class only insofar as they have to carry on a common battle against another class.' The realization that classes constitute themselves through conflict and that conflict establishes and maintains group identity has since been systematically utilized by Georges Sorel in *Reflections on Violence* and, above all, by Georg Simmel in *Conflict*.[42] It is one of those insights which, once formulated, continue to inspire successive generations of social scientists.

Among the working class, consciousness of kind had its origin in the factories of Western Europe which created through the similarity of wage and work conditions not only the class unity and the hostility towards other classes, but also the 'social passions' which were directed against an unjust and inequitable society. According to de Tocqueville, Carlyle, Engels and other perceptive writers, it was these 'social passions' of the English and French working class in the revolutionary 1840s which gave them the feeling that they were 'sleeping on a volcano'.[43] When the revolutionary tide began to ebb in the face of a new period of prosperity around the mid-century, Marx himself retired to the Reading Room of the British Museum from where he kept affirming that 'Beneath the apparently solid surface, the Revolutions of 1848 betrayed oceans of liquid matter, only needing expansion to rent into fragments continents of hard rock'.[44]

Class consciousness is something more than a set of attitudes and value commitments of which their bearers are fully aware. 'Every class', wrote Bukharin, 'sums up all the persons related in uninterrupted mutual reactions, all the "living persons" whose roots are in production and whose thoughts may reach into the skies.'[45] Class consciousness includes a distinctive ideology, a view of the world and a programme of action whose aim is to uphold, to change or to overthrow the existing state of affairs.

Marx attached considerable importance to the third criterion. A class which has not developed a class consciousness exists only 'in itself', that is, as an aggregate of persons, and thus constitutes a class potentially but not actually. Marx contrasted such a potentially existing class with a class 'for itself', a class conscious of its identity, interests and social role. Neither the French working class during the 1848 revolution nor the French peasantry at the time of the *coup d'état* of Louis Bonaparte were full-fledged classes; they were classes 'in themselves' not 'for themselves'.

The third criterion is also a source of considerable difficulties for the Marxian theory of social class. The concept of class consciousness is based on the assumption that a 'common situation' determines uniquely a 'common interest', both economic and social—the assumption which Marx actually adopts.[46] We know today that this assumption should be given up. The members of a class, as determined by the first criterion, may differ considerably in the awareness of their position within the larger society and support mutually exclusive conceptions of social and political action. To put it differently, the characteristics which determine an economic class are not, as a rule, co-extensive with the characteristics which describe the social and political outlook of the members of the class; an economic class may overlap two or more classes in the ideological sense (that is, as determined by the third criterion). A class which satisfies all three criteria is a class 'for itself' and a class *par excellence* in the Marxian sense. But empirically such a class can never exist, for its members are bound to have incompatible ideologies and consequently are not, strictly speaking, a class for itself. In order to avoid this contradiction we would have to assume that if a class satisfies the first two criteria, it is only probable that its members would share a common ideology.

Apart from the sociological concept of social class as defined by the three criteria, we find in Marx a different concept of social class, which, as it occurs in Marx's historical writings, may be called historical. Many writers, Aron and Ossowski in particular, have drawn attention to the fact that the number of social classes in *The Class Struggles in France, 1848 to 1850* or *Revolution and Counter-Revolution in Germany*[47] cannot be accommodated within the concept of social class used in the *Manifesto of the Communist Party* or *Capital*. In the first of these works Marx listed six classes (financial bourgeoisie, industrial bourgeoisie, petty bourgeoisie, peasant class, proletarian class, and *Lumpenproletariat*, which corresponds to the peasant-workers in the present day industrializing countries), and in the second work even seven (the feudal nobility, the bourgeoisie, petty bourgeoisie, rich and middle peasants, poor peasants, agricultural labourers and industrial workers). These groups are not distinguished according to the criteria for the existence of social class which are laid down beforehand and applied to historical data available to the author. They are major social groups, the chief actors on the historical scene, as observed by Marx or Engels. They are not distinguished entirely arbitrarily, for they appear as groups of distinct economic and/or

B*

political interests which are also manifest in their common social
and/or political attitudes and in the role they play in the development of events. It is clear, however, that the criteria by which they
are distinguished, without being entirely arbitrary, are of Marx's
own choice, that is, they were adopted according to his requirement at that time and the kind of analysis he wished to give. But
when the term 'class' is used that way, both the defining characteristics and number of classes change from one case to another.
They are bound to be as numerous and variable as the historical
situations to which they are applied. For instance, bankers,
industrialists and land-owners can be considered as a single class
or as several, depending upon the demands of the enquiry. The
peasantry can be treated in the same way and considered either as
one class or as divided against itself as Lenin saw it.[48]

The two concepts of social class in Marx—the sociological and
historical—set a problem of whether they are reconcilable at all,
and if they are, in what way we should relate them. One could
argue that only classes in the sociological sense are genuinely
Marxian classes and that classes in the historical sense are merely
Weberian status groups, determined by occupation and style of
life. Alternatively, the classes in the historical sense could be
regarded as transitional, intermediate or mixed classes, as it were,
historical epiphenomena which are eventually bound to disappear
in order to join either the bourgeoisie or the working class. On this
assumption, only the bourgeoisie and the working class are 'true'
classes in Marx's sense, for they only can ultimately become classes
for themselves and be active agents of long-range historical
change. Historically, these are matters for speculation because
there is no indication in Marx as to how he himself would solve
the problem he set for others.


## THE ORIGINS AND ASSUMPTIONS OF
## HISTORICAL MATERIALISM

In the second decade of the nineteenth century, after the armies of
Napoleon had finally been defeated by the European coalition, a
new idea was born in the fertile brains of the French, and was
eagerly discussed in the journals *Le Censeur européen* (*The European
Censor*), *L'Industrie* (*The Industry*), and *L'Organisateur* (*The*

*Organizer*). They announced the irreducible distinction between the 'military and theological' and 'industrial and scientific' regimes and were convinced that in Europe a new industrial society was in process of formation in the very bosom of the old military system. This idea found in Saint-Simon its most enthusiastic protagonist. Auguste Comte, Amand Bazard and B. P. Enfantin elaborated Saint-Simon's views which were then transplanted to England and adopted by H. T. Buckle and Herbert Spencer.[49] It was Marx, however, who in the materialist conception of history made the most fruitful use of them.

The distinction between the two types of society was based on the assumption that the first need for man is to secure his subsistence. He can do so either by (*a*) taking advantage of the bounty of nature or by (*b*) plundering his fellow-men or by (*c*) the produce of his industry. Man tried all these ways in turn. The first way did not increase wealth, could dispense with political organization and, as a matter of fact, preceded it. The second, based on the rule of man over man, was a necessary step for societies to take in order to escape from primitive barbarism and advance towards civilization. But it resulted in perpetual war, pillage and the corrupting division of society into masters and slaves, rulers and ruled. Only the third way was acceptable, because it allowed man to live in peace, develop all his faculties, and produce everything needed for his happiness. Therefore, as Saint-Simon put it, 'politics is the science of production'.[50] Government is unavoidable as long as the old feudal system survives. A well-ordered industrial society, however, will not be governed but administered. Governmental rule implies the use of force which makes the ruled obey the authority. Administrative or industrial rule does not impose arbitrary orders; it simply declares what it is proper to do or not to do, what is in the nature of things and has, therefore, to be voluntarily obeyed. Society is destined to pass from governmental rule to administrative rule because in the industrial society the main concern of man is to produce in order to satisfy human needs. The industrial leaders need not command as the military leaders did; they would use persuasion and induce men to concur, for their own benefit, in the productive activity. Whereas a superior class lived at the expense of an inferior one and the 'exploitation of man by man' was a characteristic phenomenon of the military society, in the industrial society the exploitation of man by man would be replaced by 'the exploitation of the terrestrial globe by men in association'.[51]

The first formulation of historical materialism in *The German Ideology* and *The Poverty of Philosophy* (including the important letter to P. V. Annenkov) is firmly grounded in the Saint-Simonist views of society and history. Marx shares with the Saint-Simonists the assumption that the production of the means of subsistence is the basic fact to be taken into account in any analysis of social life. It is the most basic fact because the production of the means of subsistence is temporarily prior to all other human activities and hence the way the production is organized determines man's social existence, the mutual relations of the major groups within the society, the political system under which they live, and the goals they strive for and realize. Since the means of subsistence and of satisfying other needs which are superimposed on the biological ones are scarce, there arise conflict and strife which divide society into social classes and remain the driving force of social evolution.[52] In view of the fact that the mode of production is the decisive factor in human society, Marx, like Saint-Simon, came to believe that 'politics is the science of production'. To use the phrase which Marx wrote down later but which is implicit in his youthful works, he based his view of society and history on the proposition that 'the anatomy of civil society is to be sought in political economy'.

Marx also shared and reaffirmed the Saint-Simonist belief—the 'new social science', as he called it in the *Manifesto of the Communist Party*—that the historical process is subject to law; that it passes through certain well-defined stages; that each stage is causally related to its predecessor and successor; that the succession of the developmental stages is itself governed by laws; and that the historical process constitutes progress.[53] In *The German Ideology* Marx distinguished four main epochs in the economic formation of society—the tribal, ancient communal (based on slavery), feudal, and modern capitalistic (determined by big industry and universal competition) modes of production, to which he added the Asiatic type in the famous Preface to *A Contribution to the Critique of Political Economy*.[54] To avoid misunderstanding, Marx explained that epochs in the history of society are no more separated from each other by hard and fast lines of demarcation than are geological epochs and can be described solely in terms of their general characteristics.[55] Marx himself investigated in detail only one of these forms or stages, namely, the stage of early capitalism. Recently, the Asiatic mode of production has been subject to searching investigations from the Marxian point of view.[56]

When we look at historical materialism more closely, we soon discover that it reveals not only similarities with, but also differences from, the Saint-Simonist view of society and history. Three differences seem to be particularly important.

First, historical materialism is firmly based on the assumptions of Marx's naturalistic philosophy. This philosophy gives to historical materialism a logical consistency and methodological fruitfulness which are absent in the Saint-Simonist philosophy of history. In this respect only Comte, who investigated the problems of society and history from a philosophically consistent point of view, could offer a genuine alternative to historical materialism. But Comte's detailed investigations of the industrial system fall into the period of Comte's 'second career', when he partly abandoned his own positivistic assumptions.

The second important difference lies in their respective choice of factors which were responsible for the changes in the mode of production: for Saint-Simon it was science but for Marx it was technique and technology. For Saint-Simon, 'history proves that scientific and political revolutions have alternated, that they have successively acted with respect to each other like causes and effects'. For instance, according to Saint-Simon two facts more than all others contributed to the dissolution of the feudal system, the invention of printing, which provided enormous prospects for scientific progress, and Copernicus's discovery whose influence greatly affected the power of theology.[57] For Marx, on the other hand, any alteration in the mode of production 'except in trivial matters, is solely owing to a revolution in the instruments of labour'.[58] The starting point of modern industry is the introduction of entirely new instruments of labour which attained its advanced form in the organized system of machinery in a factory. Technical improvement may first be limited to one sphere of industry but it soon involves a similar change in other spheres. 'Thus spinning by machinery made weaving by machinery a necessity, and both together made the mechanical and chemical revolution that took place in bleaching, printing, and dyeing, imperative.'[59] Since the mode of production depends on the nature of tools, the perfection of machinery, and the method of operating them, the tools and machines, the strength, attention, skill or proficiency of the labourer determine the way in which the labour process is socially organized, that is, in the Marxian terminology, the social relations of production. For instance, the change from hand-mills to steam-mills involves a change from the simplest forms of co-operation to associated labour or labour in common. 'The co-operative character of the labour process is, in the case of machinery, a technical necessity dictated by the instrument of labour itself.'[60] Similarly, the manufacturing period simplifies, improves and multiplies the implements of labour by adapting them to particular application. These implements are used to the best advantage in the hands of specialized labourers. The consequently direct dependence of labourers on each other requires their co-operation in the production of the same finished article and creates continuity, regularity and order of quite a different kind from that to be found in a handicraft. Thus, as Marx points out, the co-operative form of the production process, which is based on a division of labour, assumes its typical form in manufacturing.[61]

The general argument, using this and similar evidence, claims that as the productive forces are constantly improved, so the social relations are also in constant change. The argument seems to be sound but not without important qualifications. It seems to be sound so long as the 'social relations of production' refer solely to the organization of productive processes and labour co-operation within the factory. But Marx appears to have meant all social relations—'the sum total of the relations of production'[62]—and not only those involved in the process of production itself. We have to attach the wider meaning to the phrase 'social relations of production' because Marx himself sometimes included, explicitly, 'a definite organization of the labour of society' in its 'productive forces'.[63] In the light of this interpretation the argument reveals a logical gap, for Marx provides no evidence, as distinct from suggestive hints, to justify the statement that the productive forces determine all social relations.[64]

The question also arises why the productive forces should be constantly improved. Saint-Simon's answer was that the improvement was due, directly or indirectly, to the advancement of knowledge, by which he meant human ability to discover and invent. Marx's answer was different, pregnant with important implications, and entirely divergent from that of Saint-Simon. He suggested that men make their own history but they make it under circumstances given and transmitted from the past. The circumstances are the productive forces and social relations inherited from all preceding generations, all the accumulated tools, machines, skills, knowledge, forms of organization, and so forth, which are handed by one generation to the next. The environment, into which man is born, acts upon him and is acted upon, changes him and is changed in turn by his response. Man's intelligence and inventiveness grow and expand as he rises to the challenge and pressure of circumstances which his social ancestors made for him and which, when solved, he hands down remade to his successors. Therefore, man's nature, including his intelligence, is the result of his own labour; man is what his activity makes him. 'Life is not determined by consciousness but consciousness by life.'

The third major difference, with important and far-reaching implications, concerns the place of ideas and ideals in the human development. For Saint-Simon ideas and ideals were the moving force of co-operative association and human progress. Moral ideas, he wrote, are the only bond which can join men to society and on this account social institutions, religion, politics and education can be described as ideas in action, as a system of thought under different guises. Since every social order is an application of a philosophical system, it is impossible to institute a new order without having previously established the new philosophic system to which it must correspond.[65] In the 1840s these ideas of Saint-Simon found numerous supporters in Germany among whom the most distinguished were the so-called Young Hegelians, a group of thinkers and writers that included the brothers Bauer, Ruge, Stirner and Marx. They also believed every social order to embody a set of philosophical ideas, sociology to be a branch of philosophy, and philosophy to have both social significance and practical implications. The conceptual similarity between the Saint-Simonists and the Young Hegelians is considerable and prompted a contemporary scholar to describe the doctrine of the latter as 'Hegelized Saint-Simonism'.[66]

Marx was a Young Hegelian for a short time but as soon as he became the Editor of *Rheinische Zeitung* he moved beyond their philosophical position. He also rejected the Saint-Simonist view of the role of ideas in society and history, because, as he wrote,

'When people speak of ideas that revolutionize society, they do but express the fact that within the old society the elements of a new one have been created and that the dissolution of the old ideas keeps even pace with the dissolution of the old conditions of existence'.[67] We have seen how according to Marx men develop their productive forces and at the same time certain relations with one another, since the nature of social relations is determined by, and necessarily changes with, the growth and change of the productive forces. But when men establish relations with one another they produce also 'principles, ideas and categories' in conformity with these social relations. For, in general, ideas and ideals express those relations in conceptualized and verbalized form; they are the means by which it is possible for men to become aware of their social and historical situation. Being expressions of the social relations, ideas and ideals cannot exceed the conditions in which they arise. They change in conformity with the social relations and, ultimately, the productive forces, and are as historical and transitory as the modes of material production which they reflect. If the social relations in a society using a hand-mill are different from those prevailing in a society making use of a steam-mill, then the political systems, religious organizations, law, science and philosophy must also be different in the two societies.

Historical materialism which has so far been presented, is to be found in Marx's youthful writings. It is based on the naturalistic conception of man and the evolutionary view of society and formulates certain methodological principles for the description and explanation of social change. On this account it may be classified as a methodological rather than a metaphysical theory of society and history. It starts with the requirement that such a theory should be based on observable facts and on historical records and concludes that, once human action and interaction are described in empirical terms, social and political institutions, morality, law, religion and philosophy lose the appearance of having an independent existence. They are established, maintained, and changed by human action and interaction which are based on or reflect the social relations of production.

The second formulation of the materialist conception of history originated in the *Manifesto of the Communist Party* and was presented more systematically in the Preface to *A Contribution to the Critique of Political Economy*. In this formulation historical materialism assumes the form of a rigid, metaphysical theory of historical causation. This is the theory which explains social and historical evolution as the result of the causal determination of the ideological forms by the economic structure of society, by the conflict between the mode of production and property relations or between the productive forces and the social relations of production. This substantive materialist conception of history also substitutes the law of variation and succession of historical periods for the original hypothesis of social evolution. This law is said to be not only independent of human will and intelligence but also a determinant of them. Thus, the power of man to change his circumstances is abolished and social evolution can no longer be described as a self-generating process. As I understand it, the reified concepts of productive forces, social relations, mode of production, material base and ideological superstructure take over the function which only men can perform.[68]

Pareto's evaluation of these two formulations (or of the two possible interpretations of a single doctrine, as Pareto himself put it) succinctly distinguishes the strong points of the first and the essential weakness of the second formulation.

> If the economic interpretation of history be taken in the sense that the economic state of society entirely determines all social phenomena arising within it, we get a principle . . . from which a wealth of inferences may be so drawn as to constitute a science. The economic interpretation of history was a notable forward step for social science, bringing out as it did the contingent character of certain phenomena, such as morals and religion, which many people regarded and still regard as proclaiming absolute verities. Undoubtedly, moreover, it contains an element of truth in that it takes account of the interdependence of economic and other social factors. Its error lies in representing that interdependence as a relation of cause and effect.[69]

The Preface to *A Contribution to the Critique of Political Economy* lends itself easily to the interpretation in which the economic factor becomes the only determinant of historical development. On this account the Marxian doctrine has often been given the name of 'economic materialism' or 'economic interpretation of history'. But the view that historical materialism was ever meant to be a reductive doctrine, that is, a doctrine reducing a variety of causes to a single kind, to the economic conditions of human existence, was firmly rejected by Engels towards the end of his life. Engels assumed his own and Marx's responsibility for this misunderstanding and assigned it to their somewhat misleading exposition of the doctrine.

> Marx and I are ourselves partly to blame for the fact that the younger people sometimes lay more stress on the economic side than is due to it. We had to emphasize the main principle *vis-à-vis* our adversaries, who denied it, and we had not always the time, the place or the opportunity to allow the other elements involved in the interaction [that is, the elements of the super-structure, Z.A.J.] to come into their rights.[70]

Engels asseverated that neither Marx nor he himself ever believed in a monistic economic determinism; he denied excluding the possibility of the interaction between the sub- and super-structure or rejecting the principle of the relative independence of ideological forms. The role of the material or economic conditions of life was not prescriptive but only restrictive. Historical materialism explained the origin of ideas and did not deny that ideas once born could or did exercise influence on human action and, in general, on the course of human affairs.[71]

The rejection of a monistic economic determinism raises a more general question: 'Is historical materialism a materialistic theory at all?' There is little doubt that a geographical or biological interpretation of history, as formulated by Montesquieu or Buckle, Bagehot, Gumplowicz or Ratzenhofer respectively, deserves more justly the qualification of being materialistic than historical materialism itself. For all these theories are reductive and materialistic in the original sense of this term; they reduce all social change to the ultimate action of the physical world, to the fertility of the soil or the bounty of nature, the type of climate or the pressure of population, the struggle for domination or more precisely the Darwinian struggle for survival. The historical materialism of Marx is not a materialistic theory in this sense. It is not a reductive theory and does not select a physical or biological phenomenon for the explanation of the course of history.

Historical materialism is opposed to any supernaturalistic conception of man, society and history. As such, it emphasizes the decisive importance of natural conditions in the determination of social life and social change. But the term 'natural conditions' is not co-extensive with 'physical characteristics of man's natural environment'; it is much wider than the latter phrase. According to Marx, the physical environment as such cannot determine man's action and consciousness unless it is socially and culturally mediated. As Marx put it, 'the production of life' always involves a natural and a social relationship.[72] Any natural force must be brought under the control of society to become a socially significant fact. Man is both determined by and responsive to the circumstances, including his physical environment, which he shapes, re-shapes, and transforms by his action. Not only circumstances make men, but also men make circumstances. This approach to man and society is better described as realistic or naturalistic than as materialistic. For its basic premise is not the proposition 'only matter exists' but the assumption that a scientific study of society and history can be based on observation of the world in which men live. The material conditions, Engels explained parenthetically in one of his writings intended to popularize the Marxian views, 'are the physically sensible conditions in which society at a given period produces and exchanges its means of subsistence'.[73] When history and sociology reject philosophical speculation and rely on observation of social and economic development (the 'life-process' in the Marxian terminology), social and historical knowledge loses its speculative and ideological character and acquires the precision of natural science.

## THE ECONOMIC AND SOCIOLOGICAL THEORIES OF CAPITALISM

The study of capitalist industrial society occupies an important place in the Marxian theory of society and history. No interpretation of the Marxian thought can be sound and adequate, if it fails to account for this fact or assigns to *Capital* and other economic writings of Marx a marginal importance.

Marx owed to the founding fathers of classical economics—to Adam Smith and Say, Malthus and Ricardo—the belief that the economic order was a natural order, analogous to that of the physical universe. 'The production of wealth', wrote J. S. Mill,

'is evidently not an arbitrary thing. It has its necessary conditions.'
Political economy tries to discover the laws by which the production of wealth is determined. They are ultimate laws, that is, they
are neither made nor alterable by men. Men can only understand
their significance, conform to and be guided by them. Yet political
economy is a 'moral and social science', because it is concerned
with moral and psychological causes, which are dependent on
social relations and institutions or on the principles of human
nature.[74] The achievements of political economy suggested that
social life in general may be part of a natural order, governed by
laws beyond man's control but which he can come to know and use
to his advantage.

Furthermore, as I have mentioned earlier, Saint-Simon and his
school established the belief that in the arrangement of human
affairs the organization of production is more important and
fundamental than political institutions and forms of government.
The increased importance of industrial functions focused attention on social problems and economic relations which were
recognized as the mainspring of social life. Marx endorsed and
developed this idea in his theory of capitalistic industrialization.

The social importance of economic relations was incompatible
with the classical tradition of economic thought for which
economic life was essentially the activity of isolated individuals.
For this reason Enfantin criticized Adam Smith and his successors
for the abstract over-simplification of their investigations, for the
failure to see that political economy is concerned with 'the relations that join all members of a society together in material
production', and for the separation of the subject-matter of
political economy from the totality of social relations.[75] Marx took
up this Saint-Simonist thread and staged a powerful attack on the
analytical procedure and abstract assumptions of classical economists. For Marx, society was no mere aggregate of individuals.
Economic analysis could not ignore the social character of production and the historical nature of the structure of society. *Capital* is
neither a mere technical economic treatise, as Böhm-Bawerk
and Schumpeter held it to be, nor an 'Existentialist analysis' of the
human situation in an economy dominated by private enterprise
and competition, as some French Existentialists and theologians
maintain. *Capital* combines sociology and economics by investigat-
ing economic life within a social context, all aspects of which are

interrelated, and on this foundation it provides an alternative theory of capitalist production.

While Marx's dominant interest was the formulation of a theory of social and historical evolution, his published historical and economic studies were concerned exclusively with the capitalist mode of production. The reasons why Marx should have concentrated his attention on the early stages of capitalism hardly need mentioning. This period was directly relevant to his political activities in addition to providing the most suitable battle ground for his critical analysis of classical economics. Having been persuaded that a new industrial society was being born, he identified industrial society with the capitalist mode of production, and only late in his life had second thoughts about the truth of this proposition.[76] But he never really gave up the belief that capitalism was the only possible means to industrialization, and in Marx's lifetime there was hardly any evidence to the contrary. For this reason he told the German readers of *Capital* that the English hard way to industrial (capitalist) society was the road which the less industrially advanced nations would have to follow.

Concentration on one particular period had finally the advantage of providing the best opportunity of repudiating an important proposition of the classical and also marginal utility school economists who claimed that they discovered a universally valid theory, that is, laws which were universal in respect to the spatio-temporal scope. Marx challenged this claim and maintained that social and economic laws were regional or historical in character; they held for all human societies at a specified stage of their evolution but not at an earlier or later one. Industrial capitalist society had laws of its own which were both limited to certain conditions of time and space and different from the laws which apply to feudal or ancient society or to the socialist society of the future[77]. *Capital* provides a description of the genesis of industrial society in England, an analysis of the capitalist mode of production, of its structure and progressive change, together with the laws that hold in this type of socio-economic organization.

In his speech at the graveside of Karl Marx, Engels said that Marx made two great contributions to knowledge. He discovered 'the law of development of human history'—Engels had the materialist conception of history in mind—and 'the special law of motion governing the present-day capitalist mode of production', by which he meant the discovery of the concept of surplus value.[78] The importance of the concept of surplus value lies in the fact that it provides the mainstay for the whole elaborate system presented in *Capital*. It helps to demonstrate that the profits of the capitalist come from the exploitation of the worker; as there could be no profits without exploitation, capitalism is, by its very nature, a system of exploitation. Moreover, the concept of surplus value plays an indispensable part in demonstrating that the capitalist mode of production sows and cultivates the seeds of its own destruction; that it produces an ever increasing misery on one side, and a concentration of production and finance on the other which, together with a steadily decreasing rate of profit and an increasing instability in the capitalist economy, result in the polarization of the population into two irreconcilable classes, the bourgeoisie and proletariat; and that at this juncture the overthrow of the bourgeois political order and capitalist mode of production becomes inevitable.

What is surplus value? To answer this question we have first to ask 'What is value?'. For the economist, value is the measure which permits one commodity to be exchanged for another.[79] If the exchange is to be acceptable to both sides and equitable in this sense, the commodities exchanged must be of equal value, that is, it should be possible to buy them at the same price. 'Value' in the economic sense means the exchange value of a commodity or its price, for the latter is simply the monetary measure of value.

Marx adopted the labour theory of value of Ricardo, whose 'keen power of theoretical penetration' Marx greatly admired. Ricardo suggested that value is the amount of labour-time embodied in a product. From this point of view, capital is reducible to labour. For example, a machine tool can be regarded as the sum of accumulated labour which went into its production and which again is used in the production of various articles itself. The value of a commodity can then be expressed in terms of labour—accumulated labour and labour power—required in its production. Marx, who slightly modified Ricardo's definition, defined value as the quantity of labour socially necessary for the production of a commodity in a given state of society, that is, the average time required for its production as determined by the productive powers of labour (the state of technology, the social organization or the efficiency of labour). To put it briefly in Marx's own words, 'a commodity has a value, because it is a crystallization of social labour'.[80] The important consequence of this definition which reduces capital and land to labour inputs was the proposition that labour was the only source of all value.

This raises the question: how is it possible for a capitalist to make profit at all?—and Marx answered it by analysing what happens when the owners of the means of production (accumulated labour) and free labourers enter the commodity market. Labourers are free in the sense that they are neither slaves nor serfs as in the past; and they are labourers because they have only their labour power to sell. When labour-power is offered for exchange, it becomes a commodity, and its value, like the value of any other commodity, is determined by the amount of labour-time necessary for its production. In this case, what is exchanged is labour power and the means of subsistence necessary to maintain the labourer alive. According to this theory, wages are thus related to the value of labour power and not to the value of the commodity produced by the labour power. The reasons for such arrangements and their implications can be more clearly seen by considering an example.

Let us suppose that the value of labour power is 30/– a day and that the worker needs four hours to produce the amount of commodities equivalent to his wage. Every minute of work beyond the period of four hours (the so-called surplus labour) produces values which are not paid for and which are taken by the capitalist. Labour power invariably produces values in excess of the total cost which consists of its market price, the price of raw materials and the productive power of machines. Marx called these excess values 'surplus value', a term which he apparently adopted from the physiocrats.[81]. The profit of the capitalist is the surplus value which he appropriates from the worker. The capitalist is in a position to deprive the worker of everything he produces beyond the price of his labour because the capitalist, as the owner of the means of production, holds the commanding position on the market. The 'free' labourer, having no alternative source of livelihood, and being a pauper or virtual pauper, has to accept the conditions set by the buyer of labour power. Since the worker does receive the exchange value equivalent for his labour power—his means of subsistence—he is not defrauded. But he is at the mercy of the capitalist and the latter takes advantage of it. The worker is exploited because by selling his labour power he also surrenders his right to the surplus value which he produces and for which he does not receive anything in exchange. Moreover, he must be increasingly exploited. Since the capitalist production depends on ever increasing the amount of surplus labour, the worker has to give more and more of his labour free. Thus, his chances of being reduced to pauperism are bound to increase.[82]

Marx maintained that the theory of surplus value explained not only the high rate of economic growth under the capitalist mode of production but also the prospective economic decay and the ultimate self-destruction of capitalism.[83] As has been mentioned earlier, the mechanism of capitalist accumulation was bound to increase the unemployment and poverty of the worker whilst improving the situation and wealth of the capitalist. In this way inequality was ever growing and misery was reaching proportions beyond endurance. These predictions did not come true, and thus the theory of surplus value, from which these predictions were derived, was not confirmed by the development of events.[84] Various attempts were made later, in particular, by Rudolf Hilferding, Rosa Luxemburg and Lenin, to save the theory by the addition of new hypotheses. I cannot go into this matter now but it appears that the additional hypotheses also failed to obtain the expected confirmation.

Moreover, Eugen von Böhm-Bawerk, an Austrian economist, laid bare a serious logical flaw in the Marxian system, namely, that the third volume of *Capital* contradicts the first. Marx's theory demands that the organic composition of capital[85] determines the rate of profit; the greater the variable part of capital, the higher the rate of profit. The theory implies, therefore, that equal amounts of capital with dissimilar organic composition should yield different profits, while in fact equal amounts of capital, irrespective of their organic composition, yield equal profits. Marx was aware of this 'apparent', as he called it, 'contradiction' and promised to explain it without any modification of his assumptions in a later volume of *Capital*. This he did not succeed in doing, for the Marxian solution in the third volume of *Capital* is incompatible with the theory of surplus value presented in the first. As a matter of fact, Marx abandoned the view that prices tend to correspond to the values of commodities and recognized by implication that the labour theory of value fails to provide a theory of prices. As Mrs.

Joan Robinson put it, in the third volume of *Capital* 'common sense triumphs' over Marx's theory of value which was inspired by 'a picture of the capitalist process as a system of piracy, preying upon the very life of the workers' rather than by hard facts.[86]

The large measure of approval and support which Marxian economics continue to enjoy may, of course, be due to reasons other than its logical consistency and empirical confirmation. While the theory intended to explain the exploitation of labour under the capitalist mode of production does not achieve its objective, the failure of the explanation does not affect the hard fact of exploitation as such. This fact has still remained fresh in people's minds, is continually receiving new support in many parts of the world, and psychologically, at least, it supports the theory relating to it, however logically inadequate this theory may be. Furthermore, the Marxian theory naturally appeals to all those who share Marx's criticism of capitalism on social and moral grounds; on this account they tend to ignore or underestimate the logical flaws in the broad outlines of Marxian economics. Finally, as Pareto argued, Marx's sociological work helped to tear down the structure of classical economics which had been based on middle-class interests and adorned with ethical considerations. It clearly revealed the necessity of adding new notions to the conceptual framework of classical economics and had other manifest merits. But to ask the question:

> Whether Marx's theory of 'surplus value' is false or true is about as important as knowing whether and how baptism eradicates sin in trying to determine the social value of Christianity.

As Pareto said elsewhere, with his theory of surplus value Marx introduced 'ethical considerations into places where they did not belong', and fell victim to the same error which he exposed in classical economics.[87]

In recent times, many writers, in particular French Catholic and Existentialist writers, have concurred in the essential points of Pareto's verdict. They maintain that *Capital* is not an economic treatise but a philosophical and ethical work; that Marxian economics in general and the conception of surplus value in particular are an Existentialist analysis and a normative theory.

According to these writers, who go to the opposite extreme as compared with Böhm-Bawerk and Schumpeter, Marx does not investigate the mechanism of the market or capitalist production but a human and social situation to which the market or capitalist production gives rise.[88]

Since the consequences deriving from the theory of surplus value are disconfirmed by historical developments, the validity of the theory is doubtful and a radical modification or abandonment of it is imperative. (This is recognized explicitly or implicitly by such prominent Marxian economists as Joan Robinson and Oskar Lange.) The reconstruction or rejection of the theory of surplus value does not imply that *Capital* is no longer of any interest except to the historian of economic thought. Marx's economic theory reveals the ideological assumptions and logical flaws in the classical economic doctrines. In contrast to 'classical' and 'modern economics', which was developed in the last quarter of the nineteenth century, the Marxian theory emphasizes the social character of production and its changing historical forms. Its considerable internal consistency, as compared with earlier and later schools of economic thought, is today frequently recognized by economists. While the logical structure of *Capital* is not perfect and the laws of capitalist production fail to work 'with iron necessity towards inevitable results', *Capital* may still be considered as a work concerned with long-range trends inherent in the capitalist mode of production—such as the decline in the rate of profit, the increasing inequality of income distribution (the fall in relative wages), the concentration of production and capital in fewer and fewer hands, or the tendency for the modern corporation to grow ever larger and strive for security against the vicissitudes of the market. It can be argued that these trends are characteristic of certain stages of capitalism, and that by relentless pressure from within they are capable of transforming it (J. K. Galbraith's *The New Industrial State* provides the latest sociological and economic theory of this kind). But we cannot assert, without providing new premises and arguments, that these transformations follow the law of capitalist accumulation and lead ultimately to the expropriation of the expropriators.

The fate of the theory of surplus value does not affect Marx's contribution to the sociology of capitalism, that is, to the study of social changes which take place in an industrial capitalist society.

For in this field of enquiry Marx's views about the division of labour and its consequences for the social structure of pre-industrial and industrial society are of considerable interest. It is customary to regard Durkheim as the first vigorous and original sociological mind that worked on the division of labour. This is not entirely true; Marx not only preceded but also forestalled Durkheim in some respects. Durkheim referred to *Capital* in *The Division of Labour in Society* and was clearly familiar with Marx's ideas. Their respective views have important points in common despite the fact that for Marx division of labour was a divisive and conflict-generating factor but for Durkheim and also for Comte and Spencer it was a solidary force and one of the principal sources of social cohesion. Apart from certain specific points, their views are similar, since they both consider division of labour to be one of the most important facts of social dynamics, 'a kind of concerted action' as Spencer put it, 'which does not originate in deliberate concert'.[89] They both fully understood what Mandeville had said with admirable clarity many years earlier, namely, that when we ignore the social effects of the division of labour 'we often ascribe to the excellency of man's genius and the depth of his penetration, what is in reality owing to length of time and the experience of many generations, all of them very little differing from one another in natural parts and sagacity'.[90]

In Ferguson and Adam Smith the terms 'subdivision of tasks', 'separation of mechanical arts and professions' or 'division of labour' are used in a wide sense to denote economic divisions of labour and differentiations of rank, calling, station, or place in life, to which we would now refer as differentiations of occupation, function, and social prestige.[91] Moreover, Durkheim applied the term in a very wide sense, in which he followed Comte, to mean the specialization of tasks in general. He consequently spoke of the division of social labour (*division du travail social*), but he specifically disowned the restriction of its use to economic activities and also rejected its reduction to the propensity to barter.[92] Marx clearly distinguished between the various uses of the term, of which three are more important than others—the social division of labour (also division of labour in a society), which is subdivided into division of labour in general and in particular, and division of labour in the workshop, called also division of labour in singular or in detail. Marx's distinction between the social division of labour and that in the workshop reappears in Max Weber in his distinction between social and technical divisions of labour.[93]

The social division of labour concerns the breakdown of social production into its main divisions or *genera*, viz, agriculture, industry, commerce, etc. Unlike the other kinds of division, that in the workshop in particular, division of labour in society is common to even the most diverse economic formations. It starts naturally and spontaneously within a family, tribe or clan as the result of differences in sex, age, natural predisposition (e.g. physical strength), needs, accidents, and so forth. The social division of labour includes, therefore, not only the separation of economic but also of social functions and corresponds to the Durkheimean concept of the division of social labour.[94]

When the *genera* of labour are split into kinds or species and sub-species, we obtain the division of labour in particular. For instance, once the separation of agricultural, industrial and commercial labour within a society is accomplished, a further development within these branches leads to various divisions among individuals performing specific kinds of labour. This particular division is no longer as spontaneous and natural as the general one, for it is determined by the methods of production applied in agriculture, industry or commerce and leads to the divisions of men into slaves and free, into castes, guilds, estates or social classes.[95] Division of labour in particular is a necessary condition for the emergence of these various major groups which, in turn, condition the relations among the individuals co-operating in definite kinds of labour and which also are specifically related to each other.[96]

Finally, we have division of labour in the workshop with its two major subdivisions—division of labour in manufacture and in the factory. Only this kind of division of labour constantly divides and subdivides skills, employments or jobs into more and more narrowly circumscribed activities and is a division of labour in the purely economic sense. Division of labour in manufacture and in the workshop in general demands that the social division of labour should previously have attained a certain stage of development. On the other hand, division of labour in the workshop develops, multiplies, and transforms the nature of the social division. Division of labour in society is stimulated by the territorial division of labour and international exchange, by the development of manufacture and factory system, and it establishes in every sphere of society the all-pervading system of specialization.[97]

The social division of labour, without any trace of the particular division and division in the workshop, can exist only within the primitive family and in the tribal organization or in segmental societies in Durkheim's sense.[98] In *Capital* Marx described an Asian instance of segmental societies which in his view are characterized by the unchangeableness of their economic structure, sharply contrasting with the constant dissolution and reconstruction of Asiatic States and dynasties.[99] The particular division in a society is established with the separation of town and country, which is a long historical process; its crystallization may take as long as several centuries. This division appeared in the ancient communal formations, based on slavery, and in the caste and guild systems of production in more recent times. The separation between town and country leads to the separation of material (manual) and mental labour, which is reflected in the appearance of the class of priests and ideologists as representatives of purely mental labour. The division of material and mental labour meant that from then onwards the enjoyment and the burden of labour devolved on different groups of individuals. Like the separation between town and country, it is a lengthy historical process which in Europe only reached completion in capitalism.[100]

Division of labour in the workshop appeared in mid-sixteenth century Europe together with manufacture, of which it is the distinguishing principle. Manufacture retained the character of a handicraft, because under this form of production each operation, whether complex or simple, was to be done by hand. Manufacture led to the invention of machines and their large-scale application in factories. Since manufacture and modern industry are only successive stages of the capitalist mode of production, one can say that division of labour in the workshop is a special creation of capitalism alone.[101]

The question now arises, 'What are the causes which explain the development and the variations of the division of labour in society?' The answer is, the increase in population, by which Marx means both its absolute number and density, density being relative to the technical state of society. A relatively thinly populated country like the United States has a denser population than the more numerously populated India, because the former country has well-developed and the latter poorly-developed means of communication. The relativity of density with respect to technical progress introduces implicitly the concept of moral density in the Durkheimean sense, that is, the frequency of interaction among individuals which is inseparable from the increase in population or material density. Thus Marx's answer to the question, 'What makes the division of labour develop?' is the same as that given later by Durkheim, namely, material and moral density.[102]

While the various kinds of division of labour have the same cause, this cause is not invariably the sufficient condition for its variation; it is also the wider social context within which division of labour takes place that accounts for it. Division of labour may be affected either by the exchange of commodities among societies which have different modes of production and different products for exchange, or by the action of causes inherent in a given society itself. In the latter case, the material and moral density is one such cause and the property relations are another. The difference in property relations enhances the distinction between division of labour in society and division of labour in the workshop. The former implies the dispersion of the means of production among independent producers who act under pressure of their mutual interests, that is, competition; and the latter implies their concentration in the hands of the capitalist, with an undisputed authority over labour-power. For this reason the social division of labour, which develops more or less spontaneously, is anarchic, but division in the workshop is despotic. Labourers, crowded into the factory, are organized like privates of the industrial army who are placed under the command of a hierarchy of sergeants and officers.[103]

The social division of labour, both general and particular, and division in the workshop differ in kind rather than in degree. Marx agreed with all his predecessors that division of labour constitutes an important factor in the increasing rate of economic growth. But he concentrated more on the disadvantages than on the advantages of division of labour. What the others had to say on this matter he said better, more emphatically, and with greater humanity, supporting his rhetoric with a wealth of detailed knowledge. There was no doubt in his mind that the productive power of labour is augmented, above all, by a greater division of labour and continual improvement of machinery. Within the capitalist mode of production 'the division of labour is necessarily followed by greater division of labour, the application of machinery by still greater application of machinery'.[104] But the social and psychological, or even biological, effects of the ever increasing use of machinery and division of labour were disastrous. Since division of labour in the workshop makes the worker develop one single faculty at the expense of all others, it 'attacks the individual at the very roots of his life'.[105] This part of Marx's work, which is too well known to need recapitulation, is something more than a historical document for it was meant to refer to the future. While the relevant parts of *Capital* describe the conditions of industrial work in England around the middle of the last century, they also constitute a set of forecasts based on observed trends. Recent publications supply evidence that not all these forecasts have failed. They indicate that the division of labour has now become the atomization of labour, 'reducing it to a single movement' and causing undue fatigue, physiological and neurological damage; that workers feel themselves bound to their jobs by minute subdivision and the absence of any special training; and that despite the awareness of the harm inflicted by the specialization of industrial jobs, the present trend, which results from a search for speed and greater efficiency, is likely to continue unabated.[106]

The central point of the general argument is the statement that as we pass from manufacture to modern machine industry the psychologically and socially harmful effects of division of labour in the workshop grow in scope and intensity. In the manufacturing period division of labour crippled the body and mind of the worker but at least created new skills. In the factory system, however, the crippling effects became more intense, no new skills arose and the old ones were thrown overboard by machinery. Again this statement was meant to be both descriptive and predictive. The basis of the forecast was the assumption that modern industry, by replacing a detailed function of a worker with a mechanical process, tended towards a constant reduction in the number of workers. Moreover, as division of labour in the factory increases, each labour process is resolved into its constituent elements, and labour is simplified by 'scientific management'. Modern industry tended to substitute a simple skill for a more complex one and to reduce all operations in the factory to the same low level of what is no longer any form of skill but a dexterity in performing a few repetitive movements. The work of a machine operative in a modern factory could be learnt by anybody within a short period of time. The increasing simplicity of operations was bound to result in a greater mobility of labour which in turn, together with the redundancy caused by increased use of machinery, compelled the workers to compete among themselves. The replacement of the labour of men by 'cheap labour', the work of women and children, completed this picture.

If the Marxian forecasts about the consequences of division of labour in the factory came true, the labour force in a highly advanced industrial country would consist—apart from a huge industrial reserve army of unemployed—of the following three divisions: a numerically unimportant group of highly skilled workers, such as engineers or mechanics, who look after the factory equipment; machine operatives whose skill is low, easily acquired and replaceable; and unskilled labourers or mere machine minders, comprising some proportion of women and children. Marx's description of the labour force in the period of manufacture bears a closer resemblance to the present state of affairs than that concerned with the workers in modern industry.

It is often said that for Marx the separation and specialization of industrial jobs was an absolute evil and that its abolition, the liberation of men from the 'enslaving subordination of the individual to the division of labour' was one of the defining characteristics of communist society.[107] There is in *The German Ideology* the often quoted passage about the communist society of the future where society regulates production and makes it possible for everybody to do one thing today and another tomorrow, to hunt, fish or rear sheep at different times of the day to suit his inclination, without ever becoming a hunter, fisherman or shepherd. According to this interpretation, a complete man would achieve all-round development of all his abilities by escaping subjection to the division of labour (the communist society of the future was to consist of such universally specialized people). There are a few passages in *The German Ideology*, but only in this work of 1845-6, which support the view that Marx cherished the ideal of the complete man.[108] It fitted in very well with the romantic concept of work as 'life's primary want' and as the expression of man's 'true nature' which was widespread in the nineteenth century, particularly among Utopian and anarchic socialists. Moreover, it was an effective means of reinforcing Marx's critique of capitalism.

The ideal of a total or a complete man is, however, an impossible goal. It is not logically impossible, for it does not involve any contradiction, but granted the nature of man and society, it is impossible for all practical purposes. It was evident that despite its severely limiting and damaging effects on man, the specialization of skills and division of occupations was inseparable from technical progress and economic growth. It was inseparable not only from the capitalist mode of production but from any advanced form of production, irrespective of the class structure of society. Marx emphasized in the *Manifesto of the Communist Party* and *Capital* that division of labour in manufacture[109] creates a superior organization of labour, develops new productive forces in the society, and increases the social productive power of workers. Historically it was a progress and a necessary phase in the economic development of society; the creation of the inexhaustible productive powers of modern industry fulfilled the first condition of the emancipation of Labour.[110]. On the other hand, it turned out to be a more refined and civilized method of exploitation because the increased wealth benefited the capitalist, and not the worker, thus strengthening the authority of capital over labour. The use made of the division of labour rather than the division of labour in itself became the main target of Marx's criticism.

Once the inevitability of the division of labour is accepted, the ideal of the complete man in *The German Ideology* is no longer tenable. As a matter of fact Marx abandoned it explicitly in the third volume of *Capital*.[111] Work, he wrote there, is an inescapable necessity, an everlasting, nature-imposed condition of human existence, common to all social formations and all possible modes of production. 'Work', Marx wrote elsewhere, 'cannot become a play'.[112] Since man is never in a position to become entirely emancipated from it, he can gain freedom only in so far as he is capable of restricting as much as possible the determination of his whole life by this realm of necessity, by bringing it under his control instead of being controlled by it. The harmful and disadvantageous effects of an advanced technology can be allayed by the reduction of working hours,[113] the increase and creative use of leisure,[114] technological training which befits the worker for a variety of labour,[115] and restraints on the division of labour when-

C

ever it goes wild. Marx maintained that leisure (free time), to which he attached an increasing importance and which he defined as both spare time and the time devoted to higher activities, could transform the worker into a different individual. The true economy, Marx wrote, consisted in the saving of labour time which reduced the cost and increased the forces of production. The saving in labour time, entirely appropriated by the capitalist, should be used to extend the free time of the worker.[116]

The division of labour gives rise to certain moral issues, of which both Marx and Durkheim were fully aware.[117] The development of man, Durkheim wrote, can be conceived in two entirely different ways. We can see the ideal in the perfect man, a 'thorough and complete human being, one quite sufficient unto himself'; and we can see it in a man who lacks the brilliance and selfish dilettantism of the other but is a part of society because he is dependent on others; he devotes himself to restricted tasks, and does his duty with vigour, competence and productive strength. We have reasons to believe that the former conception of man is not compatible with the division of labour in society, but the latter is. Durkheim points out that it is not by any means self-evident why the former conception should be more elevated than the latter. 'An ideal is not more elevated because more transcendent, but because it leads us to vaster perspectives'.

Durkheim's clear-cut distinctions enable us to clarify Marx's views on the matter. In his youth Marx cherished the ideal of a perfect and complete man but rejected or at least restricted it so much in his maturity that he may be said to have endorsed the alternative ideal. The Utopia of *The German Ideology* is replaced by the concept of man who lives fully through realization of his particular talents and by being useful and productive to society and his fellow-men.

## SOCIAL CLASS, POLITICAL POWER AND THE STATE

Like other branches of sociology, the sociology of politics is a field of diverse and loosely related studies which share the characteristic of being concerned with the distribution and the exercise of power in society. Political sociology differs from political science in its approach rather than in subject matter. While political science examines the formal institutions and their relations to society, political sociology investigates how these institutions come to command power and how they are affected by society.[118]

Marx had a consuming interest in political power and made a determined effort to discover the roots and mechanism of power in society. His interest is reflected in his life-long political activities which were devoted to educating and organizing the international working class movement as an effective political force; in his criticism of the Utopians and in his struggle with Proudhon or Bakunin, whose common error was the disregard or ignorance of the role and importance of power in society; and in his historical writings with their impressive grasp of the logic of history. Marx's supreme skill in the analysis of contemporary events derived from his understanding of the regularities which determine the outcome, seemingly unpredictable, of the struggle for power among competing social classes, groups, parties or personalities.

In contrast to his overriding interest in power there is relatively little systematic reflection on power in Marx's writings. This may be due to his belief that the sociology of politics has no existence independently of political economy which must have reduced the importance of politics in the Weberian sense, that is, the concern with such problems as to how people strive to share power or to influence the distribution of power among the various groups within a State.[119] In this respect Marx reflected and expressed the conviction of his times that acts of government could have no lasting or profound consequences and that the decisive events took place at the level of economic and industrial organization.[120] Marx agreed that it may appear paradoxical and contrary to everyday experience to consider the decisions of government, the laws, or the ideas of historians, economists and philosophers to be less important than the prevailing system of economic relations. There would be no need for science, however, if one accepted only appearances and failed to investigate their underlying causes. 'It is also a paradox that the earth moves around the sun, and that water consists of two highly inflammable gases'. Scientific truth is always a paradox if judged by the criteria of common sense and everyday knowledge. The real motions of the planets are concealed from those who are only familiar with their apparent motions which are accessible to the senses. 'All science would be superfluous if the forms of appearance of things coincided with their essence'.[121]

It is sometimes said that because of these assumptions Marx not only failed, but also was bound to fail, as a political sociologist. He misconceived, so the argument goes, the relation between the political order and the economic order, reduced the former to the latter, and thus ignored the fact that the connection between political conflicts and social struggles is not always direct. Marx combined in his political sociology important insights with a revolutionary ideal and the Utopian tendencies in his thinking distorted his grasp of the realities of power and authority.

There are statements in Marx, in the *Manifesto of the Communist Party* in particular, which may support this assessment. Let us consider, for instance, the propositions: 'The history of all hitherto existing society is the history of class struggle', 'Political power . . . is merely the organized power of one class for oppressing another' or 'Law, morality, religion are . . . so many bourgeois prejudices, behind which lurk in ambush just as many bourgeois interests'. These propositions describe in economic terms the political organization of society, the manifestations of power or the whole world of ideas and they practically reduce the bourgeois institutions of government and culture to the economic basis. Needless to say, they become easy game for present-day political sociologists. They may provide support for Mosca's claim that Marx asserted a uniform subordination of the whole political organization to the type of economic production, or to Popper's statement that Marx considered politics to be impotent.[122] But the *Manifesto* neither was nor was intended to be a detached theoretical enquiry. It was written in haste, in the expectation of an impending revolution, and was designed to produce definite results. The *Manifesto* was a political declaration of beliefs and objectives which expressed some of Marx's important theoretical ideas but used them as ideological weapons rather than as analytical tools. They should be treated, therefore, with due caution, making allowances for the purposes they were to serve and the revolutionary fervour of the times.

Whenever it is a case of actually applying the materialist conception to the development of historical or political events, Marx does not give the slightest justification for the assertion that he reduced historical materialism to a monistic economic determinism. In his historical writings, especially *The Class Struggles in France, 1848 to 1850* and *The Eighteenth Brumaire of Louis Bonaparte*, Marx analysed the economic and social structure of France in order to discover the social forces involved in the struggle for power, to assess their relative strength, and to determine their objective as well as the nature of the conflict between them. This examination of the social situation allowed him to account for the shifting alliances of the forces engaged in the struggle, the decisive turnings in the course of events and their final outcome. He illustrated convincingly the truth of the famous proposition of *The Eighteenth Brumaire of Louis Bonaparte* that a historian and a social scientist has to distinguish the 'phrases and fancies' of the parties involved in a political struggle from their group interests and objectives founded in the economic realities of society. These studies neither present political events as a direct result of economics forces nor reduce the political order to the economic order. They are based on the assumption that the political order is not autonomous and that the question of who governs or gains the upper hand in the struggle for power is not decided solely by the imaginary or real rights, ideals, tactical ability or determination of the parties involved. The real determining factor was economic power in the sense that it constituted the necessary condition for establishing political domination and authority of one group over all others. If this necessary condition was absent, the class or party struggling for power might win a battle but would be bound to lose the war. Only if we confuse a necessary condition with a sufficient condition, does historical materialism become, through our own error, a reductive doctrine.

In his writings concerned with the French upheavals in the mid-nineteenth century Marx made it abundantly clear that power over the market, the power based on ownership of the means of production, was not the only one he observed and recognized. Dahrendorf, a German sociologist, is right when he claims that some of Marx's statements are or seem to be derived from the proposition 'economic power is *eo ipso* political power', but he fails to notice that this proposition does not imply 'political power is *eo ipso* economic power'—an important distinction. Furthermore, the proposition 'economic power is *eo ipso* political power, would hold in the circumstances in which only the two principal classes —the propertied and the propertyless class—remain on the scene to fight out their final battle. Otherwise Marx's views seem to be that the two concepts—political and economic power—overlap. Not all political power but only 'political power, properly so called, is merely the organized power of one class for oppressing another'.[123] This overlapping relation implies that there are instances of property (for instance, small landed property) with which no political power is associated, and conversely forms of political power which are not conjoined with property. Witnessing the developments of early capitalist industrialism Marx must have been impressed by the close connection between economic and political power, the political helplessnes of the working class and the undisputed political authority of the owners of the means of production. But when he scrutinized the contemporary political events or analysed the dramatic historical conflicts of his time, he did not go to the extremes of which he has been accused. He firmly held to the assumption that economic power is the most significant factor to be taken into account in every analysis of power relations and that there is a connection between the class structure of a society and its political system, between social classes and political parties, between social and political struggles. This is a reasonable and fruitful assumption and it has since been applied to great advantage.

Since Marx, there has been a considerable increase in our knowledge of power, which we owe to many thinkers but, above all, to Max Weber.[124] Weber stated explicitly that neither economic nor economically conditioned power is identical with power as such; he kept economic power and political power distinct; he recognized the fact that economic power may be acquired as the consequence of power existing on other grounds and that men may strive for it for its own sake; he showed the variety of sources and forms of power; and he established the distinction between different modes of social stratification on the one hand (by economic interest and social prestige which in turn are related to occupation and style of life), and the distribution of political power on the other. We now accept the fact that power is heterogeneous in its origin and multiform in its manifestations. We speak of temporal, spiritual, political, economic, military, administrative, governmental, organizational and many other species of power. We readily subdivide each of these species and talk of the political power of the workers, the capitalists and the middle classes; of the economic power of organized labour and employers; of the spiritual power of the churches, the ideologists and intellectuals; of the administrative power of the bureaucracy or police. The diversity of irreducible power groups in advanced industrial societies seems to have no limits. The post-Weberian concept of power is incomparably richer than the Marxian and offers considerable analytical advantages. But there must be some other advantages in the simpler Marxian view of power, for we resort to it whenever we want to discover where the 'real' power in society is to be found. This suggests that the improvement of our conceptual framework for the description of the phenomena of power has perhaps not been matched by its explanatory capacity.

Although Marx's political sociology can and should be exonerated from some standard forms of criticism, it should be conceded that it suffers from a certain inherent weakness. For instance, Marx's doctrine of the State is highly vulnerable and inadequate. It is one thing to assert, as Marx did, that on the whole the division into those who own property and the propertyless is co-extensive with the division into rulers and ruled, and quite a different one to consider this provisional proposition as conclusive evidence for the claim that the State is an instrument of class domination and class exploitation. Historical evidence and the world in which Marx lived provided some evidence in support of Marx's claim. But it did not provide evidence that the State was only an instrument by which one class exploited the others. The State may be, and probably was indeed, used for this purpose. Locke said as much when he defined political power 'to be the right of making laws . . . for the regulating and preserving of property' and Adam Smith supported him in this respect, claiming that 'civil government . . . is in reality instituted for the defence of the rich against the poor, or of those who have some property against those who have none at all'.[125] Lorenz von Stein wrote in 1850 that 'the ruling class of society must necessarily strive in its own interest to seize the control of governmental power'. It controls state administration because it controls public offices. It can hold them with the exclusion of others by stipulating the qualifications on which the appointment depends and which only the members of the ruling class satisfy.[126] Historically and sociologically it is always enlightening to relate the action of a government to the prevailing class structure, class interests and class conflicts.

But not all actions and functions of the State can be explained by the assumption that state power is an organization of the propertied class, an instrument by which one group dominates others or which is used by the rulers to the disadvantage of the ruled. If we make the Spencerian distinction between those laws which derive their obligation from the will of the governing agency and those which derive it from the consensus of individual interests, we should concede that every government performs certain functions which are advantageous to all. For instance, it keeps peace between groups with antagonistic interests, provides security from foreign aggression, and carries out an ever increasing number of services without which a contemporary society would degenerate into chaos within a few days. Engels himself recognized this fact (as did Marx in *The German Ideology*), although he did not allow it to modify his more extreme view of the State. He agreed that it is not possible to 'have organization without authority'—where 'authority' means the 'imposition of the will of another upon ours'—and that a certain degree of authority and subordination are things which 'independently of all social organization' are always necessary. Elsewhere Engels argued that as society grows and advances, groups of conflicting interests (not necessarily classes in the Marxian sense) arise within it and then a power becomes necessary to moderate and keep the antagonism within the bounds of social order. As John Plamenatz suggested, the proposition that the State is a necessary condition of class exploitation is nearer the truth than the other, more extreme, proposition that the State is nothing but an instrument of class rule, although only the latter provides the premise for the conclusion 'if there is no exploitation of class by class, there is no need for the State and the State disappears'.[127] As it stands, the Marxian doctrine of the State is guilty of a similar ideological distortion of social reality to the classical doctrine which described the function of the State as securing the good of society as a whole.

Even more important are the objections which can be raised against Marx's basic assumption that the political order is determined, in the qualified sense, by class relations and, in particular, by the dominant class. This proposition may be true in a polarized social world, dichotomously divided into two hostile camps. It is evident, however, that historically class relations did not evolve in this direction. Owing to the moderating influence which the improved material conditions, the extension of political and social rights, and manifest vertical social mobility have exercised on class antagonism, social classes have become, in conformity with certain Marxian class-determining criteria, less cohesive and stable groups.[128] The growing complexity of class differentiation, which blurs inter-class boundary lines, tends to invalidate the Marxian proposition that the division into the property owning class and the propertyless class is co-extensive with the division into the ruling class and the class of the ruled. Furthermore, the concept of the ruling class (in the Marxian sense) cannot be accepted uncritically, for a class never rules, irrespective of whether the bourgeoisie or the proletariat is the ruling class. Only men can govern and then the question arises as to how they are chosen and dismissed, that is, how the relationships between the rulers and the ruled are determined. These considerations make it clear that Marx's qualified proposition concerning the connection between class structure and political system leaves unsolved a large number of important problems. These problems have to be investigated by new methods because the Marxian approach provides no clue to their solution.

In the history of beliefs about the structure of society and the relationship between wealth and power two schools of thought can be distinguished. One says that wealth gives power and the other that power gives wealth. The Marxian sociology of politics belongs, in principle, to the first tradition. As far as I am aware, Ludwig Gumplowicz was first to formulate the second tradition in sociological terms. According to Gumplowicz, political power is the source of economic privileges, for private property presupposes the power to enforce obedience and to organize the social framework, of which private property is part.[129]

Universal suffrage and literacy, the appearance of large-scale political parties, the growing public and state administration, the responsibility of the government for the maintenance of economic growth, and the ever increasing use of mass media of communication tend to give precedence to political power over wealth. This precedence has been further strengthened by the new circumstances which in the last fifty years have arisen, to varying extent, all over the world and which have given to political authorities the opportunity and power of effectively altering the class structure by their own decisions. As Ossowski pointed out, in such situations social

c*

classes are no longer a spontaneous creation, but a product of human design, and 'class conflicts give way to other forms of social antagonism'.[130] If class consciousness is a necessary condition for a class 'in itself' to become a class 'for itself', and the workers or other major social groups are prevented from acquiring it by governmental decrees and other means of social control, it is the ruling groups, their composition, internal rules and ideology which come to determine class relations, instead of the former being determined by the latter. To use Aron's felicitous formulation, 'it is not the state of the productive forces but the state of the political forces . . . which is the main cause of the varying characteristics of each type of society, the cause of the rise or fall of one type of society or another'.[131]

The changes and continuing trends in this direction have given rise to the formulation of the theory of political *élites*, whose leading theorists—G. Mosca, V. Pareto, and R. Michels—are known as the Machiavellians or the realist school of political scientists. According to this theory, in all societies there are always two classes of people, a class that rules and a class that is ruled. The first class, which is a minority, monopolizes power and enjoys its advantages; the second, which constitutes an enormous majority, is directed and controlled by the first, either by legal or arbitrary means. That minorities rule majorities is a natural and inevitable occurrence; a minority is organized, for the very reason that it is a minority, and being organized is bound to dominate the unorganized majority. Only if we confuse the state of law with the state of fact and forget that the latter alone has a bearing on social reality, may we fail to see that every society is governed by an *élite*. It is the composition and structure of the *élite* that determines the political system and the level of civilization of different peoples. The changes in, and the circulation of, *élites* are two of the major factors of social change. Mosca and Pareto subscribed to a pluralistic theory of history, and it was not therefore their intention to reduce social change to the changes in, and to the circulation of, *élites*. The *élite* only determines the relation between the State and society, and through the State shapes the society itself.[132]

It is undeniable that the theory of political *élites* provides, with respect to Marx, an alternative theoretical solution of the problem concerning the relationship between power and wealth. It does not reject the Marxian approach altogether but accommodates it within its own conceptual framework, making wealth one of the main roads of access to the political class (in Mosca's sense) or political *élite*.

Different views have been taken of the relation between the two theories of power. Some believe that the Machiavellians offer a successful challenge to Marx's political sociology, for they are able to explain all facts accounted for by Marx in addition to those which must be left unexplained as long as we remain satisfied with the Marxian conceptual framework. Therefore, the *élite* theory is more comprehensive and methodologically fruitful than the Marxian theory.[133] According to others, this is an entirely unjustifiable evaluation, for the Marxian theory still retains a considerable explanatory power. Moreover, the Machiavellians misinterpret the concept of democracy and democratic forms of government in order to defend an essentially inegalitarian society. Consequently, their ideologically motivated challenge to the Marxian theory cannot be regarded as successful in reaching its objective.[134] Finally, there is the view that the Marxian theory of power and the theory of political *élites* need not be necessarily mutually exclusive. Michels, who did more than either Mosca or Pareto to examine the Marxian political sociology from the point of view of the *élite* theory, came to the conclusion that the latter 'far from conflicting with or replacing the materialist conception of history, completes that conception and reinforces it'.[135] The circulation of *élites* in Pareto's sense can best be explained by economic and social changes which Marx considered to be the primary factor of social evolution. Pareto himself indicated that 'in virtue of class-circulation, the governing *élite* is always in a state of slow and continuous transformation'.[136]

What is worth noting for our present purpose is the point on which the three assessments are in agreement. All three of them recognize that Marx made a lasting contribution to political sociology, which the alternative theory also assimilates rather than supersedes. On the other hand, they have established the point that Marx's theory of power is no longer sufficient. A decisive step forward seems to have been made by locating power in, or deriving it from, formal organizations. Since we associate power with organizations rather than with a particular kind of them, as Marx did, we can study not only power which an organization commands but also the ways in which individuals acquire power within an organization.[137] We then discover, following in the Machiavellians' footsteps, that different organizations may produce different kinds of leaders. Thus our approach to the study of power, as compared with Marx's, has been entirely changed, for we have become aware of the ubiquity of power. But if we seem to be able to see further and wider than Marx did, we owe it to the fact— which many of his present-day detractors and intellectual inferiors superciliously deny—that we all take advantage of his important insights.

## MARX'S CONTRIBUTION TO SOCIOLOGY

Marx contributed greatly to theoretical sociology but he cannot be credited with a full-fledged sociological theory.[138] His theoretical achievements can be divided into the three main categories of philosophical foundations, theoretical orientations, and a sociological conceptual framework.

Marx formulated the philosophical assumptions of the naturalistic school of thought in the social sciences. Whether a social scientist supports the naturalistic or the anti-naturalistic trend depends on his views about the nature of the subject-matter with which the social sciences are concerned. Marx was not a materialist, and he did not claim that social phenomena are ontologically reducible to or identical with physical phenomena. But he argued that the data of all sciences are obtained and investigated by the same procedures. We come to know the data in all sciences through sense experience —observation or experiment—and we organize and evaluate this knowledge by means of a common scientific method which is determined by the nature of the human organism and related to man's social and natural environment. Like all other sciences, sociology has to do with the formulation and validation of empirically significant propositions. There is no reason to separate knowledge of the physical and social or cultural world.[139]

According to Marx, society is prior to individuals and sociology is therefore prior to psychology. The social sciences are concerned with the phenomena of human interaction, that is, of the reciprocal and interdependent behaviour of individuals and groups. This assumption can be called the 'thesis of interactionism' and is today adopted by many social scientists irrespective of whether they support the naturalistic or anti-naturalistic school of thought. From this point of view, which implies an evolutionary outlook on society, society is the totality of social relations established and constantly transformed by interaction. For Marx, evolutionary change was a self-generating process, conforming to laws whose discovery was an important task of sociology. Social laws state relationships between kinds of interaction and are independent of the action of individuals. All these basic assumptions have become so familiar to successive generations of social scientists that they tend to be taken for granted.

On this naturalistic philosophical foundation are based three theoretical orientations, that is, broad postulates, admitting both a substantive and a methodological interpretation.[140] Theoretical orientations may indicate types of variables or relationships, which are considered both fruitful and indispensable for the investigation of all kinds of social phenomena. They define a general approach to, or a way of viewing society, and imply that the social scientist can ignore a certain type or types of facts only at the risk of succumbing to misleading conceptions.

The first and most important Marxian orientation is the belief that conflict is the dominant process or relationship (conflict always presupposes a relationship), and that conflict has both divisive and solidary consequences. This orientation can be described as an even more general principle of the persistence of conflict; as Max Weber put it, 'conflict cannot be excluded from social life'.[141] Individuals and groups always make rival and incompatible claims to scarce resources, to wealth, power or prestige. Progress results from the struggle between various groups. A society free from conflicts would be a stagnating or already stationary society.

The second theoretical orientation postulates a universal interdependence and, consequently, a certain kind of unity, among all the parts of any given society. Each part of a society is determined by the system to which it belongs and in turn itself determines other parts of this system. This orientation can be called the 'postulate of functionalism' because it underlies functional analysis in contemporary sociology and social anthropology. But while functional analysis overlooks or even neglects conflict altogether—for Talcott Parsons conflict is exclusively a disruptive phenomenon and a denial of social order—the postulate of functionalism is nevertheless compatible with the idea of society being based on conflicting groups. Conflict and functional dependence are two complementary aspects of one and the same process.

According to the third theoretical orientation, macro-sociological structures and laws can claim validity only within a specified period of time and, therefore, must be considered historically. A sociological description is inadequate unless it includes the historical dimension of the phenomena under investigation. As Marx himself put it, sociology, like political economy, becomes mythology when it ignores change and development.

Theoretical orientations are expressed in terms of certain key concepts which are used for the formulation of problems or applied as tools of sociological analysis. There is therefore a close connection between theoretical orientations and conceptual frameworks, and this is certainly true in the case of Marx.

The Marxian frame of reference consists of macro-sociological concepts, among which that of the economic formation of society (*ökonomische Gesellschaftsformation*) is the most fundamental. The term itself may be misleading if it is understood to imply that formations of society are forms of purely economic and industrial organization, in other words, things apart and artificially isolated from the rest of social life. While the social relations of production are basic to the structure of any society, its total formation must be effected on multiple social and cultural levels.

In the description and analysis of social formations the two concepts of productive forces, including technology, and class structure are the most significant. Since Marx considered class structure as the key to the understanding of the structure of society, the investigation of society from the standpoint of class relations constitutes the starting point of any fruitful social enquiry. The terms 'class differentiation' and 'class structure', as used by Marx, do not refer solely to the class composition of a population. They imply relations of dependence, subordination and power; and power involves material force, authority, political domination and intellectual supremacy. As the analysis of society from the standpoint of class structure covers such an extensive network of social relations, the examination of society from this point of view remains a powerful tool of sociological analysis.

The concepts of social formation, class structure and power are perhaps the most important and significant elements of the Marxian conceptual framework. But apart from these three elements, the Marxian conceptual framework also includes other concepts such as those of progress,[142] of the historically restricted scope of social laws, of ideology and social engineering ('practice' in the Marxian terminology), all of which continue to exercise a persistent and extensive influence on sociological thought.[143]

Marx's contributions to empirical sociology are frequently entirely ignored. The only exception is historical materialism but this is usually presented as a substantive theory of history and thus part of theoretical sociology. It should, however, be remembered that historical materialism is mainly, though not exclusively, a sociological doctrine for guidance in empirical investigations of society as a whole and of social change in particular.

But Marx's contribution to empirical sociology is not limited to historical materialism. Marx was one of the first social scientists who showed that such documents as reports of Inquiry Commissions or of H.M. Factory Inspectors, Parliamentary, Inland Revenue or Public Health reports, Hansard, the National Census, various statistical publications and abstracts, and finally newspapers, periodicals and even works of fiction, provide an inexhaustible wealth of sociological knowledge. In this respect Marx may have been indebted to Engels's *The Condition of the Working Class in England*; this work of distinction combined an ecological and sociographic enquiry, based on observation and the study of various documents, with a critique of society. While Marx may have been indebted to Engels and his predecessors in sociography, to such writers as Andrew Ure, John Wade or Dr J. P. Kay, he understood the importance of the empirical approach in social enquiry and suggested its extension and improvement by the introduction of new research techniques. He himself made a wide use of statistics in the validation of sociological propositions and produced, as far as I am aware, the first questionnaire (*Enquête*) which was to help in collecting 'knowledge of the conditions in which the working class lives and works'.[144]

The selections which follow are representative of all the more important elements of Marxist thought, and have been arranged in such a way as to provide a rounded, systematic and coherent picture of his contribution to the making of a science of society.

*Part One*

*The Philosophical, Sociological
and Methodological Foundations*

# (A) Philosophical Premises

## (1) PHILOSOPHY, LANGUAGE AND REALITY

For philosophers, one of the most difficult tasks is to descend from the world of thought to the actual world. *Language* is the immediate actuality of thought. Just as philosophers have given thought an independent existence, so they had to make language into an independent realm. This is the secret of philosophical language, in which thoughts in the form of words have their own content. The problem of descending from the world of thoughts to the actual world is turned into the problem of descending from language to life.

We have shown that thoughts and ideas acquire an independent existence in consequence of the personal circumstances and relations of individuals acquiring independent existence. We have shown that exclusive, systematic occupation with these thoughts on the part of ideologists and philosophers, and hence the systematization of these thoughts, is a consequence of division of labour, and that, in particular, German philosophy is a consequence of German petty-bourgeois conditions. The philosophers would only have to dissolve their language into the ordinary language, from which it is abstracted, to recognize it as the distorted language of the actual world, and to realize that neither thoughts nor language in themselves form a realm of their own, that they are only *manifestations* of actual life.

*GI*, pp. 491–2.

It is the old illusion that changing existing conditions depends only on the good will of people, and that existing conditions consist of ideas. The alteration of consciousness divorced from actual conditions—which philosophers pursue as a profession,

71

i.e., as a *trade*—is itself a product of existing conditions and inseparable from them. This ideal rising above the world is the ideological expression of the impotence of philosophers in face of the world. Practical life every day gives the lie to their ideological bragging.

*GI*, p. 414.

## (2) THE NATURAL SCIENCES AND THE NATURAL SCIENCE OF MAN

The *natural sciences* have developed a tremendous activity and have assembled an ever-growing mass of data. But philosophy has remained alien to these sciences just as they have remained alien to philosophy. Their momentary *rapprochement* was only a *fantastic* illusion. There was a desire for union but the power to effect it was lacking. Historiography itself only takes natural science into account incidentally, regarding it as a factor making for enlightenment, for practical utility and for particular great discoveries. But natural science has penetrated all the more *practically* into human life through industry. It has transformed human life and prepared the emancipation of humanity, even though its immediate effect was to accentuate the dehumanization of man. *Industry* is the actual historical relationship of nature, and thus of natural science, to man. If industry is conceived as the *exoteric* manifestation of the essential human *faculties*, the *human* essence of nature and the *natural* essence of man can also be understood. Natural science will then abandon its abstract materialist, or rather idealist, orientation, and will become the basis of a *human* science, just as it has already become—though in an alienated form—the basis of actual human life. One basis for life and another for science is *a priori* a falsehood. Nature, as it develops in human history, in the act of genesis of human society, is the *actual* nature of man; thus nature, as it develops through industry, though in an *alienated* form, is truly *anthropological* nature.

Sense experience (*see* Feuerbach) must be the basis of all science. Science is only genuine science when it proceeds from sense experience, in the two forms of *sense perception* and *sensuous need*; i.e. only when it proceeds from nature. The whole of history is a preparation for 'man' to become an object of *sense* perception, and for the development of human needs (the needs of man as such). History itself is a *real* part of *natural history*, of the development of nature into man. Natural science will one day incorporate the science of man, just as the science of man will incorporate natural science; there will be a *single* science.

Man is the direct object of natural science, because directly *perceptible nature* is for man directly human sense experience (an identical expression) in the form of the *other person* who is directly presented to him in a sensuous way. His own sense experience only exists as human sense experience for himself through the *other person*. But *nature* is the direct object of the *science of man*. The first object for man—man himself—is nature, sense experience; and the particular sensuous human faculties, which can only find objective realization in *natural* objects, can only attain self-knowledge in the science of natural being. The element of thought itself, the element of the living manifestation of thought, language, is sensuous in character. The *social* reality of nature and *human natural science*, or the *natural science of man*, are identical expressions.

*EPM*, pp. 163–4.

## (3) NATURALISTIC ANTHROPOLOGY, POLITICAL ATHEISM AND THE CRITIQUE OF SOCIETY

For Germany, the *criticism of religion* has been largely completed; and the criticism of religion is the premise of all criticism.

The *profane* existence of error is compromised once its *celestial oratio pro aris et focis* has been refuted. Man, who has found in the fantastic reality of heaven, where he sought a supernatural being, only his own reflection, will no longer be tempted to find only the *semblance* of himself—a non-human being—where he seeks and must seek his true reality.

The basis of irreligious criticism is this: *man makes religion;* religion does not make man. Religion is indeed man's self-consciousness and self-awareness so long as he has not found himself or has lost himself again. But *man* is not an abstract being, squatting outside the world. Man is *the human world*, the state, society. This state, this society, produce religion which is an *inverted world consciousness*, because they are an *inverted world*. Religion is the general theory of this world, its encyclopaedic compendium, its logic in popular form, its spiritual *point d'honneur*, its enthusiasm, its moral sanction, its solemn complement, its general basis of consolation and justification. It is *the fantastic realization* of the human being inasmuch as the *human being* possesses no true reality. The struggle against religion is, therefore, indirectly a struggle against *that world* whose spiritual *aroma* is religion.

*Religious* suffering is at the same time an *expression* of real suffering and a *protest* against real suffering. Religion is the sigh of the oppressed creature, the sentiment of a heartless world, and the soul of soulless conditions. It is the *opium* of the people.

The abolition of religion as the *illusory* happiness of men, is a demand for their *real* happiness. The call to abandon their illusions about their condition is a *call to abandon a condition which requires illusions*. The criticism of religion is, therefore, *the embryonic criticism of this vale of tears* of which religion is the *halo*.

Criticism has plucked the imaginary flowers from the chain, not in order that man shall bear the chain without caprice or consolation but so that he shall cast off the chain and pluck the living flower. The criticism of religion disillusions man so that he will think, act and fashion his reality as a man who has lost his illusions and regained his reason; so that he will revolve about himself as his own true sun. Religion is only the illusory sun about which man revolves so long as he does not revolve about himself.

It is the *task of history*, therefore, once the *other-world of truth* has vanished, to establish the *truth of this world*. The immediate *task of philosophy*, which is in the service of history, is to unmask human self-alienation in its *secular form* now that it has been unmasked in its *sacred form*. Thus the criticism of heaven is transformed into the criticism of earth, the *criticism of religion* into the *criticism of law*, and the *criticism of theology* into the *criticism of politics*.

CHPR, pp. 43-4.

It is clear that the arm of criticism cannot replace the criticism of arms. Material force can only be overthrown by material force; but theory itself becomes a material force when it has seized the masses. Theory is capable of seizing the masses when it demonstrates *ad hominem*, and it demonstrates *ad hominem* as soon as it becomes radical. To be radical is to grasp things by the root. But for man the root is man himself. What proves beyond doubt the radicalism of German theory, and thus its practical energy, is that it begins from the resolute *positive* abolition of religion. The criticism of religion ends with the doctrine that *man is the supreme being for man*. It ends, therefore, with the *categorical imperative to overthrow all those conditions* in which man is an abased, enslaved, abandoned, contemptible being—conditions which can hardly be better described than in the exclamation of a Frenchman on the occasion of a proposed tax upon dogs: 'Wretched dogs! They want to treat you like men!'

*CHPR*, p. 52.

# (4) THE PHILOSOPHICAL SOURCES OF COMMUNISM

The French Enlightenment of the eighteenth century, in particular *French materialism*, was not only a struggle against the existing political institutions and the existing religion and theology; it was just as much an *open* struggle against *metaphysics* of the *seventeenth century*, and against all metaphysics, in particular that of *Descartes, Malebranche, Spinoza and Leibniz. Philosophy* was opposed to *metaphysics*, as *Feuerbach* in his first decisive attack on *Hegel* opposed *sober philosophy* to *drunken speculation*. Seventeenth-century *metaphysics*, beaten off the field by the French Enlightenment, to be precise, by *French materialism* of the eighteenth century, was given a *victorious and solid restoration* in *German philosophy*, particularly in *speculative German philosophy* of the nineteenth century. After *Hegel* linked it in so masterly a fashion with all subsequent metaphysics and with German idealism and founded a metaphysical universal kingdom, the attack on *speculative metaphysics* and *metaphysics in general* again corresponded, as in the eighteenth century, to the attack on theology. It will be defeated for ever by *materialism* which has now been perfected by the work of *speculation* itself and coincides with *humanism*. As *Feuerbach* represented *materialism* in the *theoretical* domain, French and English *socialism* and *communism* in the *practical* field represent *materialism* which now *coincides* with *humanism*.

There are *two trends* in *French materialism*; one traces its origin to *Descartes*, the other to *Locke*. The latter is *mainly* a *French* development and leads direct to *socialism*. The former, *mechanical* materialism, merges with what is properly French *natural science*. The two trends cross in the course of development. We have no need here to go deep into French materialism, which comes direct from *Descartes*, any more than into the French *Newton* school or the development of French natural science in general.

We shall therefore just note the following:

*Descartes* in his *physics* endowed *matter* with self-creative power and conceived *mechanical* motion as the act of its life. He completely separated his *physics* from his *metaphysics*. *Within* his physics *matter* is the only *substance*, the only basis of being and of knowledge.

*Mechanical* French materialism followed *Descartes's physics* in opposition to his metaphysics. His followers were by profession *anti-metaphysicists*, i.e. *physicists*.

The school begins with the *physician Leroy*,* reaches its zenith with the physician *Cabanis*, and the physician *Lamettrie* is its centre. Descartes was still living when Leroy, like Lamettrie in the eighteenth century, transposed the Cartesian structure of *animals* to the human soul and affirmed that the soul is a *modus of the body* and *ideas* are *mechanical motions*. Leroy even thought Descartes had kept his real opinion secret. Descartes protested. At the end of the eighteenth century *Cabanis* perfected Cartesian materialism in his treatise *Rapports du physique et du moral de l'homme.* . . .

*Metaphysics* of the seventeenth century, represented in France by *Descartes*, had *materialism* as its *antagonist* from its very birth.

* The philosopher described as 'the physician Leroy' is Henricus Regius, or Henry de Roy, of Utrecht, at one time an ardent adherent of Descartes. Marx refers to Regius's book *Fundamenta Physicae* (1646) and to Descartes's repudiation of Regius's views contained in that book. See Descartes's letter to the French translator (Father Picot) of *The Principles of Philosophy*, *Oeuvres de Descartes*, publiées par C. Adam et P. Tannery, tome IX, Paris, 1905 (1647). (Z.A.J.)

It personally opposed Descartes in *Gassendi*, the restorer of *Epicurean* materialism. French and English materialism was always closely related to *Democritus* and *Epicurus*. Cartesian metaphysics had another opponent in the *English* materialist *Hobbes*. Gassendi and Hobbes were victorious over their opponent long after their death when metaphysics was already officially dominant in all French schools.

*Voltaire* observed that the indifference of Frenchmen to the disputes between Jesuits and Jansenists in the eighteenth century was due less to philosophy than to *Law's* financial speculation.* And, in fact, the downfall of seventeenth-century metaphysics can be explained by the materialistic theory of the eighteenth century only as far as that theoretical movement itself is explained by the practical nature of French life at the time. That life was turned to the immediate present, worldly enjoyment and worldly interests, the *earthly* world. Its anti-theological, anti-metaphysical, and materialistic practice demanded corresponding anti-theological, anti-metaphysical and materialistic theories. Metaphysics had *in practice* lost all credit. Here we have only to indicate briefly the *theoretical* process.

In the seventeenth century metaphysics (cf. Descartes, Leibniz, and others) still had an element of *positive*, profane content. It made discoveries in mathematics, physics and other exact sciences which seemed to come within its pale. This appearance was done away with as early as the beginning of the eighteenth century. The positive sciences broke off from it and determined their own separate fields. The whole wealth of metaphysics was reduced to beings of thought and heavenly things, although this was the very time when real beings and earthly things began to be the centre of all interest. Metaphysics had gone stale. In the very year in which Malebranche and Arnauld, the last great French metaphysicians of the seventeenth century, died, *Helvétius* and *Condillac* were born.

The man who deprived seventeenth-century metaphysics of all *credit* in the domain of *theory* was *Pierre Bayle*. His weapon was *scepticism* which he forged out of metaphysics' own magic formulae. He at first proceeded from Cartesian metaphysics. As *Feuerbach*

* John Law (1675–1729), a Scottish financier active in France, was the founder of a bank and numerous companies with interests in Louisiana, Canada and India, all of which ended in bankruptcy. (Z.A.J.)

was driven by the fight against speculative theology to the fight against *speculative philosophy* precisely because he recognized in speculation the last prop of theology, because he had to force theology to turn back from pretended science to *coarse*, repulsive *faith*, so Bayle too was driven by religious doubt to doubt about metaphysics which was the support of that faith. He therefore critically investigated metaphysics from its very origin. He became its historian in order to write the history of its death. He mainly refuted *Spinoza* and *Leibniz*.

*Pierre Bayle* did not only prepare the reception of materialism and the philosophy of common sense in France by shattering metaphysics with his scepticism. He heralded *atheistic society*, which was soon to come into existence, by *proving* that a society consisting only of atheists is *possible*, that an atheist *can* be a respectable man and that it is not by atheism but by superstition and idolatry that man debases himself.

To quote the expression of a French writer, *Pierre Bayle* was '*the last metaphysician in the seventeenth-century sense of the word and the first philosopher in the sense of the eighteenth century.*'

Besides the negative refutation of seventeenth-century theology and metaphysics, a *positive, anti-metaphysical* system was required. A book was needed which would systematize and theoretically justify the practice of life of the time. *Locke's* treatise on the origin of human reason came from across the Channel as if in answer to a call. It was welcomed enthusiastically like a long-awaited guest.

To the question 'Was *Locke* perchance a follower of *Spinoza*?' 'Profane' history may answer:

Materialism is the son *of Great Britain by birth*. Even Britain's scholastic *Duns Scotus* wondered '*Can matter think*?'

In order to bring about that miracle he had recourse to God's omnipotence, i.e. he forced *theology* itself to preach *materialism*. In addition he was a *nominalist*. Nominalism is a main component of *English* materialism and is in general the *first expression* of materialism.

The real founder of *English materialism* and all *modern experimental* science was *Bacon*. For him natural science was true science and *physics* based on perception was the most excellent part of natural science. *Anaxagoras* with his *homoeomeria* and *Democritus* with his atoms are often the authorities he refers to. According to his teaching the *senses* are infallible and are the *source* of all knowledge. Science is *experimental* and consists in applying a *rational method* to the data provided by the senses. Induction, analysis, comparison, observation and experiment are the principal requisites of rational method. The first and most important of the inherent qualities of *matter* is *motion*, not only *mechanical* and *mathematical* movement, but still more *impulse, vital life-spirit, tension*, or, to use Jacob Böhme's* expression, the *throes (Qual)* of matter. The primary forms of matter are the living, individualizing *forces of being* inherent in it and producing the distinctions between the species.

In *Bacon*, its first creator, materialism contained latent and still in a naive way the germs of all-round development. Matter smiled at man with poetical sensuous brightness. The aphoristic doctrine itself, on the other hand, was full of the inconsistencies of theology.

In its further development materialism became *one-sided*. *Hobbes* was the one who *systematized Bacon's* materialism. Sensuousness lost its bloom and became the abstract sensuousness of the *geometrician*. *Physical* motion was sacrificed to the *mechanical* or *mathematical, geometry* was proclaimed the principal science. Materialism became *hostile* to *humanity*. In order to overcome the *anti-human incorporeal* spirit in its own field, materialism itself was obliged to mortify its flesh and become an *ascetic*. It appeared as a *being of reason*, but it also developed the implacable logic of reason.

If man's senses are the source of all his knowledge, Hobbes argues, proceeding from Bacon, then conception, thought, imagination, etc., are nothing but phantoms of the material world more or less divested of its sensuous form. Science can only give a name to these phantoms. One name can be applied to several phantoms. There can even be names of names. But it would be a contradiction to say, on the one hand, that all ideas have their origin in the world of the senses and to maintain, on the other hand, that a word is more than a word, that besides the beings represented, which are always individual, there exist also general beings. An *incorporeal substance* is just as much a nonsense as an *incorporeal body. Body, being, substance*, are one and the same *real* idea. One cannot separate the thought from matter *which* thinks. Matter is the

---

* Jacob Böhme (1575–1624), a cobbler by occupation, a prominent mystic and mystical writer by vocation. (Z.A.J.)

subject of all changes. The word *infinite* is *meaningless* unless it means the capacity of our mind to go on adding without end. Since only what is material is perceptible, knowable, *nothing* is known of the existence of God. I am sure only of my own existence. Every human passion is a mechanical motion ending or beginning. The objects of impulses are what is called good. Man is subject to the same laws as nature; might and freedom are identical.

Hobbes systematized Bacon, but did not give a more precise proof of his basic principle that our knowledge and our ideas have their source in the world of the senses.

*Locke* proved the principle of Bacon and Hobbes in his essay on the origin of human reason.

Just as Hobbes did away with the *theistic* prejudices in Bacon's materialism, so Collins, Dodwell, Coward, Hartley, Priestley* and others broke down the last bounds of Locke's sensualism. For materialists, at least, deism is no more than a convenient and easy way of getting rid of religion.

We have already mentioned how opportune Locke's work was for the French. Locke founded the philosophy of *bon sens*, of common sense; i.e. he said indirectly that no philosopher can be at variance with the healthy human senses and reason based on them.

Locke's *immediate* follower, *Condillac*, who also translated him into *French*, at once opposed Locke's sensualism to seventeenth-century *metaphysics*. He proved that the French had quite rightly rejected metaphysics as the mere bungling of fancy and theological prejudice. He published a refutation of the systems of *Descartes*, *Spinoza*, *Leibniz* and *Malebranche*.

In his *Essai sur l'origine des connaissances humaines* he expounded Locke's ideas and proved that not only the soul, but the senses too, not only the art of creating ideas, but also the art of sensuous perception are matters of *experience* and *habit*. The whole development of man therefore depends on *education* and *environment*. It was only by *eclectic* philosophy that Condillac was ousted from the French schools.

The difference between *French* and *English* materialism follows

* Anthony Collins (1676–1729), an English philosopher, a friend of Locke, a deist and free thinker. Henry Dodwell (1726–1784), a deist and free-thinker. William Coward (1657–1725), a physician and free-thinker. David Hartley (1705–1757), a philosopher and founder of the associationist school in psychology. Joseph Priestley (1733–1804), a chemist and a non-conformist minister reputed for his unorthodox views. (Z.A.J.)

from the difference between the two nations. The French imparted to English materialism wit, flesh and blood, and eloquence. They gave it the temperament and grace that it lacked. They *civilized* it.

In *Helvétius*, who also based himself on Locke, materialism became really French. Helvétius conceived it immediately in its application to social life (Helvétius, *De L'homme, de ses facultés intellectuelles et de son éducation*). Sensuous qualities and self-love, enjoyment and correctly understood personal interests are the bases of moral. The natural equality of human intelligence, the unity of progress of reason and progress of industry, the natural goodness of man and the omnipotence of education are the main points in his system.

In *Lamettrie's* works we find a combination of Descartes's system and English materialism. He makes use of Descartes's physics in detail. His *Man Machine* is a treatise after the model of Descartes's beast-machine. The physical part of Holbach's *Système de la nature ou des lois du monde physique et du monde moral* is also a result of the combination of French and English materialism, while the moral part is based substantially on the moral of Helvétius. *Robinet** (De la nature*), the French materialist who had the most connection with metaphysics and was therefore praised by Hegel, refers explicitly to *Leibniz*.

We need not dwell on Volney,** Dupuis,*** Diderot and others any more than on the physiocrats, having already proved the dual origin of French materialism from Descartes's physics and English materialism, and the opposition of French materialism to seventeenth-century *metaphysics* and to the metaphysics of Descartes, Spinoza, Malebranche, and Leibniz. The Germans could not see this opposition before they came into the same opposition with *speculative metaphysics*.

As *Cartesian* materialism merges into *natural science proper*, the other branch of French materialism leads direct to *socialism* and *communism*.

* Jean Battiste Robinet (1735–1820) was a materialist and hylozoist philosopher. In *D'Alembert's Dream* Diderot adopted his views and made them widely known. (Z.A.J.)
** Constantin François de Volney (1757–1820), a French philosopher who belonged to the philosophical school of thought misleadingly called the 'idéologues'. They developed and systematized the ideas of Locke, Condillac and Helvétius. (Z.A.J.)
*** Charles Dupuis (1742–1809) was a philosopher interested in the origins of religion which he traced back to a primitive astrology. (Z.A.J.)

There is no need of any great penetration to see from the teaching of materialism on the original goodness and equal intellectual endowment of men, the omnipotence of experience, habit and education, and the influence of environment on man, the great significance of industry, the justification of enjoyment, etc., how necessarily materialism is connected with communism and socialism. If man draws all his knowledge, sensation, etc., from the world of the senses and the experience gained in it, the empirical world must be arranged so that in it man experiences and gets used to what is really human and that he becomes aware of himself as man. If correctly understood interest is the principle of all moral, man's private interest must be made to coincide with the interest of humanity. If man is unfree in the materialist sense, i.e. is free not through the negative power to avoid this or that, but through the positive power to assert his true individuality, crime must not be punished in the individual, but the anti-social source of crime must be destroyed, and each man must be given social scope for the vital manifestation of his being. If man is shaped by his surroundings, his surroundings must be made human. If man is social by nature, he will develop his true nature only in society, and the power of his nature must be measured not by the power of separate individuals but by the power of society.

This and similar propositions are to be found almost literally even in the oldest French materialists. This is not the place to assess them. *Fable of the Bees: Or Private Vices, Public Benefits*, by *Mandeville*, one of the early English followers of Locke, is typical of the social tendencies of materialism. He proves that in *modern* society vice is *indispensable* and *useful*. This was by no means an apology of modern society.

*Fourier** proceeds immediately from the teaching of the French materialists. The *Babouvists*** were coarse, uncivilized materialists, but mature communism too comes *directly* from *French materialism*. The latter returned to its mother-country, *England*, in the

---

* François-Marie Fourier (1772–1837) was a Utopian socialist writer whom Marx valued highly. (Z.A.J.)
** The Babouvists were the supporters of Babeuf's doctrine. François Noël Babeuf (1760–1797) preached the abolition of private property and organized a secret organization which was to initiate a 'Republic of Equals'. The plot was discovered and Babeuf was executed together with thirty of his supporters. (Z.A.J.)

form *Helvétius* gave it. **Bentham** based his system of *correctly understood interest* on Helvétius's moral, and **Owen** proceeded from **Bentham's** system to found English communism. Exiled to England, the Frenchman Cabet* came under the influence of communist ideas there and on his return to France became the most popular, although the most superficial, representative of communism. Like Owen, the more scientific French communist, Dézamy,** Gay and others, developed the teaching of *materialism* as the teaching of *real humanism* and the *logical* basis of *communism*.

*HF*, pp. 168–77.

# (5) THE SOCIOLOGICAL BASIS OF NEW MATERIALISM

For the *practical* materialist, i.e. the *communist*, it is a question of revolutionising the existing world, of practically attacking and changing existing things. When occasionally we find such views with Feuerbach, they are never more than isolated surmises and have much too little influence on his general outlook to be considered here as anything else than embryos capable of development. Feuerbach's 'conception' of the sensuous world is confined on the one hand to mere contemplation of it, and on the other to mere feeling; he says 'Man' instead of 'real historical man'. . . . He does not see how the sensuous world around him is, not a thing given direct from all eternity, remaining ever the same, but the product of industry and of the state of society; and, indeed, in the sense that it is an historical product, the result of the activity of a whole succession of generations, each standing on the shoulders of the preceding one, developing its industry and its intercourse, modifying its social system according to the changed needs. Even the objects of the simplest 'sensuous certainty' are only given him through social development, industry and commercial intercourse.

---

* Etienne Cabet (1788–1856), author of *Voyage en Icarie* (1842), is often described as an Utopian Communist. He emigrated to the United States where he founded a Communist settlement in Nauvoo, Illinois. For details see C. Nordhoff, *The Communistic Societies of the United States*, Dover Publications, 1966, pp. 333 ff. (Z.A.J.)
** Theodore Dézamy (1803–1850) was a journalist and supporter of Utopian Communism. (Z.A.J.)

The cherry-tree, like almost all fruit-trees, was, as is well known only a few centuries ago transplanted by *commerce* into our zone and therefore only *by* this action of a definite society in a definite age it has become 'sensuous certainty' for Feuerbach.

Incidentally, when we conceive things thus, as they really are and happened, every profound philosophical problem is resolved, as will be seen even more clearly later, quite simply into an empirical fact. For instance, the important question of the relation of man to nature . . . out of which all the 'unfathomably lofty works' on 'substance' and 'self-consciousness' were born, crumbles of itself when we understand that the celebrated 'unity of man with nature' has always existed in industry and has existed in varying forms in every epoch according to the lesser or greater development of industry, just like the 'struggle' of man with nature, right up to the development of his productive powers on a corresponding basis. Industry and commerce, production and the exchange of the necessities of life, themselves determine distribution, the structure of the different social classes and are, in turn, determined by it as to the mode in which they are carried on; and so it happens that in Manchester, for instance, Feuerbach sees only factories and machines, where a hundred years ago only spinning-wheels and weaving-looms were to be seen, or in the Campagna of Rome he finds only pasture lands and swamps, where in the time of Augustus he would have found nothing but the vineyards and villas of Roman capitalists. Feuerbach speaks in particular of the perception of natural science; he mentions secrets which are disclosed only to the eye of the physicist and chemist: but where would natural science be without industry and commerce? Even this 'pure' natural science is provided with an aim, as with its material, only through trade and industry, through the sensuous activity of men. So much is this activity, this unceasing sensuous labour and creation, this production, the basis of the whole sensuous world as it now exists, that, were it interrupted only for a year, Feuerbach would not only find an enormous change in the natural world, but would very soon find that the whole world of men and his own perceptive faculty, nay his own existence, were missing. Of course, in all this the priority of external nature remains unassailed, and all this has no application to the original men produced by *generatio aequivoca* (spontaneous generation); but this differentiation has meaning only in so far

THESES ON FEUERBACH

85

as man is considered to be distinct from nature. For that matter, nature, the nature that preceded human history, is not by any means the nature in which Feuerbach lives, not the nature which today no longer exists anywhere (except perhaps on a few Australian coral islands of recent origin) and which, therefore, does not exist for Feuerbach.

Certainly Feuerbach has a great advantage over the 'pure' materialists in that he realises how man too is an 'object of the senses'. But apart from the fact that he only conceives him as an 'object of the senses', not as 'sensuous activity', because he still remains in the realm of theory and conceives of men not in their given social connection, not under their existing conditions of life, which have made them what they are, he never arrives at the really existing active men, but stops at the abstraction 'man', and gets no further than recognising 'the true, individual, corporeal man' emotionally, i.e. he knows no other 'human relationships' 'of man to man' than love and friendship, and even then idealised. He gives no criticism of the present conditions of life. Thus he never manages to conceive the sensuous world as the total living sensuous *activity* of the individuals composing it; and therefore when, for example, he sees instead of healthy men a crowd of scrofulous, over-worked and consumptive starvelings, he is compelled to take refuge in the 'higher perception' and in the ideal 'compensation in the species', and thus to relapse into idealism at the very point where the communist materialist sees the necessity, and at the same time the condition, of a transformation both of industry and of the social structure.

As far as Feuerbach is a materialist he does not deal with history, and as far as he considers history he is not a materialist. With him materialism and history diverge completely, a fact which incidentally is already obvious from what has been said.

*GI*, pp. 56-9.

6) THESES ON FEUERBACH*

I

The chief defect of all hitherto existing materialism—that of Feuerbach included—is that the thing [*Gegenstand*], reality,

D

sensuousness, is conceived only in the form of the *object* [*Objekt*] o
of *contemplation* [*Anschauung*], but not as *human sensuous activity*
*practice*, not subjectively. Hence it happened that the *active* side
in contradistinction to materialism, was developed by idealism—
but only abstractly, since, of course, idealism does not know real
sensuous activity as such. Feuerbach wants sensuous objects, really
differentiated from the thought objects, but he does not conceive
human activity itself as *objective* [*gegenständliche*] activity. Hence
in the *Essence of Christianity*, he regards the theoretical attitude a
the only genuinely human attitude, while practice is conceived and
fixed only in its dirty-judaical form of appearance. Hence he doe
not grasp the significance of 'revolutionary', of 'practical-critical,'
activity.

## II

The question whether objective [*gegenständliche*] truth can be
attributed to human thinking is not a question of theory but is a
*practical* question. In practice man must prove the truth, that is
the reality and power, the this-sidedness [*Diesseitigkeit*] of his
thinking. The dispute over the reality or non-reality of thinking
which is isolated from practice is a purely *scholastic* question.

## III

The materialist doctrine that men are products of circumstances
and upbringing, and that, therefore, changed men are products o
other circumstances and changed upbringing, forgets that it is men
that change circumstances and that the educator himself needs
educating. Hence, this doctrine necessarily arrives at dividing
society into two parts, of which one is superior to society (in
Robert Owen, for example).

* There are two slightly different versions of the *Theses on Feuerbach*. The
first, which Marx wrote in 1845, was never published during his lifetime
Engels discovered it among Marx's papers and, since it consisted of 'notes
hurriedly scribbled down for later elaboration', edited it for publication in 188
(in the Appendix to the separate edition of his *Ludwig Feuerbach and the End
of Classical German Philosophy*). The present translation is based on Engels'
text which was checked with the manuscript of Marx. The two versions of the
*Theses on Feuerbach* in German can be found in *MEW*, B.3, and in English
translation in *The German Ideology*. (Z.A.J.)

The coincidence of the changing of circumstances and of human activity can be conceived and rationally understood only as *revolutionizing practice*.

## IV

Feuerbach starts out from the fact of religious self-alienation, the duplication of the world into a religious, imaginary world and a real one. His work consists in the dissolution of the religious world into its secular basis. He overlooks the fact that after completing this work, the chief thing still remains to be done. For the fact that the secular foundation detaches itself from itself and establishes itself in the clouds as an independent realm is really only to be explained by the self-cleavage and self-contradictoriness of this secular basis. The latter must itself, therefore, first be understood in its contradiction and then, by the removal of the contradiction, revolutionized in practice. Thus, for instance, once the earthly family is discovered to be the secret of the holy family, the former must then itself be criticized in theory and revolutionized in practice.

## V

Feuerbach, not satisfied with *abstract thinking*, appeals to *sensuous contemplation*; but he does not conceive sensuousness as *practical*, human-sensuous activity.

## VI

Feuerbach resolves the religious essence into the *human* essence. But the human essence is no abstraction inherent in each single individual. In its reality it is the ensemble of the social relations.

Feuerbach, who does not enter upon a criticism of this real essence, is consequently compelled:

(*a*) To abstract from the historical process and to fix the religious sentiment [*Gemüt*] as something by itself and to presuppose an abstract—*isolated*—human individual.

(b) The human essence, therefore, can with him be comprehended only as 'genus,' as an internal, dumb generality which
merely *naturally* unites the many individuals.

# VII

Feuerbach, consequently, does not see that the 'religious sentiment' is itself a *social product*, and that the abstract individual
whom he analyses belongs in reality to a particular form of
society.

# VIII

Social life is essentially *practical*. All mysteries which mislead
theory to mysticism find their rational solution in human practice
and in the comprehension of this practice.

# IX

The highest point attained by *contemplative* materialism, that is
materialism which does not understand sensuousness as practical
activity, is the contemplation of single individuals in 'civil society'.

# X

The standpoint of the old materialism is '*civil*' society; the
standpoint of the new is *human* society, or socialized humanity.

# XI

The philosophers have only *interpreted* the world, in various ways;
the point, however, is to *change* it.

*TF*, pp. 365–7.

# (7) PHILOSOPHY AND SOCIAL CHANGE

Philosophy, above all German philosophy, has a propensity to solitude, to systematical seclusion, to dispassionate self-contemplation which opposes it from the outset in its estrangement to the quick-witted and alive-to-events newspapers whose only delight is in information. Philosophy, taken in its systematic development, is unpopular; its secret weaving within itself seems to the layman to be an occupation as overstrained as it is unpractical; it is considered as a professor of magic whose incantations sound pompous because they are unintelligible.

Philosophy, in accordance with its character, has never made the first step towards replacing the ascetic priestly vestments by the light conventional garb of the newspapers. But philosophers do not grow out of the soil like mushrooms, they are the product of their time and of their people, whose most subtle, precious and invisible sap circulates in philosophical ideas. The same spirit that builds railways by the hands of the workers builds philosophical systems in the brain of the philosophers. Philosophy does not stand outside the world any more than man's brain is outside of him because it is not in his stomach; but, of course, philosophy is in the world with its brain before it stands on the earth with its feet, whereas many another human sphere has long been rooted in the earth by its feet and plucks the fruits of the world with its hands before it has any idea that the 'head' also belongs to the world or that this world is the world of the head.

Because every true philosophy is the spiritual quintessence of its time, the time must come when philosophy not only internally by its content but externally by its appearance comes into contact and mutual reaction with the real contemporary world. Philosophy then ceases to be a definite system in presence of other definite systems, it becomes philosophy generally, in presence of the world, it becomes the philosophy of the world of the present. The formal features which attest that philosophy has achieved that importance, that it is the living soul of culture, that philosophy is becoming worldly and the world philosophical, were the same in all times: any history book will show, repeated with stereotyped fidelity, the simplest rituals which unmistakably mark philosophy's introduction into drawing-rooms and priests' studies, the editorial offices of newspapers and the antichambers of courts, into the hatred and the love of the people of the time. Philosophy is introduced into the world by the clamour of its enemies who betray their internal infection by their desperate appeals for help against the blaze of ideas. These cries of its enemies mean as much for philosophy as the first cry of a child for the anxious ear of the mother, they are the cry of life of the ideas which have burst open the orderly hieroglyphic husk of the system and become citizens of the world.

*LAKZ*, pp. 30–1.

# (B)  *Sociological Premises*

## (1) THE PRINCIPLE OF EMPIRICISM

The premises from which we begin are not arbitrary ones, not dogmas, but real premises from which abstraction can only be made in the imagination. They are the real individuals, their activity and the material conditions under which they live, both those which they find already existing and those produced by their activity. These premises can thus be verified in a purely empirical way.

The first premise of all human history is, of course, the existence of living human individuals.[1] Thus the first fact to be established is the physical organization of these individuals and their consequent relation to the rest of nature. Of course, we cannot here go either into the actual physical nature of man, or into the natural conditions in which man finds himself—geological, oro-hydrographical,* climatic and so on.[2] The writing of history must always

---

* 'Oro-hydrographical conditions' means conditions determined by mountains and seas, rivers and other water. (Z.A.J.)
[1] (The following passage is crossed out in the manuscript:) The first *historical* act of these individuals distinguishing them from animals is not that they think, but that they begin to *produce their means of subsistence*.
[2] (The following passage is crossed out in the manuscript:) Not only the original, spontaneous organization of men, especially racial differences, depends on these conditions but also the entire further development, or lack of development, of men up to the present time.

set out from these natural bases and their modification in the course of history through the action of men.

Men can be distinguished from animals by consciousness, by religion or anything else you like. They themselves begin to distinguish themselves from animals as soon as they begin to *produce* their means of subsistence, a step which is conditioned by their physical organization. By producing their means of subsistence men are indirectly producing their actual material life.

The way in which men produce their means of subsistence depends first of all on the nature of the actual means of subsistence they find in existence and have to reproduce. This mode of production must not be considered simply as being the reproduction of the physical existence of the individuals. Rather it is a definite form of activity of these individuals, a definite form of expressing their life, a definite *mode of life* on their part. As individuals express their life, so they are. What they are, therefore, coincides with their production, both with *what* they produce and with *how* they produce. The nature of individuals thus depends on the material conditions determining their production.

This production only makes its appearance with the *increase of population*. In its turn this presupposes the *intercourse* [*Verkehr*] of individuals with one another. The form of this intercourse is again determined by production.

The relations of different nations among themselves depend upon the extent to which each has developed its productive forces, the division of labour and internal intercourse. This statement is generally recognized. But not only the relation of one nation to others, but also the whole internal structure of the nation itself depends on the stage of development reached by its production and its internal and external intercourse. How far the productive forces of a nation are developed is shown most manifestly by the degree to which the division of labour has been carried. Each new productive force, in so far as it is not merely a quantitative extension of productive forces already known (for instance the bringing into cultivation of fresh land), causes a further development of the division of labour.

The division of labour inside a nation leads at first to the separation of industrial and commercial from agricultural labour, and hence to the separation of *town* and *country* and to the conflict of their interests. Its further development leads to the separation of commercial from industrial labour. At the same time through the division of labour inside these various branches there develop various divisions among the individuals co-operating in definite kinds of labour. The relative position of these individual groups is determined by the methods employed in agriculture, industry and commerce (patriarchalism, slavery, estates, classes). These same conditions are to be seen (given a more developed inter-course) in the relations of different nations to one another.

The various stages of development in the division of labour are just so many different forms of ownership, i.e. the existing stage in the division of labour determines also the relations of individuals to one another with reference to the material, instru-ment, and product of labour.

*GI*, pp. 31–3.

The fact is . . . that definite individuals who are productively active in a definite way enter into these definite social and political relations. Empirical observation must in each separate instance bring out empirically, and without any mystification and specula-tion, the connection of the social and political structure with production. The social structure and the State are continually evolving out of the life-process of definite individuals, but of individuals, not as they may appear in their own or other people's imagination, but as they *really* are; i.e., as they operate, produce materially, and hence as they work under definite material limits, presuppositions and conditions independent of their will.[1]

The production of ideas, of conceptions, of consciousnesss, is at first directly interwoven with the material activity and the material intercourse of men, the language of real life. Conceiving,

---

[1] (The following passage is crossed out in the manuscript:) The ideas which these individuals form are ideas either about their relation to nature or about their mutual relations or about their own nature. It is evident that in all these cases their ideas are the conscious expression—real or illusory—of their real relationships and activities, of their production and intercourse and of their social and political organization. The opposite assumption is only possible if in addition to the spirit of the real, materially evolvéd individuals a separate spirit is presupposed. If the conscious expression of the real relations of these indivi-duals is illusory, if in their imagination they turn reality upside-down, then this in its turn is the result of the limited material mode of activity and their limited social relations arising from it.

thinking, the mental intercourse of men, appear at this stage as the direct efflux of their material behaviour. The same applies to mental production as expressed in the language of politics, laws, morality, religion, metaphysics, etc., of a people. Men are the producers of their conceptions, ideas, etc.—real, active men, as they are conditioned by a definite development of their productive forces and of the intercourse corresponding to these, up to its furthest forms. Consciousness can never be anything else than conscious existence, and the existence of men is their actual life-process. If in all ideology men and their circumstances appear upside-down as in a *camera obscura*, this phenomenon arises just as much from their historical life-process as the inversion of objects on the retina does from their physical life-process.

In direct contrast to German philosophy which descends from heaven to earth, here we ascend from earth to heaven. That is to say, we do not set out from what men say, imagine, conceive, nor from men as narrated, thought of, imagined, conceived, in order to arrive at men in the flesh. We set out from real, active men, and on the basis of their real life-process we demonstrate the development of the ideological reflexes and echoes of this life-process. The phantoms formed in the human brain are also, necessarily, sublimates of their material life-process, which is empirically verifiable and bound to material premises. Morality, religion, metaphysics, all the rest of ideology and their corresponding forms of consciousness, thus no longer retain the semblance of independence. They have no history, no development; but men, developing their material production and their material intercourse, alter, along with this their real existence, their thinking and the products of their thinking. Life is not determined by consciousness, but consciousness by life. In the first method of approach the starting-point is consciousness taken as the living individual; in the second method, which conforms to real life, it is the real living individuals themselves, and consciousness is considered solely as *their* consciousness.

This method of approach is not devoid of premises. It starts out from the real premises and does not abandon them for a moment. Its premises are men, not in any fantastic isolation and rigidity, but in their actual, empirically perceptible process of development under definite conditions. As soon as this active life-process is described, history ceases to be a collection of dead facts

D*

as it is with the empiricists (themselves still abstract), or an imagined activity of imagined subjects, as with the idealists.

Where speculation ends—in real life—there real, positive science begins: the representation of the practical activity, of the practical process of development of men. Empty talk about consciousness ceases, and real knowledge has to take its place. When reality is depicted, philosophy as an independent branch of knowledge loses its medium of existence. At the best its place can only be taken by a summing-up of the most general results, abstractions which arise from the observation of the historical development of men. Viewed apart from real history, these abstractions have in themselves no value whatsoever. They can only serve to facilitate the arrangement of historical material, to indicate the sequence of its separate strata. But they by no means afford a recipe or schema, as does philosophy, for neatly trimming the epochs of history. On the contrary, our difficulties begin only when we set about the observation and the arrangement—the real depiction—of our historical material, whether of a past epoch or of the present. The removal of these difficulties is governed by premises which it is quite impossible to state here, but which only the study of the actual life-process and the activity of the individuals of each epoch will make evident.

*GI*, pp. 36–9.

## (2) HISTORY AS THE STUDY OF SOCIAL EVOLUTION

We must begin by stating the first premise of all human existence and, therefore, of all history, the premise, namely, that men must be in a position to live in order to be able to 'make history'. But life involves before everything else eating and drinking, a habitation, clothing and many other things. The first historical act is thus the production of the means to satisfy these needs, the production of material life itself. And indeed this is an historical act, a fundamental condition of all history, which today, as thousands of years ago, must daily and hourly be fulfilled merely in order to sustain human life. . . . Therefore in any interpretation of history one has first of all to observe this fundamental fact in all its significance and all its implications and to accord it its due importance. It is well known that the Germans have never done this, and they have never, therefore, had an *earthly* basis for history and consequently never a historian. The French and the English, even if they have conceived the relation of this fact with so-called history only in an extremely one-sided fashion, particularly as long as they remained in the toils of political ideology, have nevertheless made the first attempts to give the writing of history a materialistic basis by being the first to write histories of civil society, of commerce and industry.

The second point is that the satisfaction of the first need (the action of satisfying, and the instruments of satisfaction which has been acquired) leads to new needs; and this production of new needs is the first historical act. Here we recognize immediately the spiritual ancestry of the great historical wisdom of the Germans who, when they run out of positive material and when they can serve up neither theological nor political nor literary rubbish, assert that this is not history at all, but the 'prehistoric era'. They do not, however, enlighten us as to how we proceed from this nonsensical 'prehistory' to history proper; although, on the other hand, in their historical speculation they seize upon this 'prehistory' with especial eagerness because they imagine themselves safe there from interference on the part of 'crude facts', and, at the same time, because there they can give full rein to their speculative impulse and set up and knock down hypotheses by the thousand.

The third circumstance which, from the very outset, enters into historical development, is that men, who daily remake their own life, begin to make other men, to propagate their kind: the relation between man and woman, parents and children, the *family*. The family, which to begin with is the only social relationship, becomes later, when increased needs create new social relations and the increased population new needs, a subordinate one (except in Germany), and must then be treated and analysed according to the existing empirical data, not according to 'the concept of the family', as is the custom in Germany.[1] These three aspects of social

1 The building of houses. With savages each family has as a matter of course its own cave or hut like the separate family tent of the nomads. This separate domestic economy is made only the more necessary by the further development of private property. With the agricultural peoples a communal domestic economy is just as impossible as a communal cultivation of the soil. A great advance was the building of towns. In all previous periods, however, the abolition of individual economy, which is inseparable from the abolition of private

activity are not of course to be taken as three different stages, but just as three aspects or, to make it clear to the Germans, three 'moments', which have existed simultaneously since the dawn of history and the first men, and which still assert themselves in history today.

The production of life, both of one's own in labour and of fresh life in procreation, now appears as a double relationship: on the one hand as a natural, on the other as a social relationship. By social we understand the co-operation of several individuals, no matter under what conditions, in what manner and to what end. It follows from this that a certain mode of production, or industrial stage, is always combined with a certain mode of co-operation, or social stage, and this mode of co-operation is itself a 'productive force'. Further, that the multitude of productive forces accessible to men determines the nature of society, hence, that the 'history of humanity' must always be studied and treated in relation to the history of industry and exchange. But it is also clear how in Germany it is impossible to write this sort of history, because the Germans lack not only the necessary power of comprehension and the material but also the 'evidence of their senses', for across the Rhine you cannot have any experience of these things since history has stopped happening. Thus it is quite obvious from the start that there exists a materialistic connection of men with one another, which is determined by their needs and their mode of production, and which is as old as men themselves. This connection is ever taking on new forms, and thus presents a 'history' independently of the existence of any political or religious nonsense which would especially hold men together.

Only now, after having considered four moments, four aspects of the primary historical relationships, do we find that man also

property, was impossible for the simple reason that the material conditions governing it were not present. The setting-up of a communal domestic economy presupposes the development of machinery, of the use of natural forces and of many other productive forces, e.g., of water-supplies, of gas-lighting, steam-heating, etc., the removal (of the antagonism) of town and country. Without these conditions a communal economy would not in itself form a new productive force; lacking any material basis and resting on a purely theoretical foundation, it would be a mere freak and would end in nothing more than a monastic economy.—What was possible can be seen in the towns brought about by condensation and the erection of communal buildings for various definite purposes (prisons, barracks, etc.). That the abolition of individual economy is inseparable from the abolition of the family is self-evident.

possesses 'consciousness';[1] but, even so, not inherent, not 'pure' consciousness. From the start the 'spirit' is afflicted with the curse of being 'burdened' with matter, which here makes its appearance in the form of agitated layers of air, sounds, in short, of language. Language is as old as consciousness, language *is* practical consciousness that exists also for other men, and for that reason alone it really exists for me personally as well; language, like consciousness, only arises from the need, the necessity, of intercourse with other men.[2] Where there exists a relationship, it exists for me: the animal does not enter into '*relations*' with anything, it does not enter into any relation at all. For the animal, its relation to others does not exist as a relation. Consciousness is, therefore, from the very beginning a social product, and remains so as long as men exist at all. Consciousness is at first, of course, merely consciousness concerning the *immediate* sensuous environment and consciousness of the limited connection with other persons and things outside the individual who is growing self-conscious. At the same time it is consciousness of nature, which first appears to men as a completely alien, all-powerful and unassailable force, with which men's relations are purely animal and by which they are overawed like beasts; it is thus a purely animal consciousness of nature (natural religion).

We see here immediately: this natural religion or this particular relation of men to nature is determined by the form of society and vice versa. Here, as everywhere, the identity of nature and man appears in such a way that the restricted relation of men to nature determines their restricted relation to one another, and their restricted relation to one another determines men's restricted relation to nature, just because nature is as yet hardly modified historically; and, on the other hand, man's consciousness of the necessity of associating with the individuals around him is the beginning of the consciousness that he is living in society at all. This beginning is as animal as social life itself at this stage. It is mere herd-consciousness, and at this point man is only distinguished from sheep by the fact that with him consciousness takes

[1] (Marginal note by Marx:) Men have history because they must *produce* their life, and because they must produce it moreover in a *certain* way: this is determined by their physical organization; their consciousness is determined in just the same way.

[2] (The following words are crossed out in the manuscript:) My relationship to my surroundings is my consciousness.

the place of instinct or that his instinct is a conscious one. This sheep-like or tribal consciousness receives its further development and extension through increased productivity, the increase of needs, and, what is fundamental to both of these, the increase of population. With these there develops the division of labour, which was originally nothing but the division of labour in the sexual act, then that division of labour which develops spontaneously or 'naturally' by virtue of natural predisposition (e.g., physical strength), needs, accidents, etc., etc. Division of labour only becomes truly such from the moment when a division of material and mental labour appears.[1] From this moment onwards consciousness *can* really flatter itself that it is something other than consciousness of existing practice, that it *really* represents something without representing something real; from now on consciousness is in a position to emancipate itself from the world and to proceed to the formation of 'pure' theory, theology, philosophy, ethics, etc. But even if this theory, theology, philosophy, ethics, etc., comes into contradiction with the existing relations, this can only occur because existing social relations have come into contradiction with existing forces of production; this, moreover, can also occur in a particular national sphere of relations through the appearance of the contradiction, not within the national orbit, but between this national consciousness and the practice of other nations,[2] i.e., between the national and the general consciousness of a nation (as we see it now in Germany).

Moreover, it is quite immaterial what consciousness starts to do on its own: out of all such muck we get only the one inference that these three moments, the forces of production, the state of society, and consciousness, can and must come into contradiction with one another, because the *division of labour* implies the possibility, nay the fact, that intellectual and material activity—enjoyment and labour, production and consumption—devolve on different individuals, and that the only possibility of their not coming into contradiction lies in the negation in its turn of the division of labour. It is self-evident, moreover, that 'spectres', 'bonds', 'the higher being', 'concept', 'scruple', are merely the idealistic, spiritual expression, the conception apparently of the isolated individual, the image of very empirical fetters and limitations, within which the

[1] (Marginal note by Marx:) The first form of ideologists, *priests*, is concurrent.
[2] (Marginal note by Marx:) *Religion*. The Germans and *ideology* as such.

mode of production of life and the form of intercourse coupled with it move.

With the division of labour, in which all these contradictions are implicit, and which in its turn is based on the natural division of labour in the family and the separation of society into individual families opposed to one another, is given simultaneously the *distribution*, and indeed the *unequal* distribution, both quantitative and qualitative, of labour and its products, hence property: the nucleus, the first form, of which lies in the family, where wife and children are the slaves of the husband. This latent slavery in the family, though still very crude, is the first property, but even at this early stage it corresponds perfectly to the definition of modern economists who call it the power of disposing of the labour-power of others. Division of labour and private property are, moreover, identical expressions: in the one the same thing is affirmed with reference to activity as is affirmed in the other with reference to the product of the activity.

*GI*, pp. 39–44.

## (3) THE INDIVIDUAL AND SOCIETY

Social activity and social mind by no means exist *only* in the form of activity or mind which is directly communal. Nevertheless, communal activity and mind, i.e. activity and mind which express and confirm themselves directly in a *real association* with other men, occur everywhere where this direct expression of sociability arises from the content of the activity or corresponds to the nature of mind.

Even when I carry out *scientific* work, etc., an activity which I can seldom conduct in direct association with other men, I perform a *social*, because *human*, act. It is not only the material of my activity—such as the language itself which the thinker uses— which is given to me as a social product. My *own existence* is a social activity. For this reason, what I myself produce I produce for society, and with the consciousness of acting as a social being. . . .

It is above all necessary to avoid postulating 'society' once again as an abstraction confronting the individual. The individual *is* the *social being*. The manifestation of his life—even when it does not appear directly in the form of a communal manifestation, accomplished in association with other men—is, therefore, a manifestation and affirmation of *social life*. Individual human life and species-life are not different things, even though the mode of existence of individual life is necessarily either a more *specific* or a more *general* mode of species-life, or that of species-life a *specific* or more *general* mode of individual life.

*EPM*, pp. 157–8.


Individuals have always and in all circumstances 'started out *from themselves*', but since they were not *unique* in the sense of not needing any connections with one another, and since their *needs*, consequently their nature and the method of satisfying their needs, connected them with one another (relations between the sexes, exchange, division of labour), they *had to* enter into relations with one another. Further, since they entered into association with one another not as pure Egos, but as individuals at a definite stage of development of their productive forces and requirements, and since this association, in its turn, determined production and needs, it was, therefore, precisely the personal, individual behaviour of individuals, their behaviour to one another as individuals, that created the existing conditions and daily reproduces them anew. They entered into association with one another as what they were, they started out 'from themselves', as they were, irrespective of their 'outlook on life'. This 'outlook on life'—even the warped one of the philosophers—could, of course, only be determined by their actual life. Hence it certainly follows that the development of an individual is determined by the development of all the others with whom he is directly or indirectly associated, and that the different generations of individuals entering into relation with one another are connected with one another, that the physical existence of the later generations is determined by that of their predecessors, and that these later generations inherit the productive forces and forms of association accumulated by their predecessors, their own mutual relations being determined thereby. In short, it is clear that a development occurs and that the history of a single individual cannot possibly be separated from the history of preceding or contemporary individuals, but is determined by this history.

*GI*, pp. 481–2.

To begin with, the subject of our enquiry concerns *material production*. The starting point is naturally individuals producing in society, and hence the socially determined production by individuals. The individual and isolated hunter or fisherman who forms the starting point with Smith and Ricardo, belongs to the insipid illusions of the eighteenth century. They are Robinsonades which do not by any means represent, as historians of culture imagine, a reaction against over-refinement and a return to a misrepresented natural life. They are no more based on such naturalism than is Rousseau's *contrat social* which by means of a contract brings individuals, independent of each other by nature, into mutual relation and connection. They are the fiction and only the aesthetic fiction of the small and great Robinsonades. They are, moreover, the anticipation of 'bourgeois society', which had been in the course of development since the sixteenth century and had made gigantic strides towards maturity in the eighteenth. In this society of free competition the individual appears free from the bonds of nature, etc., which in former epochs of history made him a part of a definite, limited human aggregation. To the prophets of the eighteenth century, on whose shoulders Smith and Ricardo are still standing, this eighteenth-century individual, constituting the joint product of the dissolution of the feudal form of society and of the new forces of production which had developed since the sixteenth century, appears as an ideal whose existence belongs to the past; not as a result of history, but as its starting point. Since that individual appeared to be in conformity with nature, according to their conception of human nature, he was not a product of history, but of nature. This illusion has been characteristic of every new epoch in the past. Stcuart,* who in certain respects opposed the eighteenth century and, as an aristocrat, stood more firmly on historical ground, escaped this simplicity of view.

The further back we go into history, the more the individual and, therefore, the producing individual seems to depend on and constitute a part of a larger whole: at first it is, quite naturally, the family and the clan,** which is but an enlarged family; later on, it is the community growing up in its different forms out of the clash

* Sir James Steuart (1712–1780), whose *Inquiry into the Principles of Political Oeconomy* (1767) Marx carefully studied. (Z.A.J.)
** For Marx's analysis of the social and economic organization of the Scottish-Gaelic clans see 'Election—Financial Clouds—The Duchess of Sutherland and Slavery', *NYDT*, 9 February 1853. (Z.A.J.)

and the amalgamation of clans. It is but in the eighteenth century, in 'bourgeois society', that the different forms of social bond confront the individual as a mere means to his private ends, as an outward necessity. But the period in which this view of the isolated individual becomes prevalent, is the very one in which the social relations (general from this point view) have reached the highest state of development. Man is in the most literal sense of the word a *zoon politikon*, not only a social animal, but an animal which can develop into an individual only in society. Production by isolated individuals outside society—something which might happen exceptionally to a civilized man who by accident got into the wilderness and already potentially possessed within himself the forces of society—is as great an absurdity as the idea of the development of language without individuals living together and talking to one another.* We need not dwell on this any longer. It would not be necessary to touch upon this point at all, were not the vagary which had some justification and significance with respect to the people of the eighteenth century transplanted in all earnest into the field of the contemporary political economy by Bastiat, Carey, Proudhon and others.** Proudhon and others naturally find it very pleasant, when they do not know the historical origin of a certain economic relation, to give it a historico-philosophical explanation by going into mythology. Adam or Prometheus hit upon the scheme cut and dried, whereupon it was adopted, etc. Nothing is more tediously dry than indulging in fancies *locus communis*.

*GKPÖ*, pp. 5–6; *CPE-I*, pp. 265–8 [revised translation]

* Marx's view about language seems to have been shared by other thinkers at the beginning of the nineteenth century. For instance, according to M. de Bonald, language could not have been invented by an individual nor a group of individuals, for a human society could no more exist without language than a human individual without society (de Bonald used this argument to support his theistic metaphysics). See M. de Bonald, *Recherches philosophiques sur les premiers objets des connaissances morales*, Oeuvres de M. de Bonald, Paris, 1882, pp. 60 ff. (I owe this observation to my colleague, Mr J. A. Beckford). The view about the social origin and the importance of language for the very existence of human society was later forgotten by the so-called comparative philologists and was rediscovered by such social anthropologists as E. Sapir and B. Malinowski (Z.A.J.)
** Frédéric Bastiat (1801–1850), a French economist, a friend of Cobden and a supporter of free trade; Henry Charles Carey (1793–1879), an American economist; Pierre-Joseph Proudhon (1809–1865), the founder of anarchic socialism; all are writers whose views Marx frequently criticized. (Z.A.J.)

# (4) THE SOCIAL WORLD IS A MAN-MADE WORLD

Nothing is more inaccurate than the way in which the economists as well as the Socialists examine society with regard to its economic conditions. For instance, Proudhon says against Bastiat that 'for society there is no difference between capital and product. For the individuals this difference is entirely subjective'.[1] Thus, he calls precisely the social—subjective, and the subjective abstraction —society. The difference between product and capital consists precisely in the fact that product as capital signifies a definite relation which belongs to a historical form of society. The so-called enquiry from the standpoint of society simply amounts to overlooking the differences which precisely express social relations (the relations of the bourgeois society). Society does not consist of individuals but it represents the sum of relations, in which these individuals stand to each other, and of the connections between them.* As if anyone would ever say: from the standpoint of society there are no slaves and no citizens; they are both men. On the contrary, they are men outside society. To be a slave and to be a citizen are social determinations, the relationships of men A and B. Man A as such is not a slave. He is a slave in and through society. What Proudhon maintains here about capital and product means, according to him, that from the standpoint of society there is no difference between capitalists and workers, a difference which exists precisely from the standpoint of society only.

*GKPÖ*, pp. 175–6.

# (5) THE SOCIAL NATURE OF PRODUCTION AND THE HISTORICAL CHARACTER OF SOCIAL LAWS

All production is appropriation of nature by the individual within and through a definite form of society. In that sense it is a taut-

---

* 'Society, that is, the man in his social relations' (*GKPÖ*, p. 600). (Z.A.J.)
[1] F. Bastiat et P.-J. Proudhon, *Gratuité du crédit. Discussion entre M. Fr. Bastiat et M. Proudhon*, Paris, 1850.

ology* to say that property (appropriation) is a condition of production. But it becomes ridiculous, when from that one jumps at once to a definite form of property, *e.g.*, private property (which implies, besides, as a prerequisite the existence of an opposite form, viz., absence of property). History points rather to common property (*e.g.*, among the Hindoos, Slavs, ancient Celts, etc.) as the primitive form, which still plays an important part at a much later period as communal property. The question as to whether wealth grows more rapidly under this or that form of property, is not even raised here as yet. But that there can be no such a thing as production, nor, consequently, society, where property does not exist in any form, is a tautology. Appropriation which does not appropriate is a *contradictio in subjecto*.

*GKPÖ*, p. 9; *CPE-I*, p. 273.

Whenever we speak . . . of production, we always have in mind production at a certain stage of social development, production by social individuals. Hence, it might seem that in order to speak of production at all, we must either trace the historical process of development through its various phases, or declare at the outset that we are dealing with a certain historical period, e.g., with modern capitalistic production which, as a matter of fact, con-stitutes the subject proper of this work. But all periods of produc-tion have certain characteristics in common, that is, common determining attributes. *Production in general* is an abstraction, but it is an intelligible abstraction, in so far as it singles out and fixes the common features, thereby saving us repetition. However, these general features which have been abstracted by comparison as common to all, are themselves a highly articulated structure that can be divided into various attributes. Some of these attributes belong to all periods, others are common to a few. Some of them are common to the most modern as well as to the most ancient periods. No production is conceivable without them; but while even the most completely developed languages have laws and attributes in common with the least developed ones, what is

---

* Marx uses the word 'tautology' but means what we now call 'analytical propo-sition', that is, a proposition which is true or false by virtue of the meaning of the words which occur in it. An analytical proposition is a proposition about language and has no empirical significance. (Z.A.J.)

characteristic of their development is the points of departure from the general and common. The attributes which govern production at a given time must be distinguished from the general ones in order to avoid losing sight of the essential points of difference. This general uniformity is due to the fact that the subject, mankind, and the object, nature, remain the same. The failure to remember this one fact is the source of all the wisdom of modern economists who are trying to prove the eternal nature and harmony of existing social conditions. Thus they say, e.g., that no production is possible without some instruments of production, let that instrument be only the hand; that none is possible without past accumulated labour, even if that labour consists of mere skill which has been accumulated and concentrated in the hand of the savage by repeated exercise. Capital is, among other things, also an instrument of production, also past objectified labour. Hence capital is a universal, eternal natural relation which is true if we disregard the specific properties which turn an 'instrument of production' and 'stored up labour' into capital. The entire history of the relations of production appears to a man like Carey, e.g., as a malicious perversion for which governments are responsible.

*GKPÖ*, pp. 6–7; *CPE-I*, pp. 268–70 [revised translation].

# (C)  *The Methodological Rules*

## (1) THE METHOD OF POLITICAL ECONOMY

When we consider a given country from the standpoint of political economy, we begin with population and its division into classes, its distribution in urban, rural and maritime areas and in various branches of production; then we study its exports and imports, annual production and consumption, price of commodities, and so forth.

The correct procedure seems to involve commencing with the real and concrete, with the objectively valid assumptions of any problem. For instance, in the case of political economy, one would begin with population which is the basis and the agent responsible for the entire process of social production. However, on closer examination this proves to be wrong. Population is an abstraction if we ignore, e.g., the classes of which it consists. These classes, again, are but empty words unless we know what the elements are on which they are based, such as wage-labour, capital, etc. These imply, in their turn, exchange, division of labour, prices, etc. For instance, capital does not mean anything without wage-labour, value, money, price, etc. If we start out, therefore, with population, we have only a chaotic conception of the whole, but by dividing it into less comprehensive attributes we will analytically arrive at progressively simpler concepts; thus we shall be proceeding from what was perceived as concrete to finer and finer abstractions until we get at the simplest attributes. At this point, we would start on our return journey until we finally came back to population, but this time not as a chaotic conception of a whole, but as a rich totality of many attributes and relations. The former method is the one which, historically speaking, political economy adopted at its inception. For instance, the economists of the seventeenth century always started out with the living whole, with population, nation, State, several States, and so forth, but in the end they invariably discovered, by means of analysis, certain determining, abstract and general relations, such as division of labour, money, value, etc. As soon as these separate aspects had been more or less established by abstraction, there arose the system of political economy which started from simple conceptions, such as labour, division of labour, demand, exchange value, and concluded with State, international exchange and world market. Clearly the latter method is scientifically correct. The concrete is concrete, because it is composed of many attributes, i.e., it is a unity of manifold elements. In our thought, it therefore appears as a process of synthesis, as a result, and not as a starting point, although it is the actual starting point and, therefore, also the origin of perception and general ideas. In the former method the complete conception passes into an abstract attribute; in the latter, the abstract attributes lead to the reconstruction of the concrete subject in the course of reasoning. Hegel succumbed to the illusion, therefore, of considering the real as the result of self-concentrated, self-absorbed and spontaneously operating thought, while the method of advancing from the abstract to the concrete is but a way of thinking by which the concrete is grasped and is reconstructed in our mind as a concrete. It is by no means, however, the process which itself generates the concrete. For instance, the simplest economic category, say, exchange value, implies the existence of population, and more significantly a population that is producing under certain relations of production; it also implies the existence of certain types of family, community or State, etc. It can have no other existence except as an abstract partial relation (*einseitige Beziehung*) within an already given concrete and living whole.

*GKPÖ*, pp. 21–2; *CPE-I*, pp. 292–4 [revised translation].

## (2) THE NATURE OF SOCIAL ENQUIRY AND SOCIAL LAWS

Every beginning is difficult, holds in all sciences. To understand the first chapter, especially the section that contains the analysis of commodities, will, therefore, present the greatest difficulty. That which concerns more especially the analysis of the substance of value and the magnitude of value, I have, as much as it was possible, popularized.[1] The value-form, whose full developed shape is the money-form, is very elementary and simple. Nevertheless, the human mind has for more than 2,000 years sought in vain to get to the bottom of it, whilst on the other hand, to the successful analysis of much more composite and complex forms, there has been at least an approximation. Why? Because the body, as an organic whole, is more easy of study than are the cells of that body. In the analysis of economic forms, moreover, neither microscopes nor chemical reagents are of use. The force of abstraction must replace both. But in bourgeois society the commodity-form of the product of labour—or the value-form of the commodity—is the

[1] This is the more necessary, as even the section of Ferdinand Lassalle's work against Schulze-Delitzsch, in which he professes to give 'the intellectual quintessence' of my explanations on these subjects, contains important mistakes. If Ferdinand Lassalle has borrowed almost literally from my writings, and without any acknowledgment, all the general theoretical propositions in his economic works, e.g., those on the historical character of capital, on the connection between the conditions of production and the mode of production, &c., &c., even to the terminology created by me, this may perhaps be due to purposes of propaganda. I am here, of course, not speaking of his detailed working out and application of these propositions, with which I have nothing to do.

economic cell-form. To the superficial observer, the analysis of
these forms seems to turn upon minutiae. It does in fact deal with
minutiae, but they are of the same order as those dealt with in
microscopic anatomy.

With the exception of the section on value-form, therefore, this
volume cannot stand accused on the score of difficulty. I presuppose, of course, a reader who is willing to learn something new
and therefore to think for himself.

The physicist either observes physical phenomena where they
occur in their most typical form and most free from disturbing
influence, or, wherever possible, he makes experiments under conditions that assure the occurrence of the phenomenon in its nor-
mality. In this work I have to examine the capitalist mode of
production, and the conditions of production and exchange
corresponding to that mode. Up to the present time, their classic
ground is England. That is the reason why England is used as the
chief illustration in the development of my theoretical ideas. If,
however, the German reader shrugs his shoulders at the condition
of the English industrial and agricultural labourers, or in optimist
fashion comforts himself with the thought that in Germany things
are not nearly so bad, I must plainly tell him: *De te fabula
narratur!*\*

Intrinsically, it is not a question of the higher or lower degree
of development of the social antagonisms that result from the
natural laws of capitalist production. It is a question of these laws
themselves, of these tendencies working with iron necessity
towards inevitable results. The country that is more developed
industrially only shows, to the less developed, the image of its
own future.

But apart from this. Where capitalist production is fully
naturalized among the Germans (for instance, in the factories
proper) the condition of things is much worse than in England,
because the counterpoise of the Factory Acts is wanting. In all
other spheres, we, like all the rest of Continental Western Europe,
suffer not only from the development of capitalist production, but
also from the incompleteness of that development. Alongside of
modern evils, a whole series of inherited evils oppress us, arising
from the passive survival of antiquated modes of production, with
their inevitable train of social and political anachronisms. We suffer

\* 'It is of you that the story is told!'

not only from the living, but from the dead. *Le mort saisit le vif!*\*

The social statistics of Germany and the rest of continental Western Europe are, in comparison with those of England, wretchedly compiled. But they raise the veil just enough to let us catch a glimpse of the Medusa head behind it. We should be appalled at the state of things at home, if, as in England, our governments and parliaments appointed periodically commissions of enquiry into economic conditions; if these commissions were armed with the same plenary powers to get at the truth; if it was possible to find for this purpose men as competent, as free from partisanship and respect of persons as are the English factory-inspectors, her medical reporters on public health, her commissioners of enquiry into the exploitation of women and children, into housing and food. Perseus wore a magic cap that the monsters he hunted down might not see him. We draw the magic cap down over eyes and ears as a make-believe that there are no monsters.

Let us not deceive ourselves on this. As in the 18th century the American war of independence sounded the tocsin for the European middle-class, so in the nineteenth century the American civil war sounded it for the European working class. In England the progress of social disintegration is palpable. When it has reached a certain point, it must re-act on the continent. There it will take a form more brutal or more humane, according to the degree of development of the working-class itself. Apart from higher motives, therefore, their own most important interests dictate to the classes that are for the nonce the ruling ones, the removal of all legally removable hindrances to the free development of the working class. For this reason, as well as others, I have given so large a space in this volume to the history, the details, and the results of English factory legislation. One nation can and should learn from others. And even when a society has got upon the right track for the discovery of the natural laws of its movement—and it is the ultimate aim of this work, to lay bare the economic law of motion of modern society—it can neither clear by bold leaps, nor remove by legal enactments, the obstacles offered by the successive phases of its normal development. But it can shorten and lessen the birth-pangs.

\* The dead holds the living in his grasp!

To prevent possible misunderstanding, a word. I paint the capitalist and the landlord in no sense *couleur de rose*. But here individuals are dealt with only in so far as they are the personifications of economic categories, embodiments of particular class-relations and class-interests. My standpoint, from which the evolution of the economic formation of society is viewed as a process of natural history, can less than any other make the individual responsible for relations whose creature he socially remains, however much he may subjectively raise himself above them.

In the domain of Political Economy, free scientific enquiry meets not merely the same enemies as in all other domains. The peculiar nature of the material it deals with summons as foes into the field of battle the most violent, mean and malignant passions of the human breast, the Furies of private interest. The English Established Church, e.g., will more readily pardon an attack on 38 of its 39 articles than on 1/39 of its income. Nowadays atheism itself is *culpa levis*,* as compared with criticism of existing property relations. Nevertheless, there is an unmistakable advance. I refer, e.g., to the bluebook published within the last few weeks: *Correspondence with Her Majesty's Missions Abroad, regarding Industrial Questions and Trades' Unions*. The representatives of the English Crown in foreign countries there declare in so many words that in Germany, in France, to be brief, in all the civilized states of the European continent, a radical change in the existing relations between capital and labour is as evident and inevitable as in England. At the same time, on the other side of the Atlantic Ocean, Mr Wade, Vice-President of the United States, declared in public meetings that, after the abolition of slavery, a radical change of the relations of capital and of property in land is next upon the order of the day. These are signs of the times not to be hidden by purple mantels or black cassocks. They do not signify that tomorrow a miracle will happen. They show that, within the ruling classes themselves, a foreboding is dawning, that the present society is no solid crystal, but an organism capable of change, and is constantly changing.

*C I-P*, pp. 7–10.

---

* Light offence.

## (3) THE EVOLUTIONARY APPROACH AND ITS LIMITATIONS

Bourgeois society is the most highly developed and most highly differentiated historical organization of production. The categories, in which its productive relations are expressed, and the understanding of its structure enable us also to gain an insight into the structure and the relations of production which had prevailed in all the previous forms of society. Bourgeois society has sprung from the ruins of their constituent elements and persists in retaining some of their partly unsurmounted remnants; some features which in previous societies had been present in only incipient form have achieved their full expression in bourgeois society. The anatomy of the human being is the key to the anatomy of the ape. But the intimation of a higher animal in lower ones can be understood only if the animal of the higher order is already known. The bourgeois economy furnishes a key to ancient economy, etc. This is, however, by no means true of the method of those economists who blot out all historical differences and see the bourgeois form in all forms of society. One can understand the nature of tribute, tithes, etc. after one has learned the nature of ground rent. But they must not be considered identical.

Furthermore, since bourgeois society itself is merely a form of development containing antagonistic elements, some relations belonging to earlier forms of society are frequently to be found within it but in a crippled state or as a travesty of their former self, for instance, as communal property. While it may be said, therefore, that the categories of the bourgeois economy contain what is true of all other forms of society, the statement is to be taken *cum grano salis*. They may contain these in a developed or crippled or caricatured form, but always in an essentially different one. The so-called historical development consists generally in the process whereby the last form considers its predecessors as stages leading up to itself and perceives them always from one viewpoint only, since it is very seldom and only in quite specific conditions that it is capable of criticizing itself; of course, we are not speaking here of those historical periods which appear to their own contemporaries as periods of decay. The Christian religion became capable of assisting us in an objective understanding of past mythologies only when it was ready to a certain extent, *dynamei* [potentially] as it were, for self-criticism. Similarly, bourgeois political economy only came to understand feudal, ancient, and oriental societies when self-criticism of bourgeois society had begun. In so far as bourgeois political economy had not assumed the nature of mythology by identifying the bourgeois system entirely with the past, its criticism of the feudal system, against which it still had to struggle, resembled Christian criticism of paganism or Protestant criticism of Catholicism.

> *GKPÖ*, pp. 25–6; *CPE-I*, pp. 300–1 [revised translation].

## (4) THE RESTRICTED SCOPE OF SOCIAL LAWS AND THE UBIQUITY OF CHANGE

That the method employed in *Das Kapital* has been little understood, is shown by the various conceptions, contradictory one to another, that have been formed of it.

Thus the Paris *Revue Positiviste** reproaches me in that, on the one hand, I treat economics metaphysically, and on the other hand —imagine!—confine myself to the mere critical analysis of actual facts, instead of writing receipts (Comtist ones?) for the cook-shops of the future. In answer to the reproach *in re* metaphysics, Professor Sieber has it 'In so far as it deals with actual theory, the method of Marx is the deductive method of the whole English school, a school whose failings and virtues are common to the best theoretic economists.'** M. Block—'Les théoriciens du socialisme en Allemagne' (*Journal des Economistes*, July–August, 1872)— makes the discovery that my method is analytic and says, 'Par cet ouvrage M. Marx se classe parmi les esprits analytiques les plus éminents.'*** German reviews, of course, shriek out at 'Hegelian sophistics'. The *European Messenger* of St Petersburg, in an article dealing exclusively with the method of *Das Kapital* (May

---

* Marx refers to the journal *La Philosophie Positive* which was founded by É. Littré and G. Wyrouboff in 1867. The review appeared in the issue November–December 1868. (Z.A.J.)
** The quotation comes from N. I. Sieber, *David Ricardo's Theory of Value and of Capital*, Kiev, 1871 (in Russian). Sieber was professor of political economy at the University of Kiev. See *C* I, p. 16. (Z.A.J.)
*** 'This work classes Mr Marx among the most eminent analytical minds.'

number, 1872, pp. 427–36),* finds my method of enquiry severely realistic, but my method of presentation, unfortunately, German-dialectical. It says, 'At first sight, if the judgment is based on the external form of the presentation of the subject, Marx is the most ideal of ideal philosophers, always in the German, i.e., the bad sense of the word. But in point of fact he is infinitely more realistic than all his forerunners in the work of economic criticism. He can in no sense be called an idealist.' I cannot answer the writer better than by aid of a few extracts from his own criticism, which may interest some of my readers to whom the Russian original is inaccessible.

After a quotation from the preface to my *Critique of Political Economy*, Berlin, 1859, pp. 4–7,** where I discuss the materialistic basis of my method, the writer goes on: 'The one thing which is of moment to Marx, is to find the law of the phenomena with whose investigation he is concerned; and not only is that law of moment to him, which governs these phenomena, in so far as they have a definite form and mutual connection within a given historical period. Of still greater moment to him is the law of their variation, of their development, i.e., of their transition from one form into another, from one series of connections into a different one. This law once discovered, he investigates in detail the effects in which it manifests itself in social life. Consequently, Marx only troubles himself about one thing: to show, by rigid scientific investigation, the necessity of successive determinate orders of social conditions, and to establish, as impartially as possible, the facts that serve him for fundamental starting points. For this it is quite enough, if he proves, at the same time, both the necessity of the present order of things, and the necessity of another order into which the first must inevitably pass over; and this all the same, whether men believe or do not believe it, whether they are conscious or unconscious of it. Marx treats the social movement as a process of natural history, governed by laws not only independent of human will, consciousness and intelligence, but rather, on the contrary, determining that will, consciousness and intelligence. . . . If in the history of civilization the conscious element plays a part so subordinate, then it is self-evident that a critical inquiry whose

* Marx refers to an article written by I. I. Kaufman, professor of political economy at the University of St Petersburg.
** See pp. 197–9 of this volume.

subject-matter is civilization, can, less than anything else, have for its basis any form of, or any result of, consciousness. That is to say, that not the idea, but the material phenomenon alone can serve as its starting-point. Such an enquiry will confine itself to the confrontation and the comparison of a fact, not with ideas but with another fact. For this inquiry, the one thing of moment is, that both facts be investigated as accurately as possible, and that they actually form, each with respect to the other, different momenta of an evolution; but most important of all is the rigid analysis of the series of successions, of the sequences and concatenations in which the different stages of such an evolution present themselves. But it will be said, the general laws of economic life are one and the same, no matter whether they are applied to the present or the past. This Marx directly denies. According to him, such abstract laws do not exist. On the contrary, in his opinion every historical period has laws of its own. . . . As soon as society has outlived a given period of development, and is passing over from one given stage to another, it begins to be subject also to other laws. In a word, economic life offers us a phenomenon analogous to the history of evolution in other branches of biology. The old economists misunderstood the nature of economic laws when they likened them to the laws of physics and chemistry. A more thorough analysis of phenomena shows that social organisms differ among themselves as fundamentally as plants or animals. Nay, one and the same phenomenon falls under quite different laws in consequence of the different structure of those organisms as a whole, of the variations of their individual organs, of the different conditions in which those organs function, etc. Marx, e.g., denies that the law of population is the same at all times and in all places. He asserts, on the contrary, that every stage of development has its own law of population. . . . With the varying degree of development of productive power, social conditions and the laws governing them vary too. Whilst Marx sets himself the task of following and explaining from this point of view the economic system established by the sway of capital, he is only formulating, in a strictly scientific manner, the aim that every accurate investigation into economic life must have. The scientific value of such an inquiry lies in the disclosing of the special laws that regulate the origin, existence, development, death of a given social organism and its replacement by another and higher one. And it is this value that, in point of fact, Marx's book has.'

Whilst the writer pictures what he takes to be actually my method, in this striking and (as far as concerns my own application of it) generous way, what else is he picturing but the dialectic method?

Of course the method of presentation must differ in form from that of inquiry. The latter has to appropriate the material in detail to analyse its different forms of development, to trace out their inner connection. Only after this work is done, can the actual movement be adequately described. If this is done successfully, if the life of the subject-matter is ideally reflected as in a mirror, then it may appear as if we had before us a mere *a priori* construction.

My dialectic method is not only different from the Hegelian, but is its direct opposite. To Hegel, the life-process of the human brain, i.e., the process of thinking, which, under the name of 'the Idea', he even transforms into an independent subject, is the demiurgos of the real world, and the real world is only the external, phenomenal form of 'the Idea'. With me, on the contary, the ideal is nothing else than the material world reflected by the human mind, and translated into forms of thought.

The mystifying side of Hegelian dialectic I criticized nearly thirty years ago, at a time when it was still the fashion. But just as I was working at the first volume of *Das Kapital*, it was the good pleasure of the peevish, arrogant, mediocre *Epigonoi* who now talk large in cultured Germany, to treat Hegel in the same way as the brave Moses Mendelssohn in Lessing's time treated Spinoza, i.e., as a 'dead dog'. I therefore openly avowed myself the pupil of that mighty thinker, and even here and there, in the chapter on the theory of value, coquetted with the modes of expression peculiar to him. The mystification which dialectic suffers in Hegel's hands, by no means prevents him from being the first to present its general form of working in a comprehensive and conscious manner. With him it is standing on its head. It must be turned right side up again, if you would discover the rational kernel within the mystical shell.

In its mystified form, dialectic became the fashion in Germany, because it seemed to transfigure and to glorify the existing state of things. In its rational form it is a scandal and abomination to bourgeoisdom and its doctrinaire professors, because it includes in its comprehension an affirmative recognition of the existing state of things, at the same time also, the recognition of the negation of that state, of its inevitable breaking up; because it regards every historically developed social form as in fluid movement, and therefore takes into account its transient nature not less than its momentary existence; because it lets nothing impose upon it, and is in its essence critical and revolutionary.

The contradictions inherent in the movement of capitalist society impress themselves upon the practical bourgeois most strikingly in the changes of the periodic cycle, through which modern industry runs, and whose crowning point is the universal crisis. That crisis is once again approaching, although as yet but in its preliminary stage; and by the universality of its theatre and the intensity of its action it will drum dialectics even into the heads of the mushroom-upstarts of the new, holy Prusso-German empire.

*C I-A*, pp.17–20.

## (5) THE SO-CALLED TRUE SOCIALISM AND THE CONCEPT OF IDEOLOGY

The relation between German socialism and the proletarian movement in France and England is the same as that which we found in the first volume between German liberalism, as it has hitherto existed, and the movement of the French and English bourgeoisie.* Alongside the German communists, a number of writers have appeared who have absorbed a few French and English communist ideas and amalgamated them with their own German philosophical premises. These 'socialists' or 'true socialists', as they call themselves, consider foreign communist literature not as the expression and the product of a real movement but as purely theoretical writings which have been evolved—in the same way as they imagine the German philosophical systems to have been evolved— by a process of 'pure thought'. It never occurs to them that, even when these writings do preach a system, they spring from the practical needs, the whole conditions of life of a particular class in particular countries. They innocently take on trust the illusion, cherished by some of these literary party representatives, that they

---

* Marx refers to a preceding chapter entitled *Political Liberalism*. See *GI*, pp. 206–20. (Z.A.J.)

are concerned with the 'most reasonable' social order instead of with the needs of a particular class and time. The real state of affairs escapes these true socialists, steeped as they are in their German ideology. Their activity in face of the 'unscientific' French and English consists primarily in holding up the superficiality and the 'crude' empiricism of these foreigners to the scorn of the German public, in singing the praise of 'German science' and declaring that its mission is to reveal for the first time the *truth* of communism and socialism, the absolute, *true* socialism. They immediately set to work discharging this mission as representatives of 'German science', although they are in most cases almost as little familiar with 'German science' as they are with the original writings of the French and English, which they know only from the compilations of Stein, Oelckers,* etc. And what is the '*truth*' which they impart to socialism and communism? Since they find the ideas contained in socialist and communist literature quite unintelligible—partly by reason of their ignorance even of the literary connections, partly on account of their above-mentioned misunderstanding of socialist and communist literature—they attempt to clarify them by invoking the German ideology and notably that of Hegel and Feuerbach. They detach the communist systems, critical and polemical writings from the real movement, of which they are but the expression, and force them into an arbitrary connection with German philosophy. They detach the conscious-ness of certain historically conditioned spheres of life from these spheres and evaluate it in terms of true, absolute, i.e., German philosophical consciousness. With perfect consistency they trans-form the relations of these particular individuals into relations of 'Man'; they interpret the thoughts of these particular individuals concerning their own relations as thoughts about 'Man'. In so doing, they have abandoned the realm of real history and returned to the realm of ideology, and since they are ignorant of the real connection, they can without difficulty fabricate some fantastic relationship with the help of the 'absolute' or some other ideologi-cal method. This translation of French ideas into the language of

* Lorenz von Stein (1815–1890) was the author of an influential book *Der Socialismus und Communismus des heutigen Frankreichs*, first published in 1842 and reprinted in an enlarged edition in 1848. Theodor Oelckers (1816–1869) was a celebrity of the day. His book *Die Bewegung des Socialismus und Com-munismus*, to which Marx refers, was published in 1844. (Z.A.J.)

E

the German ideologists and this arbitrarily constructed relationship between communism and German ideology, then, constitute so-called 'true socialism', which is loudly proclaimed, in the terms used by the Tories for the English constitution, to be 'the pride of the nation and the envy of all neighbours'.

Thus true socialism is nothing but the transfiguration of proletarian communism, and of its kindred parties and sects in France and England, within the heaven of the German mind and, as we shall also see, of the German sentiment. True socialism, which claims to be based on 'science', is primarily another esoteric science; its theoretical literature is only for the few who are initiated into the mysteries of the 'thinking mind'. But it has an exoteric literature as well; the very fact that it is concerned with social exoteric relations means that it must carry on some form of propaganda. In this exoteric literature it no longer appeals to the German 'thinking mind' but to the German 'sentiment'. This is all the easier since true socialism, concerned no longer with real human beings but with 'Man', has lost all revolutionary enthusiasm and proclaims instead the universal love of mankind. It turns as a result not to the proletarians but to the two most numerous classes of men in Germany, to the petty bourgeoisie with its philanthropic illusions and to the ideologists of this very same petty bourgeoisie: the philosophers and their disciples; it turns, in general, to that 'common', or uncommon, consciousness which at present rules in Germany.

The formation of this hybrid sect and the attempt to reconcile communism with the ideas prevailing at the time were necessary consequences of the actually existing conditions in Germany. The fact that a number of German communists, proceeding from a philosophical standpoint, should have arrived at communism by way of this transition was as necessary as the fact that others, unable to extricate themselves from this ideology, should go on preaching true socialism to the bitter end. We have, therefore, no means of knowing whether those true socialists whose works, criticized here, have been written some time ago, still maintain their position or whether they have advanced beyond it. We are not at all concerned with the individuals; we are merely considering the printed evidence of a tendency which is inevitable in a country so stagnant as Germany.

But in addition true socialism has provided an opening, which has been used by a host of Young-German literary men,* quacks and quill-drivers of all sorts, to exploit the social movement. The lack of any *real*, passionate, practical party conflict in Germany meant that even the social movement was at first a *merely* literary one. True socialism is a perfect example of a social literary movement that has come into being without any real party interests and now, after the formation of the communist party, it intends to persist in its despite. It goes without saying that since the appearance of a real communist party in Germany, the public of the true socialists will be more and more limited to the petty bourgeoisie and the sterile and broken-down literary hacks who represent it.

*GI*, pp. 501–3.

---

* Young Germany (*Junges Deutschland*) was a group of writers led by Karl Gutzkow, Theodor Mund, and Rudolf Wienbarg who were active in the 1830s and were influenced by Heine and Börne. Engels was their admirer for a short time. For details see P. Demetz, *Marx, Engels and the Poets: Origins of Marxist Literary Criticism*, Chicago, 1967. (Z.A.J.)

# Part Two

# Alienation: Its Sources and Manifestations

# (1) HEGEL'S CONCEPT OF ALIENATION

The outstanding achievement of Hegel's *Phenomenology**—the dialectic of negativity as the moving and creating principle—is, first, that Hegel grasps the self-creation of man as a process, objectification as loss of the object, as alienation and transcendence of this alienation, and that he, therefore, grasps the nature of *labour*, and conceives objective man (true, because real man) as the result of his *own labour*. The *real*, active orientation of man to himself as a species-being, or the affirmation of himself as a real species-being (i.e. as a human being) is only possible so far as he really brings forth all his *species-powers* (which is only possible through the co-operative endeavours of mankind and as an outcome of history) and treats these powers as objects, which can only be done at first in the form of alienation. . . .

For the present, let us make these preliminary observations: Hegel's standpoint is that of modern political economy. He conceives *labour* as the *essence*, the self-confirming essence of man; he observes only the positive side of labour, not its negative side. Labour is *man's coming to be for himself* within *alienation*, or as an *alienated* man. Labour as Hegel understands and recognizes it is *abstract mental* labour. Thus, that which above all constitutes the *essence* of philosophy, the *alienation of man knowing himself*, or *alienated* science *thinking* itself, Hegel grasps as its essence. Consequently, he is able to bring together the separate elements of earlier philosophy and to present his own as the philosophy.

*EPM*, pp. 202–3.

# (2) ALIENATED LABOUR

We have begun from the presuppositions of political economy. We have accepted its terminology and its laws. We presupposed private property; the separation of labour, capital, and land, as also of wages, profit, and rent; the division of labour; competition; the concept of exchange value, etc. From political economy itself, in

* Marx refers to Hegel's *Phänomenologie des Geistes* (*The Phenomenology of Mind*), a work which was very influential and admired in Germany in the first half of the nineteenth century. (Z.A.J.)

its own words, we have shown that the worker sinks to the level of a commodity, and to a most miserable commodity; that the misery of the worker increases with the power and volume of his production; that the necessary result of competition is the accumulation of capital in a few hands, and thus a restoration of monopoly in a more terrible form; and finally that the distinction between capitalist and landlord, and between agricultural labourer and industrial worker, must disappear, and the whole of society divide into the two classes of property *owners* and *propertyless* workers.

Political economy begins with the fact of private property; it does not explain it. It conceives the *material* process of private property, as this occurs in reality, in general and abstract formulas which then serve it as laws. It does not *comprehend* these laws; that is, it does not show how they arise out of the nature of private property. Political economy provides no explanation of the basis for the distinction of labour from capital, of capital from land. When, for example, the relation of wages to profits is defined, this is explained in terms of the interests of capitalists; in other words, what should be explained is assumed. Similarly, competition is referred to at every point and is explained in terms of external conditions. Political economy tells us nothing about the extent to which these external and apparently accidental conditions are simply the expression of a necessary development. We have seen how exchange itself seems an accidental fact. The only motive forces which political economy recognizes are *avarice* and the *war between the avaricious, competition.*

Just because political economy fails to understand the interconnexions within this movement it was possible to oppose the doctrine of competition to that of monopoly, the doctrine of freedom of the crafts to that of the guilds, the doctrine of the division of landed property to that of the great estates; for competition, freedom of crafts, and the division of landed property were conceived only as accidental consequences brought about by will and force, rather than as necessary, inevitable, and natural consequences of monopoly, the guild system, and feudal property.

Thus we have now to grasp the real connexion between this whole system of alienation—private property, acquisitiveness, the separation of labour, capital and land, exchange and competition, value and the devaluation of man, monopoly and competition—and the system of *money.*

Let us not begin our explanation, as does the economist, from a legendary primordial condition. Such a primordial condition does not explain anything; it merely removes the question into a grey and nebulous distance. It asserts as a fact or event what it should deduce, namely, the necessary relation between two things; for example, between the division of labour and exchange. In the same way theology explains the origin of evil by the fall of man; that is, it asserts as a historical fact what it should explain.

We shall begin from a *contemporary* economic fact. The worker becomes poorer the more wealth he produces and the more his production increases in power and extent. The worker becomes an ever cheaper commodity the more goods he creates. The *devaluation* of the human world increases in direct relation to the *increase in value* of the world of things. Labour does not only create goods; it also produces itself and the worker as a *commodity*, and indeed in the same proportion as it produces goods.

This fact simply implies that the object produced by labour, its product, now stands opposed to it as an *alien being*, as a *power independent* of the producer. The product of labour is labour which has been embodied in an object and turned into a physical thing; this product is an *objectification* of labour. The performance of work is at the same time its objectification. The performance of work appears in the sphere of political economy as a *vitiation* of the worker, objectification as a *loss* and as *servitude to the object*, and appropriation as *alienation*.

So much does the performance of work appear as vitiation that the worker is vitiated to the point of starvation. So much does objectification appear as loss of the object that the worker is deprived of the most essential things not only of life but also of work. Labour itself becomes an object which he can acquire only by the greatest effort and with unpredictable interruptions. So much does the appropriation of the object appear as alienation that the more objects the worker produces the fewer he can possess and the more he falls under the domination of his product, of capital.

All these consequences follow from the fact that the worker is related to the *product of his labour* as to an *alien* object. For it is clear on this presupposition that the more the worker expends himself in work the more powerful becomes the world of objects which he creates in face of himself, the poorer he becomes in his inner life, and the less he belongs to himself. It is just the same as

E*

in religion. The more of himself man attributes to God the less he has left in himself. The worker puts his life into the object, and his life then belongs no longer to himself but to the object. The greater his activity, therefore, the less he possesses. What is embodied in the product of his labour is no longer his own. The greater this product is, therefore, the more he is diminished. The *alienation* of the worker in his product means not only that his labour becomes an object, assumes an *external* existence, but that it exists independently, *outside himself*, and alien to him, and that it stands opposed to him as an autonomous power. The life which he has given to the object sets itself against him as an alien and hostile force.

Let us now examine more closely the phenomenon of *objectification*; the worker's production and the *alienation* and *loss* of the object it produces, which is involved in it. The worker can create nothing without *nature*, without the *sensuous external world*. The latter is the material in which his labour is realized, in which it is active, out of which and through which it produces things.

But just as nature affords the *means of existence* of labour, in the sense that labour cannot *live* without objects upon which it can be exercised, so also it provides the *means of existence* in a narrower sense; namely the means of physical existence for the *worker* himself. Thus, the more the worker *appropriates* the external world of sensuous nature by his labour the more he deprives himself of *means of existence*, in two respects: first, that the sensuous external world becomes progressively less an object belonging to his labour or a means of existence of his labour, and secondly, that it becomes progressively less a means of existence in the direct sense, a means for the physical subsistence of the worker.

In both respects, therefore, the worker becomes a slave of the object; first, in that he receives an *object of work*, i.e. receives *work*, and secondly, in that he receives *means of subsistence*. Thus the object enables him to exist, first as a *worker* and secondly, as a *physical subject*. The culmination of this enslavement is that he can only maintain himself as a *physical subject* so far as he is a *worker*, and that it is only as a *physical subject* that he is a worker.

(The alienation of the worker in his object is expressed as follows in the laws of political economy: the more the worker produces the less he has to consume; the more value he creates the more worthless he becomes; the more refined his product the more crude and misshapen the worker; the more civilized the product the more barbarous the worker; the more powerful the work the more feeble the worker; the more the work manifests intelligence the more the worker declines in intelligence and becomes a slave of nature.)

*Political economy conceals the alienation in the nature of labour in so far as it does not examine the direct relationship between the worker (work) and production.* Labour certainly produces marvels for the rich but it produces privation for the worker. It produces palaces, but hovels for the worker. It produces beauty, but deformity for the worker. It replaces labour by machinery, but it casts some of the workers back into a barbarous kind of work and turns the others into machines. It produces intelligence, but also stupidity and cretinism for the workers.

*The direct relationship of labour to its products is the relationship of the worker to the objects of his production.* The relationship of property owners to the objects of production and to production itself is merely a *consequence* of this first relationship and confirms it. We shall consider this second aspect later.

Thus, when we ask what is the important relationship of labour, we are concerned with the relationship of the *worker* to production.

So far we have considered the alienation of the worker only from one aspect; namely, *his relationship to the products of his labour.* However, alienation appears not merely in the result but also in the *process of production*, within *productive activity* itself. How could the worker stand in an alien relationship to the product of his activity if he did not alienate himself in the act of production itself? The product is indeed only the *résumé* of activity, of production. Consequently, if the product of labour is alienation, production itself must be active alienation—the alienation of activity and the activity of alienation. The alienation of the object of labour merely summarizes the alienation in the work activity itself.

What constitutes the alienation of labour? First, that the work is *external* to the worker, that it is not part of his nature; and that, consequently, he does not fulfil himself in his work but denies himself, has a feeling of misery rather than well-being, does not develop freely his mental and physical energies but is physically exhausted and mentally debased. The worker, therefore, feels himself at home only during his leisure time, whereas at work he feels homeless. His work is not voluntary but imposed, *forced labour*. It is not the satisfaction of a need, but only a *means* for satisfying other needs. Its alien character is clearly shown by the fact that as soon as there is no physical or other compulsion it is avoided like the plague. External labour, labour in which man alienates himself, is a labour of self-sacrifice, or mortification. Finally, the external character of work for the worker is shown by the fact that it is not his own work but work for someone else, that in work he does not belong to himself but to another person.

Just as in religion the spontaneous activity of human fantasy, of the human brain and heart, reacts independently as an alien activity of gods or devils upon the individual, so the activity of the worker is not his own spontaneous activity. It is another's activity and a loss of his own spontaneity.

We arrive at the result that man (the worker) feels himself to be freely active only in his animal functions—eating, drinking and pro-creating, or at most also in his dwelling and in personal adornment —while in his human functions he is reduced to an animal. The animal becomes human and the human becomes animal.

Eating, drinking and procreating are of course also genuine human functions. But abstractly considered, apart from the environment of human activities, and turned into final and sole ends, they are animal functions.

We have now considered the act of alienation of practical human activity, labour, from two aspects: (1) the relationship of the worker to the *product of labour* as an alien object which dominates him. This relationship is at the same time the relationship to the sensuous external world, to natural objects, as an alien and hostile world; (2) the relationship of labour to the *act of production* within *labour*. This is the relationship of the worker to his own activity as something alien and not belonging to him, activity as suffering (passivity), strength as powerlessness, creation as emasculation, the *personal* physical and mental energy of the worker, his personal life (for what is life but activity?), as an activity which is directed against himself, independent of him and not belonging to him. This is *self-alienation* as against the above-mentioned alienation of the *thing*.

We have now to infer a third characteristic of *alienated labour* from the two we have considered.

Man is a species-being not only in the sense that he makes the community (his own as well as those of other things) his object both practically and theoretically, but also (and this is simply another expression for the same thing) in the sense that he treats himself as the present, living species, as a *universal* and consequently free being.

Species-life, for man as for animals, has its physical basis in the fact that man (like animals) lives from inorganic nature, and since man is more universal than an animal so the range of inorganic nature from which he lives is more universal. Plants, animals, minerals, air, light, etc. constitute, from the theoretical aspect, a part of human consciousness as objects of natural science and art; they are man's spiritual inorganic nature, his intellectual means of life, which he must first prepare for enjoyment and perpetuation. So also, from the practical aspect, they form a part of human life and activity. In practice man lives only from these natural products, whether in the form of food, heating, clothing, housing, etc. The universality of man appears in practice in the universality which makes the whole of nature into his inorganic body: (1) as a direct means of life; and equally (2) as the material object and instrument of his life activity. Nature is the inorganic body of man; that is to say nature, excluding the human body itself. To say that man *lives* from nature means that nature is his *body* with which he must remain in a continuous interchange in order not to die. The statement that the physical and mental life of man, and nature, are interdependent means simply that nature is interdependent with itself, for man is a part of nature.

Since alienated labour: (1) alienates nature from man; and (2) alienates man from himself, from his own active function, his life activity; so it alienates him from the species. It makes *species-life* into a means of individual life. In the first place it alienates species-life and individual life, and secondly, it turns the latter, as an abstraction, into the purpose of the former, also in its abstract and alienated form.

For labour, *life activity*, *productive life*, now appear to man only as *means* for the satisfaction of a need, the need to maintain his physical existence. Productive life is, however, species-life. It is life creating life. In the type of life activity resides the whole character of a species, its species-character; and free, conscious activity is the species-character of human beings. Life itself appears only as a *means of life*.

The animal is one with its life activity. It does not distinguish the activity from itself. It is *its activity*. But man makes his life activity itself an object of his will and consciousness. He has a conscious life activity. It is not a determination with which he is completely identified. Conscious life activity distinguishes man from the life activity of animals. Only for this reason is he a species-being. Or rather, he is only a self-conscious being, i.e., his own life is an object for him, because he is a species-being. Only for this reason is his activity free activity. Alienated labour reverses the relationship, in that man because he is a self-conscious being makes his life activity, his being, only a means for his *existence*.

The practical construction of an *objective world*, the *manipulation* of inorganic nature, is the confirmation of man as a conscious species-being, i.e. a being who treats the species as his own being or himself as a species-being. Of course, animals also produce. They construct nests, dwellings, as in the case of bees, beavers, ants, etc. But they only produce what is strictly necessary for themselves or their young. They produce only in a single direction, while man produces universally. They produce only under the compulsion of direct physical needs, while man produces when he is free from physical need and only truly produces in freedom from such need. Animals produce only themselves, while man reproduces the whole of nature. The products of animal production belong directly to their physical bodies, while man is free in face of his product. Animals construct only in accordance with the standards and needs of the species to which they belong, while man knows how to produce in accordance with the standards of every species and knows how to apply the appropriate standard to the object. Thus man constructs also in accordance with the laws of beauty.

It is just in his work upon the objective world that man really proves himself as a *species-being*. This production is his active species-life. By means of it nature appears as *his* work and his reality. The object of labour is, therefore, the *objectification of man's species-life*; for he no longer reproduces himself merely intellectually, as in consciousness, but actively and in a real sense, and he sees his own reflection in a world which he has constructed. While, therefore, alienated labour takes away the object of production from man, it also takes away his *species-life*, his real objectivity as a species-being, and changes his advantage over animals into a disadvantage in so far as his inorganic body, nature, is taken from him.

Just as alienated labour transforms free and self-directed activity into a means, so it transforms the species-life of man into a means of physical existence.

Consciousness, which man has from his species, is transformed through alienation so that species-life becomes only a means for him. (3) Thus alienated labour turns the *species-life of man*, and also nature as his mental species-property, into an *alien* being and into a *means* for his *individual existence*. It alienates from man his own body, external nature, his mental life and his *human* life. (4) A direct consequence of the alienation of man from the product of his labour, from his life activity and from his species-life, is that *man is alienated* from other *men*. When man confronts himself he also confronts *other* men. What is true of man's relationship to his work, to the product of his work and to himself, is also true of his relationship to other men, to their labour and to the objects of their labour.

In general, the statement that man is alienated from his species-life means that each man is alienated from others, and that each of the others is likewise alienated from human life.

Human alienation, and above all the relation of man to himself, is first realized and expressed in the relationship between each man and other men. Thus in the relationship of alienated labour every man regards other men according to the standards and relationships in which he finds himself placed as a worker.

We began with an economic fact, the alienation of the worker and his production. We have expressed this fact in conceptual terms as *alienated labour*, and in analysing the concept we have merely analysed an economic fact.

Let us now examine further how this concept of alienated labour must express and reveal itself in reality. If the product of labour is alien to me and confronts me as an alien power, to whom does it belong? If my own activity does not belong to me but is an alien, forced activity, to whom does it belong? To a being *other* than myself. And who is this being? The *gods*? It is apparent in the earliest stages of advanced production, e.g., temple building, etc. in Egypt, India, Mexico, and in the service rendered to gods, that the product belonged to the gods. But the gods alone were never the lords of labour. And no more was *nature*. What a contradiction it would be if the more man subjugates nature by his labour, and the more the marvels of the gods are rendered superfluous by the marvels of industry, the more he should abstain from his joy in producing and his enjoyment of the product for love of these powers.

The *alien* being to whom labour and the product of labour belong, to whose service labour is devoted, and to whose enjoyment the product of labour goes, can only be *man* himself. If the product of labour does not belong to the worker, but confronts him as an alien power, this can only be because it belongs to *a man other than the worker*. If his activity is a torment to him it must be a source of *enjoyment* and pleasure to another. Not the gods, nor nature, but only man himself can be this alien power over men.

Consider the earlier statement that the relation of man to himself is first *realized*, *objectified*, through his relation to other men. If he is related to the product of his labour, his objectified labour, as to an *alien*, hostile, powerful and independent object, he is related in such a way that another alien, hostile, powerful and independent man is the lord of this object. If he is related to his own activity as to unfree activity, then he is related to it as activity in the service, and under the domination, coercion and yoke, of another man.

Every self-alienation of man, from himself and from nature, appears in the relation which he postulates between other men and himself and nature. Thus religious self-alienation is necessarily exemplified in the relation between laity and priest, or, since it is here a question of the spiritual world, between the laity and a mediator. In the real world of practice this self-alienation can only be expressed in the real, practical relation of man to his fellow men. The medium through which alienation occurs is itself a *practical* one. Through alienated labour, therefore, man not only produces his relation to the object and to the process of production as to alien and hostile men; he also produces the relation of other men to his production and his product, and the relation between himself and other men. Just as he creates his own production as a vitiation, a punishment, and his own product as a loss, as a product which does not belong to him, so he creates the domination of the non-producer over production and its product. As he alienates his own activity, so he bestows upon the stranger an activity which is not his own.

We have so far considered this relation only from the side of the worker, and later on we shall consider it also from the side of the non-worker.

Thus, through alienated labour the worker creates the relation of another man, who does not work and is outside the work process, to this labour. The relation of the worker to work also produces the relation of the capitalist (or whatever one likes to call the lord of labour) to work. *Private property* is, therefore, the product, the necessary result, of *alienated labour*, of the external relation of the worker to nature and to himself.

*Private property* is thus derived from the analysis of the concept of *alienated labour*; that is, alienated man, alienated labour, alienated life, and estranged man.

We have, of course, derived the concept of *alienated labour* (*alienated life*) from political economy, from an analysis of the *movement of private property*. But the analysis of this concept shows that although private property appears to be the basis and cause of alienated labour, it is rather a consequence of the latter, just as the gods are *fundamentally* not the cause but the product of confusions of human reason. At a later stage, however, there is a reciprocal influence.

Only in the final stage of the development of private property is its secret revealed, namely, that it is on one hand the *product* of alienated labour, and on the other hand the *means* by which labour is alienated, *the realization of this alienation*.

*EPM*, pp. 120–31.


# (3) THE SOCIAL ORIGINS OF ALIENATION AND ITS ABOLITION\*

The division of labour implies the contradiction between the interest of the separate individual or the individual family and the communal interest of all individuals who have intercourse with one another. And indeed, this communal interest does not exist merely in the imagination, as the 'general interest', but first of all in reality, as the mutual interdependence of the individuals among whom the labour is divided. And finally, the division of labour offers us the first example of how, as long as man remains in natural society, that is, as long as a cleavage exists between the particular and the common interest, as long, therefore, as activity

\* Cf. *GI*, pp. 483–4. (Z.A.J.)

is not voluntarily, but naturally, divided, man's own deed becomes an alien power opposed to him, which enslaves him instead of being controlled by him. For as soon as the distribution of labour comes into being, each man has a particular, exclusive sphere of activity, which is forced upon him and from which he cannot escape. He is a hunter, a fisherman, a shepherd, or a Critical Critic, and must remain so if he does not want to lose his means of livelihood; while in communist society, where nobody has one exclusive sphere of activity but each can become accomplished in any branch he wishes, society regulates the general production and thus makes it possible for me to do one thing today and another tomorrow, to hunt in the morning, fish in the afternoon, rear cattle in the evening, criticize after dinner, just as I have a mind, without ever becoming hunter, fisherman, shepherd or critic. This fixation of social activity, this consolidation of what we ourselves produce into an objective power above us, growing out of our control, thwarting our expectations, bringing to naught our calculations, is one of the chief factors in historical development up till now.

And out of this very contradiction between the interest of the individual and that of the community the latter takes an independent form as the *State*, divorced from the real interests of individual and community, and at the same time as an illusory communal life, always based, however, on the real ties existing in every family and tribal conglomeration—such as flesh and bood, language, division of labour on a larger scale, and other interests—and especially, as we shall enlarge upon later, on the classes, already determined by the division of labour, which in every such mass of men separate out, and of which one dominates all the others. It follows from this that all struggles within the State, the struggle between democracy, aristocracy, and monarchy, the struggle for the franchise, etc., etc., are merely the illusory forms in which the real struggles of the different classes are fought out among one another (of this the German theoreticians have not the faintest inkling, although they have received a sufficient introduction to the subject in the *Deutsch-Französische Jahrbücher* and *Die heilige Familie**). Further, it follows that every class which is struggling

---

* *Deutsch-Französische Jahrbücher* is the title of a short-lived journal which appeared in Paris in 1844 under the joint editorship of Marx and Arnold Ruge. *Die heilige Familie* is Marx's own work, to which Engels contributed a few pages and which is known in English translation as *The Holy Family*. (Z.A.J.)

for mastery, even when its domination, as is the case with the proletariat, postulates the abolition of the old form of society in its entirety and of domination itself, must first conquer for itself political power in order to represent its interest in turn as the general interest, which in the first moment it is forced to do. Just because individuals seek *only* their particular interest, which for them does not coincide with their communal interest (in fact the general is the illusory form of communal life), the latter will be imposed on them as an interest 'alien' to them, and 'independent' of them, as in its turn a particular, peculiar 'general' interest; or they themselves must remain within this discord, as in democracy. On the other hand, too, the *practical* struggle of these particular interests, which constantly *really* run counter to the communal and illusory communal interests, makes *practical* intervention and control necessary through the illusory 'general' interest in the form of the State. The social power, i.e., the multiplied productive force, which arises through the co-operation of different individuals as it is determined by the division of labour, appears to these individuals, since their co-operation is not voluntary but has come about naturally, not as their own united power, but as an alien force existing outside them, of the origin and goal of which they are ignorant, which they thus cannot control, which on the contrary passes through a peculiar series of phases and stages independent of the will and the action of man, nay even being the prime governor of these.

This '*estrangement*' (to use a term which will be comprehensible to the philosophers) can, of course, only be abolished given two *practical* premises. For it to become an 'intolerable' power, i.e., a power against which men make a revolution, it must necessarily have rendered the great mass of humanity 'propertyless', and produced, at the same time, the contradiction of an existing world of wealth and culture, both of which conditions presuppose a great increase in productive power, a high degree of its development. And, on the other hand, this development of productive forces (which itself implies the actual empirical existence of men in their *world-historical*, instead of local, being) is an absolutely necessary practical premise because without it *want* is merely made general, and with *destitution* the struggle for necessities and all the old filthy business would necessarily be reproduced; and furthermore, because only with this universal development of

productive forces is a *universal* intercourse between men established, which produces in all nations simultaneously the phenomenon of the 'propertyless' mass (universal competition), makes
each nation dependent on the revolutions of the others, and finally
has put *world-historical*, empirically universal individuals in place
of local ones. Without this, (1) communism could only exist as a
local event; (2) the *forces* of intercourse themselves could not have
developed as *universal*, hence intolerable powers: they would have
remained home-bred conditions surrounded by superstition; and
(3) each extension of intercourse would abolish local communism.
Empirically, communism is only possible as the act of the dominant
peoples 'all at once' and simultaneously, which presupposes the
universal development of productive forces and the world intercourse bound up with communisms. . . .

Communism is for us not a *state of affairs* which is to be established, an *ideal* to which reality [will] have to adjust itself. We call
communism the *real* movement which abolishes the present state
of things. The conditions of this movement result from the
premises now in existence. Moreover, the mass of *propertyless*
workers—the utterly precarious position of labour-power on a
mass scale cut off from capital or from even a limited satisfaction
and, therefore, no longer merely temporarily deprived of work itself
as a secure source of life—presupposes the *world market* through
competition. The proletariat can thus only exist *world-historically*,
just as communism, its activity, can only have a 'world-historical'
existence. World-historical existence of individuals, i.e., existence
of individuals which is directly linked up with world history.

GI, pp. 44–7.

*Communism* is the *positive* abolition of *private property*, of human
*self-alienation*, and thus the real *appropriation* of *human* nature
through and for man. It is, therefore, the return of man himself as a
*social*, i.e. really human, being, a complete and conscious return
which assimilates all the wealth of previous development. Communism as a fully developed naturalism is humanism and as a
fully developed humanism is naturalism. It is the *definitive*
resolution of the antagonism between man and nature, and between
man and man. It is the true solution of the conflict between existence

and essence, between objectification and self-affirmation, between freedom and necessity, between individual and species. It is the solution of the riddle of history and knows itself to be this solution. . . .

The material, directly *perceptible* private property is the material and sensuous expression of *alienated human* life. Its movement—production and consumption—is the *sensuous* manifestation of the movement of all previous production, i.e., the realization or reality of man. Religion, the family, the state, law, morality, science, art, etc. are only *particular* forms of production and come under its general law. The positive supersession of *private property*, as the appropriation of *human* life, is, therefore, the positive supersession of all alienation, and the return of man from religion, the family, the State, etc. to his *human*, i.e., social life. Religious alienation as such occurs only in the sphere of *consciousness*, in the inner life of man, but economic alienation is that of *real life* and its supersession, therefore, affects both aspects.

*EPM*, pp. 155–6.

# Part Three

## Social Classes, Class Differentiation and Class Struggle

# (A)  The Theoretical Framework

## 1) THE ORIGIN OF SOCIAL CLASSES AND THE CLASS DETERMINATION OF THE INDIVIDUAL

In the Middle Ages the citizens in each town were compelled to unite against the landed nobility to save their skins. The extension of trade, the establishment of communications, led the separate towns to get to know other towns, which had asserted the same interests in the struggle with the same antagonist. Out of the many local corporations of burghers there arose only gradually the burgher *class*. The conditions of life of the individual burghers became, on account of their contradiction to the existing relationships and of the mode of labour determined by these, conditions which were common to them all and independent of each individual. The burghers had created the conditions in so far as they had torn themselves free from feudal ties, and were created by them in so far as they were determined by their antagonism to the feudal system which they found in existence. When the individual towns began to enter into associations, these common conditions developed into class conditions. The same conditions, the same contradiction, the same interests necessarily called forth on the whole similar customs everywhere .The bourgeoisie itself, with its conditions, develops only gradually, splits according to the division of labour into various fractions and finally absorbs all propertied classes it finds in existence[1] (while it develops the majority of the earlier propertyless and a part of the hitherto propertied classes into a new class, the proletariat) in the measure in which all property found in existence is transformed into

(Marginal note by Marx:) To begin with it absorbs the branches of labour directly belonging to the State and then all ± (more or less) ideological estates.

industrial or commercial capital. The separate individuals form a class only in so far as they have to carry on a common battle against another class; otherwise they are on hostile terms with each other as competitors. On the other hand, the class in its turn achieves an independent existence over against the individuals, so that the latter find their conditions of existence predestined, and hence have their position in life and their personal development assigned to them by their class, and become subsumed under it. This is the same phenomenon as the subjection of the separate individuals to the division of labour and can only be removed by the abolition of private property and of labour itself. We have already indicated several times how this subsuming of individuals under the class brings with it their subjection to all kinds of ideas, etc.

*GI*, pp. 68–9.

This subsuming of individuals under definite classes cannot be abolished until a class has taken shape, which has no longer any particular class interest to assert against the ruling class.

*GI*, p. 93

It is quite 'possible' that particular individuals are not 'always' determined by the class to which they belong. This circumstance decides as little the outcome of the class struggle as the defection of a few aristocrats, who went over to the *tiers-état*, decided the outcome of the French Revolution. Furthermore, these aristocrats joined at least *a* class, namely the revolutionary class, the bourgeoisie. But Herr Heinzen makes all classes vanish in the presence of the imposing idea of 'humanity'.

If, however, Herr Heinzen believes that *whole classes*, which are based on *economic* conditions, independent of their will, and which because of these conditions are placed in the most antagonistic opposition to each other, can extricate themselves from their real relations through the characteristic of 'humanity' inherent in all men, then how easy must it be for *one single* prince to rise, owing to 'humanity', above his 'princedom', his 'princely craft'?

*MCCM*, pp. 349–50.

## (2) THE PROPERTIED CLASS AND THE PROLETARIAT

Proletariat and wealth are opposites; as such they form a single whole. They are both forms of the world of private property. The question is what place each occupies in the antithesis. It is not sufficient to declare them two sides of a single whole.

Private property as private property, as wealth, is compelled to maintain *itself*, and thereby its opposite, the proletariat, in *existence*. That is the *positive* side of the contradiction, self-satisfied private property.

The proletariat, on the other hand, is compelled as proletariat to abolish itself and thereby its opposite, the condition for its existence, what makes it the proletariat, i.e., private property. That is the *negative* side of the contradiction, its restlessness within its very self, dissolved and self-dissolving private property.

The propertied class and the class of the proletariat present the same human self-alienation. But the former class finds in this self-alienation its confirmation and its good, *its own power*: it has in it a *semblance* of human existence. The class of the proletariat feels annihilated in its self-alienation; it sees in it its own power-lessness and the reality of an inhuman existence. In the words of Hegel, the class of the proletariat is in *indignation* at that abasement, an indignation to which it is necessarily driven by the contradiction between its human *nature* and its condition of life, which is the outright, decisive and comprehensive negation of that nature.

Within this antithesis the private owner is therefore the *conservative* side, the proletarian, the *destructive* side. From the former arises the action of preserving the antithesis, from the latter, that of annihilating it.

Indeed private property, too, drives itself in its economic movement towards its own dissolution, only, however, through a development which does not depend on it, of which it is uncon-scious and which takes place against its will, through the very nature of things; only inasmuch as it produces the proletariat *as* proletariat, that misery conscious of its spiritual and physical misery, that dehumanization conscious of its dehumanization and therefore self-abolishing. The proletariat executes the sentence that private property pronounced on itself by begetting the proletariat, just as it carries out the sentence that wage-labour pronounced on itself by bringing forth wealth for others and misery for itself. When the proletariat is victorious, it by no means becomes the absolute side of society, for it is victorious only by abolishing itself and its opposite. Then the proletariat disappears as well as the opposite which determines it, private property.

When socialist writers ascribe this historic role to the proletariat, it is not, as Critical Criticism* pretends to think, because they consider the proletarians as *gods*. Rather the contrary. Since the abstraction of all humanity, even of the *semblance* of humanity, is practically complete in the full-grown proletariat; since the conditions of life of the proletariat sum up all the conditions of life of society today in all their inhuman acuity; since man has lost himself in the proletariat, yet at the same time has not only gained theoretical consciousness of that loss, but through urgent, no longer disguisable, absolutely imperative *need*—that practical expression of *necessity*—is driven directly to revolt against that inhumanity; it follows that the proletariat can and must free itself. But it cannot free itself without abolishing the conditions of its own life. It cannot abolish the conditions of its own life without abolishing *all* the inhuman conditions of life of society today which are summed up in its own situation. Not in vain does it go through the stern but steeling school of *labour*. The question is not what this or that proletarian, or even the whole of the proletariat at the moment *considers* as its aim. The question is *what the proletariat is*, and what, consequent on that *being*, it will be compelled to do. Its aim and historical action is irrevocably and obviously demonstrated in its own life situation as well as in the whole organization of bourgeois society today. There is no need to dwell here upon the fact that a large part of the English and French proletariat is already *conscious* of its historic task and is constantly working to develop that consciousness into complete clarity.

*HF*, pp. 51–3.

* 'Critical Criticism' is the name which Marx gave to the ideas advocated in the monthly *Allgemeine Literatur Zeitung*. The monthly was edited by his former friend Bruno Bauer in the years 1843–4. (Z.A.J.)

# (3) INCOME AND CLASS MEMBERSHIP

'Crude'* common sense transforms class differences into 'differences in the size of the purse' and class antagonism into 'quarrels between crafts'. The size of the purse is a purely quantitative difference, by means of which any two individuals of *the same class* may be incited against each other at will. It is known that medieval *guilds* opposed each other 'according to their *craft*'. However, it is equally well known that modern class differences are not based by any means on 'craft'. Rather the division of labour produces most *diverse* kinds of work within *the same class*.

*MCCM*, p. 349.

# (4) A NOTE ON THE CONCEPT OF CLASS

The owners merely of labour-power, owners of capital, and land-owners, whose respective sources of income are wages, profits and ground-rent, in other words, wage-labourers, capitalists and land-owners, constitute then three big classes of modern society based upon the capitalist mode of production.

In England, modern society is indisputably most highly and classically developed in economic structure. Nevertheless, even here the stratification of classes does not appear in its pure form. Middle and intermediate strata even here obliterate lines of demarcation everywhere (although incomparably less in rural districts than in the cities). However, this is immaterial for our analysis. We have seen that the continual tendency and law of

* In the original 'der "grobianisch" Menschenverstand'. Marx used the adjective 'grobianisch' to suggest that Karl Heinzen, the butt of his polemical wrath, was a representative of the style characteristic of *die grobianische Literatur* ('vulgarity' Literature) of the sixteenth century. *Die grobianische Literatur* was, as Marx put it, 'plebeian in form and philistine in content', 'vulgar, boastful, bragging and arrogant', to give a few qualifications in terms of which Marx described Heinzen's prose.

Carl Heinzen (1809–1880), a German radical journalist, preferred, like Marx, living abroad to leading a silent existence in Germany. In Belgium he wrote for *Deutsche-Brüsseler Zeitung*, a paper founded by German political refugees, in which he got involved in bitter polemics with Marx and Engels. Heinzen emigrated to the United States where he remained a determined opponent of Marxian socialism. (Z.A.J.)

development of the capitalist mode of production is more and more to divorce the means of production from labour, and more and more to concentrate the scattered means of production into large groups, thereby transforming labour into wage-labour and the means of production into capital. And to this tendency, on the other hand, corresponds the independent separation of landed property from capital and labour, or the transformation of all landed property into the form of landed property corresponding to the capitalist mode of production.

The first question to be answered is this: What constitutes a class?—and the reply to this follows naturally from the reply to another question, namely: What makes wage-labourers, capitalists and landlords constitute the three great social classes?

At first glance—the identity of revenues and sources of revenue. There are three great social groups whose members, the individuals forming them, live on wages, profit and ground-rent respectively, on the realization of their labour-power, their capital, and their landed property.

However, from this standpoint, physicians and officials, e.g., would also constitute two classes, for they belong to two distinct social groups, the members of each of these groups receiving their revenue from one and the same source. The same would also be true of the infinite fragmentation of interest and rank into which the division of social labour splits labourers as well as capitalists and landlords—the latter, e.g., into owners of vineyards, farm owners, owners of forests, mine owners and owners of fisheries.

C III, pp. 862–3.

## (5) MARX ON HIS CONTRIBUTION TO THE THEORY OF SOCIAL CLASSES

In your place I should in general remark to the democratic gentlemen that they would do better first to acquaint themselves with bourgeois literature before they presume to yap at the opponents of it. For instance, these gentlemen should study the historical works of Thierry, Guizot, John Wade,* and others in order to

* Augustin Thierry (1795–1856), Comte's predecessor as Saint-Simon's secretary, was a prominent historian and author of *Histoire de la conquête de*

enlighten themselves as to the past 'history of classes'. Before they try to criticize the critique of political economy they should acquaint themselves with the fundamentals of political economy. One has only to open Ricardo's great *opus*, for example, to find these opening words of his Preface on the first page:

'The produce of the earth—all that is derived from its surface by the united application of labour, machinery, and capital—is divided among *three classes* of the community; namely, the proprietor of the land, the owner of the stock or capital necessary for its cultivation, and the labourers by whose industry it is cultivated.'[1]

How far bourgeois society in the United States still is from being mature enough to make the class struggle obvious and comprehensible is most strikingly proved by *H. C. Carey* (of Philadelphia),* the only American economist of importance. He attacks *Ricardo*, the most classic representative (interpreter) of the bourgeoisie and the most stoical adversary of the proletariat, as a man whose works are an arsenal for Anarchists, Socialists, and all the enemies of the bourgeois order of society. He reproaches not only him but Malthus, Mill, Say, Torrens, Wakefield, McCulloch, Senior, Whately, R. Jones, and others, the master-minds among the economists of Europe, with rending society asunder and preparing civil war because they show that the economic bases of the different classes are bound to give rise to a necessary and ever-growing antagonism among them. He tried to refute them, not indeed like the fatuous Heinzen** by connecting the existence of classes with the existence of *political* privileges and *monopolies*, but by attempting to make out that *economic* conditions—rent (landed property), *profit* (capital), and wages (wage labour)—instead of being conditions of struggle and

*Angleterre par les Normands* (1825) and *Essai sur la formation et les progrès de l'histoire du tiers état* (1853). Marx called him 'the father of the "class struggle" in French historiography' (Letter to Engels of 27 July 1854).

François Guizot (1787–1874), a historian and politician, who in his *Histoire de la révolution d'Angleterre* (1826–7) presented the English Revolution as a struggle between the monarchy and aristocracy on the one hand, and the middle class on the other.

John Wade (1788–1875), an industrious writer, was connected with the press throughout his life. He published many books, among them *History of the Middle and Working Classes* (1833) which went into three editions. (Z.A.J.)

* See footnote, p. 102.
* See footnote, p. 145.
[1] David Ricardo, *Principles of Political Economy and Taxation*, Preface.

antagonism are rather conditions of association and harmony
All he proves, of course, is that he is taking the 'undeveloped
conditions of the United States for 'normal conditions'.

And now as to myself, no credit is due to me for discovering
the existence of classes in modern society or the struggle between
them. Long before me bourgeois historians had described the
historical development of this class struggle and bourgeois
economists the economic anatomy of the classes. What I did that
was new was to prove: (1) that the *existence of classes* is only
bound up with *particular historical phases in the development of
production*, (2) that the class struggle necessarily leads to the
*dictatorship of the proletariat*, (3) that this dictatorship itself only
constitutes the transition to the *abolition of all classes* and to
*classless society*. Ignorant louts like Heinzen, who deny not merely
the class struggle but even the existence of classes, only prove
that, despite all their blood-curdling yelps and the humanitarian
airs they give themselves, they regard the social conditions under
which the bourgeoisie rules as the final product, the *non plus
ultra* of history, and that they are only the servitors of the bourgeoisie. And the less these louts realize the greatness and transient
necessity of the bourgeois regime itself the more disgusting is
their servitude.

Marx's letter to J. Weydemeyer* of 5 March 1852, *SC*, pp. 84–6.


## (6) THE PSYCHOLOGY OF SOCIAL CLASS**

Legitimists and Orleanists, as we have said, formed the two great
factions of the party of Order. Was that which held these factions

---

* Joseph Weydemeyer (1818–1886), a journalist, was a staunch friend and
supporter of Marx whom he always tried to help, both personally and politically. After the 1848 revolution he emigrated to the United States. It was in
Weydemeyer's weekly *Die Revolution*, which appeared in New York in 1852
that *The Eighteenth Brumaire of Louis Bonaparte* was first published (in German).
(Z.A.J.)
** In two articles, 'The Elections—Tories and Whigs' and 'The Chartists'
published in the *New York Daily Tribune* of 21 and 25 August, 1952, Marx
analysed the relations between Tories, Whigs and the Free Traders along similar
lines. According to Marx, Tories and Whigs were representatives of two
sections of landed property, and the Free Traders (supporters of the Manchester

fast to their pretenders and kept them apart from one another nothing but lily and tricolour, House of Bourbon and House of Orleans, different shades of royalism, was it at all the confession of faith of royalism? Under the Bourbons, *big landed property* had governed, with its priests and lackeys; under the Orleans, high finance, large-scale industry, large-scale trade, that is, *capital*, with its retinue of lawyers, professors and smooth-tongued orators. The Legitimate Monarchy was merely the political expression of the hereditary rule of the lords of the soil, as the July Monarchy was only the political expression of the usurped rule of the bourgeois *parvenus*. What kept the two factions apart, therefore, was not any so-called principles, it was their material conditions of existence, two different kinds of property, it was the old contrast between town and country, the rivalry between capital and landed property. That at the same time old memories, personal enmities, fears and hopes, prejudices and illusions, sympathies and antipathies, convictions, articles of faith and principles bound them to one or the other royal house, who is there that denies this? Upon the different forms of property, upon the social conditions of existence, rises an entire superstructure of distinct and peculiarly formed sentiments, illusions, modes of thought and views of life. The entire class creates and forms them out of its material foundations and out of the corresponding social relations. The single individual, who derives them through tradition and upbringing, may imagine that they form the real motives and the starting point of his activity. While Orleanists and Legitimists, while each faction sought to make itself and the other believe that it was loyalty to their two royal houses which separated them, facts later proved that it was rather their divided interests which forbade the uniting of the two royal houses. And as in private life one differentiates between what a man thinks and says of himself and what he really is and does, so in historical struggles one must distinguish still more the phrases and fancies of parties from their real organism and their real interests, their conception of themselves from their reality. Orleanists and Legitimists found themselves

School in economics and promoters of various reforms in Parliament) were the spokesmen for industrial capital. Since the Free Traders represented the interests of the industrial bourgeoisie, they were anxious to replace the institutions of the Old England by a modern State and to wrest political power from the hands of an hereditary aristocracy which was closely connected with landed interests. (Z.A.J.)

F

side by side in the republic, with equal claims. If each side wished to effect the *restoration* of its *own* royal house against the other, that merely signified that each of the *two great interests* into which the *bourgeoisie* is split—landed property and capital—sought to restore its own supremacy and the subordination of the other. We speak of two interests of the bourgeoisie, for large landed property, despite its feudal coquetry and pride of race, has been rendered thoroughly bourgeois by the development of modern society. Thus the Tories in England long imagined that they were enthusiastic about monarchy, the church and the beauties of the old English Constitution, until the day of danger wrung from them the confession that they are enthusiastic only about *ground rent*.

*EBLB*, pp. 247–8.


# (B) The Main Social Classes in Modern Society

## (1) THE BOURGEOISIE AND ITS REVOLUTIONARY ROLE

The bourgeoisie, historically, has played a most revolutionary part.

The bourgeoisie, wherever it has got the upper hand, has put an end to all feudal, patriarchal, idyllic relations. It has pitilessly torn asunder the motley feudal ties that bound man to his 'natural superiors', and has left remaining no other nexus between man and man than naked self-interest, than callous 'cash payment'. It has drowned the most heavenly ecstasies of religious fervour, of chivalrous enthusiasm, of philistine sentimentalism, in the icy water of egotistical calculation. It has resolved personal worth into exchange value, and in place of the numberless indefeasible chartered freedoms, has set up that single, unconscionable freedom—Free Trade. In one word, for exploitation, veiled by religious and political illusions, it has substituted naked, shameless, direct, brutal exploitation.

The bourgeoisie has stripped of its halo every occupation hitherto honoured and looked up to with reverent awe. It has converted the physician, the lawyer, the priest, the poet, the man of science, into its paid wage-labourers.

The bourgeoisie has torn away from the family its sentimental veil, and has reduced the family relation to a mere money relation.

The bourgeoisie has disclosed how it came to pass that the brutal display of vigour in the Middle Ages, which Reactionists so much admire, found its fitting complement in the most slothful indolence. It has been the first to shew what man's activity can bring about. It has accomplished wonders far surpassing Egyptian pyramids, Roman aqueducts, and Gothic cathedrals; it has conducted expeditions that put in the shade all former Exoduses of nations and crusades.

The bourgeoisie cannot exist without constantly revolutionizing the instruments of production, and thereby the relations of production, and with them the whole relations of society. Conservation of the old modes of production in unaltered form, was, on the contrary, the first condition of existence for all earlier industrial classes. Constant revolutionizing of production, uninterrupted disturbance of all social conditions, everlasting uncertainty and agitation distinguish the bourgeois epoch from all earlier ones. All fixed, fast-frozen relations, with their train of ancient and venerable prejudices and opinions, are swept away, all new-formed ones become antiquated before they can ossify. All that is solid melts into air, all that is holy is profaned, and man is at last compelled to face with sober senses, his real conditions of life, and his relations with his kind.

The need of a constantly expanding market for its products chases the bourgeoisie over the whole surface of the globe. It must nestle everywhere, settle everywhere, establish connexions everywhere.

The bourgeoisie has through its exploitation of the world-market given a cosmopolitan character to production and consumption in every country. To the great chagrin of Reactionists, it has drawn from under the feet of industry the national ground on which it stood. All old-established national industries have been destroyed or are daily being destroyed. They are dislodged by new industries, whose introduction becomes a life and death question for all civilised nations, by industries that no longer work up indigenous raw material, but raw material drawn from the remotes zones; industries whose products are consumed, not only at home but in every quarter of the globe. In place of the old wants satisfied by the productions of the country, we find new wants requiring for their satisfaction the products of distant lands an climes. In place of the old local and national seclusion and self sufficiency, we have intercourse in every direction, universal inter dependence of nations. And as in material, so also in intellectua production. The intellectual creations of individual nations be come common property. National one-sidedness and narrow mindedness become more and more impossible, and from th numerous national and local literatures, there arises a world literature.

The bourgeoisie, by the rapid improvement of all instrument of production, by the immensely facilitated means of communica tion, draws all, even the most barbarian, nations into civilization The cheap prices of its commodities are the heavy artillery wit which it batters down all Chinese walls, with which it forces th barbarians' intensely obstinate hatred of foreigners to capitulate It compels all nations, on pain of extinction, to adopt the bourgeoi mode of production; it compels them to introduce what it call civilization into their midst, i.e., to become bourgeois themselves In one word, it creates a world after its own image.

The bourgeoisie has subjected the country to the rule of th towns. It has created enormous cities, has greatly increased th urban population as compared with the rural, and has thus rescue a considerable part of the population from the idiocy of rural life Just as it has made the country dependent on the towns, so it ha made barbarian and semi-barbarian countries dependent on th civilized ones, nations of peasants on nations of bourgeois, th East on the West.

The bourgeoisie keeps more and more doing away with th scattered state of the population, of the means of production, an of property. It has agglomerated population, centralized means c production, and has concentrated property in a few hands. Th necessary consequence of this was political centralization. Inde pendent, or but loosely connected provinces, with separate inter ests, laws, governments and systems of taxation, became lumpe together into one nation, with one government, one code of law one national class-interest, one frontier and one customs-tariff.

The bourgeoisie, during its rule of scarce one hundred years, has created more massive and more colossal productive forces than have all preceding generations together. Subjection of Nature's forces to man, machinery, application of chemistry to industry and agriculture, steam-navigation, railways, electric telegraphs, clearing of whole continents for cultivation, canalization of rivers, whole populations conjured out of the ground—what earlier century had even a presentiment that such productive forces slumbered in the lap of social labour?

*MCP*, pp. 35–7.

## (2) THE MODERN WORKING CLASS OR THE PROLETARIANS

In proportion as the bourgeoisie, i.e., capital, is developed, in the same proportion is the proletariat, the modern working class, developed—a class of labourers, who live only so long as they find work, and who find work only so long as their labour increases capital. These labourers, who must sell themselves piecemeal, are a commodity, like every other article of commerce, and are consequently exposed to all the vicissitudes of competition, to all the fluctuations of the market.

Owing to the extensive use of machinery and to division of labour, the work of the proletarians has lost all individual character, and, consequently, all charm for the workman. He becomes an appendage of the machine, and it is only the most simple, most monotonous, and most easily acquired knack, that is required of him. Hence, the cost of production of a workman is restricted, almost entirely, to the means of subsistence that he requires for his maintenance, and for the propagation of his race. But the price of a commodity, and therefore also of labour, is equal to its cost of production. In proportion, therefore, as the repulsiveness of the work increases, the wage decreases. Nay more, in proportion as the use of machinery and division of labour increases, in the same proportion the burden of toil also increases, whether by prolongation of the working hours, by increase of the work exacted in a given time or by increased speed of the machinery, etc.

Modern industry has converted the little workshop of the patriarchal master into the great factory of the industrial capitalist.

Masses of labourers, crowded into the factory, are organized like soldiers. As privates of the industrial army they are placed under the command of a perfect hierarchy of officers and sergeants. Not only are they slaves of the bourgeois class, and of the bourgeois State; they are daily and hourly enslaved by the machine, by the over-looker, and, above all, by the individual bourgeois manufacturer himself. The more openly this despotism proclaims gain to be its end and aim, the more petty, the more hateful and the more embittering it is.

The less the skill and exertion of strength implied in manual labour, in other words, the more modern industry becomes developed, the more is the labour of men superseded by that of women. Differences of age and sex have no longer any distinctive social validity for the working class. All are instruments of labour, more or less expensive to use, according to their age and sex.

*MCP*, pp. 38–9.

Of all the classes that stand face to face with the bourgeoisie today, the proletariat alone is a really revolutionary class. The other classes decay and finally disappear in the face of modern industry; the proletariat is its special and essential product.

The lower middle class, the small manufacturer, the shopkeeper, the artisan, the peasant, all these fight against the bourgeoisie, to save from extinction their existence as fractions of the middle class. They are therefore not revolutionary, but conservative. Nay more, they are reactionary, for they try to roll back the wheel of history. If by chance they are revolutionary, they are so only in view of their impending transfer into the proletariat, they thus defend not their present, but their future interests, they desert their own standpoint to place themselves at that of the proletariat.

The 'dangerous class', the social scum, that passively rotting mass thrown off by the lowest layers of old society, may, here and there, be swept into the movement by a proletarian revolution; its conditions of life, however, prepare it far more for the part of a bribed tool of reactionary intrigue.

In the conditions of the proletariat, those of old society at large are already virtually swamped. The proletarian is without property;

his relation to his wife and children has no longer anything in common with the bourgeois family-relations; modern industrial labour, modern subjection to capital, the same in England as in France, in America as in Germany, has stripped him of every trace of national character. Law, morality, religion, are to him so many bourgeois prejudices, behind which lurk in ambush just as many bourgeois interests.

All the preceding classes that got the upper hand, sought to fortify their already acquired status by subjecting society at large to their conditions of appropriation. The proletarians cannot become masters of the productive forces of society, except by abolishing their own previous mode of appropriation, and thereby also every other previous mode of appropriation. They have nothing of their own to secure and to fortify; their mission is to destroy all previous securities for, and insurances of, individual property.

All previous historical movements were movements of minorities, or in the interest of minorities. The proletarian movement is the self-conscious, independent movement of the immense majority, in the interest of the immense majority. The proletariat, the lowest stratum of our present society, cannot stir, cannot raise itself up, without the whole superincumbent strata of official society being sprung into the air.

Though not in substance, yet in form, the struggle of the proletariat with the bourgeoisie is at first a national struggle. The proletariat of each country must, of course, first of all settle matters with its own bourgeoisie.

In depicting the most general phases of the development of the proletariat, we traced the more or less veiled civil war, raging within existing society, up to the point where that war breaks out into open revolution, and where the violent overthrow of the bourgeoisie lays the foundation for the sway of the proletariat.

Hitherto, every form of society has been based, as we have already seen, on the antagonism of oppressing and oppressed classes. But in order to oppress a class, certain conditions must be assured to it under which it can, at least, continue its slavish existence. The serf, in the period of serfdom, raised himself to membership in the commune, just as the petty bourgeois, under the yoke of feudal absolutism, managed to develop into a bourgeois. The modern labourer, on the contrary, instead of rising with the progress of industry, sinks deeper and deeper below the conditions of existence of his own class. He becomes a pauper, and pauperism develops more rapidly than population and wealth. And here it becomes evident that the bourgeoisie is unfit any longer to be the ruling class in society, and to impose its conditions of existence upon society as an over-riding law. It is unfit to rule because it is incompetent to assure an existence to its slave within his slavery, because it cannot help letting him sink into such a state that it has to feed him, instead of being fed by him. Society can no longer live under this bourgeoisie, in other words, its existence is no longer compatible with society.

The essential condition for the existence, and for the sway of the bourgeois class, is the formation and augmentation of capital; the condition for capital is wage-labour. Wage-labour rests exclusively on competition between the labourers. The advance of industry, whose involuntary promoter is the bourgeoisie, replaces the isolation of the labourers, due to competition, by their revolutionary combination, due to association. The development of Modern Industry, therefore, cuts from under its feet the very foundation on which the bourgeoisie produces and appropriates products. What the bourgeoisie, therefore, produces, above all, are its own grave-diggers. Its fall and the victory of the proletariat are equally inevitable.

*MCP*, pp. 42–3.

## (3) THE MIDDLE CLASSES

The lower strata of the middle class—the small tradespeople, shopkeepers, and retired tradesmen generally, the handicraftsmen and peasants—all these sink gradually into the proletariat, partly because their diminutive capital does not suffice for the scale on which Modern Industry is carried on, and is swamped in the competition with the large capitalists, partly because their specialized skill is rendered worthless by new methods of production. Thus the proletariat is recruited from all classes of the population.

*MCP*, pp. 39–40.

As against the coalesced bourgeoisie, a coalition between petty bourgeois and workers had been formed, the so-called *social-democratic* party. The petty bourgeois saw that they were badly rewarded after the June days of 1848, that their material interests were imperilled and that the democratic guarantees which were to ensure the effectuation of these interests were called in question by the counter-revolution. Accordingly, they came closer to the workers. On the other hand, their parliamentary representation, the *Montagne*, thrust aside during the dictatorship of the bourgeois republicans, had in the last half of the life of the Constituent Assembly reconquered its lost popularity through the struggle with Bonaparte and the royalist ministers. It had concluded an alliance with the socialist leaders. In February 1849, banquets celebrated the reconciliation. A joint programme was drafted, joint election committees were set up and joint candidates put forward. From the social demands of the proletariat the revolutionary point was broken off and a democratic turn given to them; from the democratic claims of the petty bourgeoisie the purely political form was stripped off and their socialist point thrust forward. Thus arose the *Social-Democracy*. The new *Montagne*, the result of this combination, contained, apart from some supernumeraries from the working class and some socialist sectarians, the same elements as the old *Montagne*, only numerically stronger. However, in the course of development, it had changed with the class that it represented. The peculiar character of the Social-Democracy is epitomized in the fact that democratic-republican institutions are demanded as a means, not of doing away with two extremes, capital and wage labour, but of weakening their antagonism and transforming it into harmony. However different the means proposed for the attainment of this end may be, however much it may be trimmed with more or less revolutionary notions, the content remains the same. This content is the transformation of society in a democratic way, but a transformation within the bounds of the petty bourgeoisie. Only one must not form the narrow-minded notion that the petty bourgeoisie, on principle, wishes to enforce an egoistic class interest. Rather, it believes that the *special* conditions of its emancipation are the *general* conditions within the frame of which alone modern society can be saved and the class struggle avoided. Just as little must one imagine that the democratic representatives are indeed all shopkeepers or en-

F*

thusiastic champions of shopkeepers. According to their education and their individual position they may be as far apart as heaven from earth. What makes them representatives of the petty bourgeoisie is the fact that in their minds they do not get beyond the limits which the latter do not get beyond in life, that they are consequently driven, theoretically, to the same problems and solutions to which material interest and social position drive the latter practically. This is, in general, the relationship between the *political* and *literary representatives* of a class and the class they represent.

*EBLB*, pp. 249–50.

The democrat, because he represents the petty bourgeoisie, that is, a *transition class*, in which the interests of two classes are simultaneously mutually blunted, imagines himself elevated above class antagonism generally. The democrats concede that a privileged class confronts them, but they, along with all the rest of the nation, form the *people*. What they represent is the *people's rights*; what interests them is the *people's interests*. Accordingly, when a struggle is impending, they do not need to examine the interests and positions of the different classes. They do not need to weigh their own resources too critically. They have merely to give the signal and the *people*, with all its inexhaustible resources, will fall upon the *oppressors*. Now, if in the performance their interests prove to be uninteresting and their potency impotence, then either the fault lies with pernicious sophists, who split the *indivisible people* into different hostile camps, or the army was too brutalized and blinded to comprehend that the pure aims of democracy are the best thing for it itself, or the whole thing has been wrecked by a detail in its execution, or else an unforeseen accident has this time spoilt the game. In any case, the democrat comes out of the most disgraceful defeat just as immaculate as he was innocent when he went into it, with the newly-won conviction that he is bound to win, not that he himself and his party have to give up the old standpoint, but, on the contrary, that conditions have to ripen to suit him.

*EBLB*, pp. 252–3.

# (4) THE PEASANT CLASS

The small-holding peasants form a vast mass, the members of which live in similar conditions but without entering into manifold relations with one another. Their mode of production isolates them from one another instead of bringing them into mutual intercourse. The isolation is increased by France's bad means of communication and by the poverty of the peasants. Their field of production, the small holding, admits of no division of labour in its cultivation, no application of science and, therefore, no diversity of development, no variety of talent, no wealth of social relationships. Each individual peasant family is almost self-sufficient; it itself directly produces the major part of its consumption and thus acquires its means of life more through exchange with nature than in intercourse with society. A small holding, a peasant and his family; alongside them another small holding, another peasant and another family. A few score of these make up a village, and a few score of villages make up a Department. In this way, the great mass of the French nation is formed by simple addition of homologous magnitudes, much as potatoes in a sack form a sack of potatoes. In so far as millions of families live under economic conditions of existence that separate their mode of life, their interests and their culture from those of the other classes, and put them in hostile opposition to the latter, they form a class. In so far as there is merely a local interconnection among these small-holding peasants, and the identity of their interests begets no community, no national bond and no political organization among them, they do not form a class. They are consequently incapable of enforcing their class interest in their own name, whether through a parliament or through a convention. They cannot represent themselves, they must be represented. Their representative must at the same time appear as their master, as an authority over them, as an unlimited governmental power that protects them against the other classes and sends them rain and sunshine from above. The political influence of the small-holding peasants, therefore, finds its final expression in the executive power subordinating society to itself.

*EBLB*, pp. 302-3.

The condition of the French peasants, when the republic had added new burdens to their old ones, is comprehensible. It can be seen that their exploitation differs only in *form* from the exploitation of the industrial proletariat. The exploiter is the same: *capital*. The individual capitalists exploit the individual peasants through *mortgages* and *usury*; the capitalist class exploits the peasant class through the *state taxes*. The peasant's title to property is the talisman by which capital held him hitherto under its spell, the pretext under which it set him against the industrial proletariat. Only the fall of capital can raise the peasant; only an anti-capitalist, a proletarian government can break his economic misery, his social degradation. The *constitutional republic* is the dictatorship of his united exploiters; the *social-democratic*, the *Red* republic, is the dictatorship of his allies.

*CSF*, p. 198.

In spite of the industrial and commercial prosperity that France momentarily enjoys, the mass of the people, the twenty five million peasants, suffer from a great depression. The good harvests of the last few years have forced the prices of corn much lower even than in England, and the position of the peasants under such circumstances, in debt, sucked dry by usury and crushed by taxes, must be anything but splendid. The history of the last three years has, however, provided sufficient proof that this class of the population is absolutely incapable of any revolutionary initiative.

*CSF*, pp. 209–10.

December 10, 1848,* was the day of the *peasant insurrection*. Only from this day does the February** of the French peasants date. The symbol that expressed their entry into the revolutionary movement, clumsily cunning, knavishly naive, doltishly sublime, a calculated superstition, a pathetic burlesque, a cleverly stupid anachronism, a world-historic piece of buffoonery and an

* On 10 December, 1848, Louis Bonaparte was elected the President of the Republic in a direct vote by an enormous majority. According to Marx, his election was the electoral victory of the peasants. (Z.A.J.)
** The popular rising in Paris in February, 1848, the subsequent abdication of Louis Philippe, and the formation of a Republican government. (Z.A.J.)

undecipherable hieroglyphic for the understanding of the civilized—this symbol bore the unmistakable physiognomy of the class that represents barbarism within civilization.

*CSF*, p. 159.

# (C) Class Conflict and Its Implications

## (1) THE UNIVERSALITY OF CLASS[1] DIFFERENTIATION AND CLASS STRUGGLE

The history of all hitherto-existing society[2] is the history of class struggles.

Freeman and slave, patrician and plebeian, lord and serf, guild-master[3] and journeyman, in a word, oppressor and oppressed, stood in constant opposition to one another, carried on an uninterrupted, now hidden, now open fight, a fight that each time ended, either in a revolutionary re-constitution of society at large, or in the common ruin of the contending classes.

---

[1] By bourgeoisie is meant the class of modern Capitalists, owners of the means of social production and employers of wage-labour. By proletariat, the class of modern wage-labourers who, having no means of production of their own, are reduced to selling their labour-power in order to live. [*Note by Engels to the English edition of 1888.*]

[2] That is, all *written* history. In 1847, the pre-history of society, the social organization existing previous to recorded history, was all but unknown. Since then, Haxthausen discovered common ownership of land in Russia, Maurer proved it to be the social foundation from which all Teutonic races started in history, and by and by village communities were found to be, or to have been the primitive form of society everywhere from India to Ireland. The inner organization of this primitive Communistic society was laid bare, in its typical form, by Morgan's crowning discovery of the true nature of the *gens* and its relation to the *tribe*. With the dissolution of these primaeval communities society begins to be differentiated into separate and finally antagonistic classes. I have attempted to retrace this process of dissolution in *Der Ursprung der Familie, des Privateigentums und des Staats (The Origin of the Family, Private Property and the State)*, 2nd edition, Stuttgart 1886. [*Note by Engels to the English edition of 1888.*]

[3] Guild-master, that is, a full member of a guild, a master within, not a head of a guild. [*Note by Engels to the English edition of 1888.*]

In the earlier epochs of history, we find almost everywhere a complicated arrangement of society into various orders, a manifold gradation of social rank. In ancient Rome we have patricians, knights, plebeians, slaves; in the Middle Ages, feudal lords, vassals, guild-masters, journeymen, apprentices, serfs; in almost all of these classes, again, subordinate gradations.

The modern bourgeois society that has sprouted from the ruins of feudal society has not done away with class antagonisms. It has but established new classes, new conditions of oppression, new forms of struggle in place of the old ones.

Our epoch, the epoch of the bourgeoisie, possesses, however, this distinctive feature: it has simplified the class antagonisms. Society as a whole is more and more splitting up into two great hostile camps, into two great classes directly facing each other: Bourgeoisie and Proletariat.

*MCP*, pp. 33–4.

## (2) CLASS DOMINATION: THE RULING CLASS AS A MATERIAL AND INTELLECTUAL FORCE

The ideas of the ruling class are in every epoch the ruling ideas: i.e., the class, which is the ruling *material* force of society, is at the same time its ruling *intellectual* force. The class which has the means of material production at its disposal, has control at the same time over the means of mental production, so that thereby, generally speaking, the ideas of those who lack the means of mental production are subject to it. The ruling ideas are nothing more than the ideal expression of the dominant material relationships, the dominant material relationships grasped as ideas; hence of the relationships which make the one class the ruling one, therefore, the ideas of its dominance. The individuals composing the ruling class possess among other things consciousness, and therefore think. In so far, therefore, as they rule as a class and determine the extent and compass of an epoch, it is self-evident that they do this in its whole range, hence among other things rule also as thinkers, as producers of ideas, and regulate the production and distribution of the ideas of their age: thus their ideas are the ruling ideas of the epoch. For instance, in an age and in a country where royal power, aristocracy and bourgeoisie are contending for mastery and where, therefore, mastery is shared, the doctrine of the separation of powers proves to be the dominant idea and is expressed as an 'eternal law'.

The division of labour, . . . . as one of the chief forces of history up till now, manifests itself also in the ruling class as the division of mental and material labour, so that inside this class one part appears as the thinkers of the class (its active, conceptive ideologists, who make the perfecting of the illusion of the class about itself their chief source of livelihood), while the others' attitude to these ideas and illusions is more passive and receptive, because they are in reality the active members of this class and have less time to make up illusions and ideas about themselves. Within this class this cleavage can even develop into a certain opposition and hostility between the two parts, which, however, in the case of a practical collision, in which the class itself is endangered, automatically comes to nothing, in which case there also vanishes the semblance that the ruling ideas were not the ideas of the ruling class and had a power distinct from the power of this class. The existence of revolutionary ideas in a particular period presupposes the existence of a revolutionary class . . . .

If now in considering the course of history we detach the ideas of the ruling class from the ruling class itself and attribute to them an independent existence, if we confine ourselves to saying that these or those ideas were dominant at a given time, without bothering ourselves about the conditions of production and the producers of these ideas, if we thus ignore the individuals and world conditions which are the source of the ideas, we can say, for instance, that during the time that the aristocracy was dominant, the concepts honour, loyalty, etc., were dominant, during the dominance of the bourgeoisie the concepts freedom, equality, etc. The ruling class itself on the whole imagines this to be so. This conception of history, which is common to all historians, particularly since the eighteenth century, will necessarily come up against the phenomenon that increasingly abstract ideas hold sway, i.e., ideas which increasingly take on the form of universality. For each new class which puts itself in the place of one ruling before it, is compelled, merely in order to carry through its aim, to represent its interest as the common interest of all the members of society, that is, expressed in ideal form: it has to give its ideas the form of universality, and represent them as the only rational, universally valid ones. The class making a revolution appears from the very start, if only because it is opposed to a *class*, not as a class but as the representative of the whole of society; it appears as the whole mass of society confronting the one ruling class.[1] It can do this because, to start with, its interest really is more connected with the common interest of all other non-ruling classes, because under the pressure of hitherto existing conditions its interest has not yet been able to develop as the particular interest of a particular class. Its victory, therefore, benefits also many individuals of the other classes which are not winning a dominant position, but only in so far as it now puts these individuals in a position to raise themselves into the ruling class. When the French bourgeoisie overthrew the power of the aristocracy, it thereby made it possible for many proletarians to raise themselves above the proletariat, but only in so far as they became bourgeois. Every new class, therefore, achieves its hegemony only on a broader basis than that of the class ruling previously, whereas the opposition of the non-ruling class against the new ruling class later develops all the more sharply and profoundly. Both these things determine the fact that the struggle to be waged against this new ruling class, in its turn, aims at a more decided and radical negation of the previous conditions of society than could all previous classes which sought to rule.

This whole semblance, that the rule of a certain class is only the rule of certain ideas, comes to a natural end, of course, as soon as class rule in general ceases to be the form in which society is organized, that is to say, as soon as it is no longer necessary to represent a particular interest as general or the 'general interest' as ruling.

GI, pp. 60–2.

The conditions of existence of the ruling class (determined by the development of production hitherto), which are ideally expressed in law, morality, etc., are more or less consciously transformed by the ideologists of that class into something that in

---

[1] (Marginal note by Marx:) Universality corresponds to (1) the class versus the estate, (2) the competition, world-wide intercourse, etc., (3) the great numerical strength of the ruling class, (4) the illusion of the *common* interests (in the beginning this illusion is true), (5) the delusion of the ideologists and the division of labour.

history exists independently, and which can be conceived in the consciousness of the separate individuals of that class as vocation, etc.; and which are set up as a standard of life in opposition to the individuals of the oppressed class, partly as an embellishment or realization of domination, partly as a moral means for this domination. It is to be noted here, as in general with ideologists, that they inevitably put the thing upside-down and regard their ideology both as the creative force and as the aim of all social relations, whereas it is only an expression and symptom of these relations.

*GI*, p. 461.

The more the normal form of intercourse of society, and with it the conditions of the ruling class, develop their contradiction to the advanced productive forces, and the greater the consequent split within the ruling class itself as well as the split between it and the class ruled by it, the more untrue, of course, becomes the consciousness which originally corresponded to this form of intercourse (i.e., it ceases to be the consciousness corresponding to this form of intercourse), and the more do the earlier traditional ideas of this intercourse, in which actual private interests, etc., etc., are expressed as universal interests, descend to the level of mere idealizing phrases, conscious illusion, deliberate hypocrisy. But the more their falsity is exposed by life, and the less meaning they have for consciousness itself, the more firmly are they asserted, the more hypocritical, moral and holy becomes the language of this normal society.

*GI*, pp. 316–7.

## (3) THE CLASS CONFLICT AS AN ECONOMIC AND POLITICAL STRUGGLE

The first attempts of workers to *associate* among themselves always take place in the form of combinations.

Large-scale industry concentrates in one place a crowd of people unknown to one another. Competition divides their interests. But the maintenance of wages, this common interest which they have against their boss, unites them in a common thought of resistance—*combination*. Thus combination always has a double aim, that of stopping competition among the workers, so that they can carry on general competition with the capitalist. If the first aim of resistance was merely the maintenance of wages, combinations, at first isolated, constitute themselves into groups as the capitalists in their turn unite for the purpose of repression, and in face of always united capital, the maintenance of the association becomes more necessary to them than that of wages. This is so true that English economists are amazed to see the workers sacrifice a good part of their wages in favour of associations, which, in the eyes of these economists, are established solely in favour of wages. In this struggle—a veritable civil war—all the elements necessary for a coming battle unite and develop. Once it has reached this point, association takes on a political character.

Economic conditions had first transformed the mass of the people of the country into workers. The combination of capital has created for this mass a common situation, common interests. This mass is thus already a class as against capital, but not yet for itself. In the struggle, of which we have noted only a few phases, this mass becomes united, and constitutes itself as a class for itself. The interests it defends become class interests. But the struggle of class against class is a political struggle.

In the bourgeoisie we have two phases to distinguish: that in which it constituted itself as a class under the regime of feudalism and absolute monarchy, and that in which, already constituted as a class, it overthrew feudalism and monarchy to make society into a bourgeois society. The first of these phases was the longer and necessitated the greater efforts. This too began by partial combinations against the feudal lords.

Much research has been carried out to trace the different historical phases that the bourgeoisie has passed through, from the commune up to its constitution as a class.

But when it is a question of making a precise study of strikes, combinations and other forms in which the proletarians carry out before our eyes their organization as a class, some are seized with real fear and others display a *transcendental* disdain.

An oppressed class is the vital condition for every society founded on the antagonism of classes. The emancipation of the oppressed class thus implies necessarily the creation of a new society. For the oppressed class to be able to emancipate itself it is necessary that the productive powers already acquired and the existing social relations should no longer be capable of existing side by side. Of all the instruments of production, the greatest productive power is the revolutionary class itself. The organization of revolutionary elements as a class supposes the existence of all the productive forces which could be engendered in the bosom of the old society.

Does this mean that after the fall of the old society there will be a new class domination culminating in a new political power? No.

The condition for the emancipation of the working class is the abolition of every class, just as the condition for the liberation of the third estate, of the bourgeois order, was the abolition of all estates[1] and all orders.

The working class, in the course of its development, will substitute for the old civil society an association which will exclude classes and their antagonism, and there will be no more political power properly so-called, since political power is precisely the official expression of antagonism in civil society.

Meanwhile the antagonism between the proletariat and the bourgeoisie is a struggle of class against class, a struggle which carried to its highest expression is a total revolution. Indeed, is it at all surprising that a society founded on the opposition of classes should culminate in brutal *contradiction*, the shock of body against body, as its final *dénouement*?

Do not say that social movement excludes political movement. There is never a political movement which is not at the same time social.

It is only in an order of things in which there are no more classes and class antagonisms that *social evolutions* will cease to be *political revolutions*. Till then, on the eve of every general reshuffling of society, the last word of social science will always be

*Le combat ou la mort; la lutte sanguinaire ou le néant. C'est ainsi que la question est invinciblement posée.*[2]

PP, pp. 165–8.

---

Estates here in the historical sense of the estates of feudalism, estates with definite and limited privileges. The revolution of the bourgeoisie abolished the estates and their privileges. Bourgeois society knows only *classes*. It was, therefore, absolutely in contradiction with history to describe the proletariat as the 'fourth estate'. [*Note by F. Engels to the German edition, 1885.*]

'Combat or death; bloody struggle or extinction. It is thus that the question is inexorably put.' These words come from George Sand's historical novel *Jean Ziska* (Preface). [Translator's Note.]

## (4) FREEDOM AND CLASS STRUCTURE

He* imagines that people up to now have always formed a concep
of man, and then won freedom for themselves to the extent tha
was necessary to realize this concept; that the measure of freedon
that they achieved was determined each time by their idea of th
ideal of man at the time; and on each occasion there remained ir
each individual a residue which did not correspond to this idea
and, therefore, as being 'inhuman' was either not set free or only
freed *malgré eux*.

In reality, of course, what happened was that people woi
freedom for themselves each time to the extent that was dictated
and permitted not by their ideal of man, but by the existing
productive forces. All conquests of freedom hitherto, however
have been based on restricted productive forces. The production
which these productive forces could provide was insufficient fo
the whole of society and made development possible only if some
persons satisfied their needs at the expense of others, and therefore
some—the minority—obtained the monopoly of development
while others—the majority—owing to the constant struggle to
satisfy their most essential needs, were for the time being (i.e.
until the birth of new revolutionary productive forces) excluded
from any development. Thus, society has hitherto alway
developed within the framework of a contradiction—in antiquit
the contradiction between free men and slaves, in the Middle Age
that between nobility and serfs, in modern times that between th
bourgeoisie and the proletariat. This explains, on the one hand
the abnormal, 'inhuman' means with which the oppressed clas
satisfies its needs, and, on the other hand, the narrow limits withir
which intercourse, and with it the whole ruling class, develops
Hence this restricted character of development consists not onl
in the exclusion of one class from development, but also in th
narrow-mindedness of the excluding class, and the 'inhuman' i
to be found also within the ruling class.

*GI*, pp. 474-5.

---

* Max Stirner (1806–1856), a Young Hegelian and author of *Der Einzige un
sein Eigentum* (*The Ego and His Own*). Part III of the first volume of *Th
German Ideology* is a polemic with Stirner. (Z.A.J.)

# (5) THE STABILITY OF THE RULING CLASS

What distinguishes interest-bearing capital—in so far as it is an essential element of the capitalist mode of production—from usurer's capital is by no means the nature or character of this capital itself. It is merely the altered conditions under which it operates, and consequently also the totally transformed character of the borrower who confronts the money-lender. Even when a man without fortune receives credit in his capacity of industrialist or merchant, it occurs with the expectation that he will function as capitalist and appropriate unpaid labour with the borrowed capital. He receives credit in his capacity of potential capitalist. The circumstance that a man without fortune but possessing energy, solidity, ability and business acumen may become a capitalist in this manner—and the commercial value of each individual is pretty accurately estimated under the capitalist mode of production—is greatly admired by apologists of the capitalist system. Although this circumstance continually brings an unwelcome number of new soldiers of fortune into the field and into competition with the already existing individual capitalists, it also reinforces the supremacy of capital itself, expands its base and enables it to recruit ever new forces for itself out of the substratum of society. In a similar way, the circumstance that the Catholic Church in the Middle Ages formed its hierarchy out of the best brains in the land, regardless of their estate, birth or fortune, was one of the principal means of consolidating ecclesiastical rule and suppressing the laity. The more a ruling class is able to assimilate the foremost minds of a ruled class, the more stable and dangerous becomes its rule.

*C* III, p. 587.

# (6) KNOWLEDGE AS DETERMINED BY CLASS INTERESTS

What characterizes Malthus is the *fundamental meanness* of his outlook; a meanness which only a parson could permit himself to display, a parson who looks upon human misery as the punishment for the Fall of man and stands in general need of 'an earthly vale of tears', but who at the same time, out of consideration for the benefices accruing to him, finds it most advantageous, with the help of the dogma of predestination, to 'sweeten' the sojourn of the ruling classes in the vale of tears. This meanness of outlook also reveals itself in his standards of scholarship. *First*, in his shameless and mechanical *plagiarism*. *Second*, in the *considerate*, not *inconsiderate*, conclusions which he draws from scientific premises.

Ricardo was right, for his time, in regarding the capitalist mode of production as the most advantageous for production in general, as the most advantageous for the production of wealth. He wants *production for the sake of production*, and in this [he is] *right*. Those who assert, as Ricardo's sentimental opponents have done, that production as such is not the end, forget that production for the sake of production merely means the development of human productive power, that is, *the development of the wealth of the human race as an end in itself*. If, as Sismondi* does, one sets up the welfare of the individual in opposition to this end, this is tantamount to asserting that the development of the species must be *checked* in order to ensure the welfare of the individual—for example, that wars should never be waged, since individuals are necessarily destroyed in them. Sismondi is right only as against those economists who *gloss over* this antithesis or deny it. What is not understood is that the development of the capabilities of the species *man*, although it proceeds at first at the expense of the majority of human individuals and of certain human classes, will eventually break through this antagonism and coincide with the development of the individual person, and that therefore the higher development of individuality can only be purchased through a historical process in which individuals are sacrificed. And this is to say nothing of the sterility of such edifying views, since the gains of the species in the human kingdom, as in the animal and plant kingdoms, are always made at the expense of individual advantage.**

* Jean-Charles-Léonard Simonde de Sismondi (1773–1842), a Swiss economist and historian. Marx, who owed a great deal to Sismondi's criticism of the early industrial capitalist society, described him as the head of petty-bourgeois socialism (*MCP*, pp. 53–4). (Z.A.J.)
** In the new edition of the *Theorien über den Mehrwert* the paragraph ends with the following sentence. 'This is due to the fact that the gains of the species coincide with the advantage of some particular individuals, and they also constitute the strength of these favoured members of the species.' (*TM 2*, p. 107) (Z.A.J.)

Ricardo's inconsiderateness was thus not only *scientifically honest*, but also, given his point of view, *scientifically necessary*. This means, however, that he was also entirely indifferent as to whether the development of productive power destroyed landed property or whether it destroyed the workers. If this progress reduces the value of the capital of the industrial bourgeoisie, it is just as welcome to him. If the development of the productive power of labour reduces the value of the existing fixed capital by a half, what does that matter, asks Ricardo. The productivity of human labour has doubled. Here, then, is *scientific honesty*. If Ricardo's theories taken together are in the interests of the *industrial bourgeoisie*, this is the case only *because* and in so far as the interests of this class coincide with those of production or of the productive development of human labour. Where they do not coincide but are in conflict with one another, Ricardo comes out just as *inconsiderately* against the bourgeoisie as in other cases he comes out against the proletariat and the aristocracy . . . .

But the contemptible Malthus draws from the scientifically established premises—which he always *steals*—only those conclusions which are *acceptable* and useful to the aristocracy as against the bourgeoisie and to both *as against* the proletariat. He therefore wants *production*, not *for the sake of production*, but only in so far as it maintains or consolidates[1] *the existing order of things* and serves to further the advantage of the ruling classes.

His very first book*—one of the most remarkable examples in literature of a plagiarism which was successful at the expense of the original work—had the practical aim of proving, in the interests of the then English government and landed aristocracy, that the doctrines of perfectibility of the French Revolution and of its supporters in England were 'economically' utopian. In other words, it was a panegyrical tract in favour of the existing state of affairs as against historical development, and in addition a justification of the war against revolutionary France.

His writings of 1815 on protective tariffs and ground rent** were

---

[1] In the manuscript: *aushauscht*.—(Kautsky takes *ausbauscht*, 'swells', as a slip for *ausbaut*, 'consolidates'. [R. L. Meek]

* That is, *An Essay on the Principle of Population as it Affects the Future Improvement of Society* (1798). (Z.A.J.)

** That is, *Grounds of an Opinion on the Policy of Restricting the Importation of Foreign Corn* and *An Inquiry into the Nature and Progress of Rent, and the Principles by which it is regulated*. (Z.A.J.)

intended to corroborate his earlier apology for the poverty of the producers; but in particular they were intended to defend reactionary landed property against 'enlightened', 'liberal' and 'progressive' capital, and above all to justify a retrograde piece of legislation put forward in England in the interests of the aristocracy as against the industrial bourgeoisie. Finally his *Principles of Political Economy*, directed against Ricardo, had essentially the aim of confining the absolute demands of industrial capital, and the laws according to which its productivity develops, within limits which would be 'advantageous' and 'desirable' from the point of view of the landed aristocracy, the State Church to which Malthus belonged, government officials (*Regierungspersonen*), and tax-consumers (*Steuerverzehrer*). But a man who tries to *accommodate* science to a point of view which is not derived from science itself, however erroneous it may be, but which is borrowed from outside, from *extrinsic interests* which are *foreign* to it, I call '*mean*'.

Ricardo is not mean when he places the proletarians on the same level as machinery, beasts of burden or commodities, because from his point of view 'production' demands that they should be merely machinery or beasts of burden and because in actual fact they are only commodities in capitalist production. This is stoical, objective, and scientific. In so far as it is possible without sinning against his science, Ricardo is always a philanthropist, as he was in practice.

Parson Malthus, [it is true, also] reduces the workers to beasts of burden for the sake of production, and even condemns them to live in celibacy and to die of hunger. [But] where the same demands of production reduce the landlord's 'rent', or encroach too much on the 'tithes' of the State Church or the interests of the tax-consumers, or where they sacrifice that section of the industrial bourgeoisie whose interests hinder progress to that section of the bourgeoisie which advocates the progress of production—that is, where it is a question of any interest of the aristocracy as against the bourgeoisie, or of the conservative and stagnating bourgeoisie as against the progressive bourgeoisie—in all these cases 'Parson' Malthus does not sacrifice the exclusive interests to production, but *does* his best to sacrifice the demands of production to the exclusive interests of the existing ruling classes or sections of them, and to this end he *falsifies* his scientific conclusions. That is his *scientific* meanness, his sin against science, quite apart from his

shameless and mechanical plagiarism. Malthus's scientific conclusions are *considerate* where the ruling classes in general and the
reactionary elements among these ruling classes in particular are
concerned; that is, he *falsifies* science on behalf of these interests.
His conclusions are, however, *inconsiderate* where the oppressed
classes are concerned. And it is not only that he is *inconsiderate*.
He *affects* inconsiderateness, takes a cynical pleasure in this role,
and *exaggerates* the conclusions—in so far as they are directed
against those living in poverty—to an even *greater* extent than
could be scientifically justified from his own point of view.

The hatred of the English working class against Malthus—the
'mountebank-parson',[1] as Cobbett rudely calls him—is therefore
entirely justified. The people were right here in sensing in-
stinctively that they were confronted not with a *man of science* but
with a *bought advocate*, a pleader on behalf of their enemies, a
shameless sycophant of the ruling classes . . . . .

Malthus's only merit, as against the pitiable doctrines [should
be: teachers, Z. A. J.] of harmony in bourgeois political economy,
is precisely his pointed emphasis on the disharmonies. Although
*in no instance did he discover these*, yet in every instance he clings to
them with parsonic satisfaction, amplifies them and blazons them
forth.*

Charles Darwin says in the introduction to his work *On the
Origin of Species by Means of Natural Selection, or the Preservation
of Favoured Races in the Struggle for Life:*

> In the next chapter the *Struggle for Existence*** amongst
> all organic beings throughout the world, which inevitably
> follows from the high geometrical ratio of their increase,
> will be treated of. This is the doctrine of Malthus, applied to
> the whole animal and vegetable kingdoms (1860 edn.,
> London, pp. 4–5).

In his excellent work, Darwin did not see that his discovery
of the 'geometrical' progression in the animal and vegetable
kingdoms overturns Malthus's theory. Malthus's theory is based

---

[1] In both German and English in the text. [R. L. Meek]
* '. . . yet in every instance he clings to them with the cynicism of a complac-
ent parson, amplifies and advertises them' (. . . die er aber in jedem Fall mit
pfäffisch wohlgefälligen Zynismus festhält, ausmalt und bekannt macht).
(*TM* 2, p. 110) (Z.A.J.)
** Marx's emphasis.

precisely on the fact that he opposes Wallace's* geometrical progression of human beings to the chimerical 'arithmetical' progression of animals and plants. In Darwin's work, for example in his discussion of the extinction of species, we find a natural-historical refutation of the Malthusian theory, not only of its fundamental principle but also of its details.

*TM* 2, pp. 106–10; *OM*, pp. 118–24.

* Marx refers to Robert Wallace (1697–1771), a writer on population. He is believed to have inspired Malthus. See *C* I, p. 616, n. 2.

*Part Four*

*Historical Materialism*

# (A) Early Ideas

## (1) HISTORICAL MATERIALISM AND
HISTORICAL IDEALISM*

History is nothing but the succession of the separate generations, each of which exploits the materials, the capital funds, the productive forces handed down to it by all preceding generations, and thus, on the one hand, continues the traditional activity in completely changed circumstances and, on the other, modifies the old circumstances with a completely changed activity. This can be speculatively distorted so that later history is made the goal of earlier history, e g , the goal ascribed to the discovery of America is to further the eruption of the French Revolution. Thereby history receives its own special aims and becomes 'a person ranking with other persons' (to wit: 'Self-Consciousness, Criticism, the Unique', etc.), while what is designated with the words 'destiny', 'goal', 'germ', or 'idea' of earlier history is nothing more than an abstraction formed from later history, from the active influence which earlier history exercises on later history.

*GI*, p. 59.

This conception of history depends on our ability to expound the real process of production, starting out from the material production of life itself, and to comprehend the form of inter-course connected with this and created by this mode of production

* In the following discussion Marx contrasts his own materialistic conception of history with the historical idealism of Hegel, Bruno Bauer and Max Stirner. For another sharp criticism of Hegel's view on history see *HF*, pp. 114–5. (Z.A.J.)

(i.e., civil society in its various stages), as the basis of all history; and to show it in its action as State, to explain all the different theoretical products and forms of consciousness, religion, philosophy, ethics, etc., etc., and trace their origins and growth from that basis; by which means, of course, the whole thing can be depicted in its totality (and therefore, too, the reciprocal action of these various sides on one another). It has not, like the idealistic view of history, in every period to look for a category, but remains constantly on the real *ground* of history; it does not explain practice from the idea but explains the formation of ideas from material practice; and accordingly it comes to the conclusion that all forms and products of consciousness cannot be dissolved by mental criticism, by resolution into 'self-consciousness' or transformation into 'apparitions', 'spectres', 'fancies', etc., but only by the practical overthrow of the actual social relations which gave rise to this idealistic humbug; that not criticism but revolution is the driving force of history, also of religion, of philosophy and all other types of theory. It shows that history does not end by being resolved into 'self-consciousness' as 'spirit of the spirit', but that in it at each stage there is found a material result: a sum of productive forces, a historically created relation of individuals to nature and to one another, which is handed down to each generation from its predecessor; a mass of productive forces, capital funds and conditions, which, on the one hand, is indeed modified by the new generation, but also on the other prescribes for it its conditions of life and gives it a definite development, a special character. It shows that circumstances make men just as much as men make circumstances. This sum of productive forces, capital funds and social forms of intercourse, which every individual and generation finds in existence as something given, is the real basis of what the philosophers have conceived as 'substance' and 'essence of man', and what they have deified and attacked: a real basis which is not in the least disturbed, in its effect and influence on the development of men, by the fact that these philosophers revolt against it as 'self-consciousness' and the 'Unique'. These conditions of life, which different generations find in existence, decide also whether or not the periodically recurring revolutionary convulsion will be strong enough to overthrow the basis of the entire existing system. And if these material elements of a complete revolution are not present (namely, on the one hand the existing productive forces, on the other the formation of a revolutionary mass, which revolts not only against separate conditions of society up till then, but against the very 'production of life' till then, the 'total activity' on which it was based), then, as far as practical development is concerned, it is absolutely immaterial whether the *idea* of this revolution has been expressed a hundred times already, as the history of communism proves.

In the whole conception of history up to the present this real basis of history has either been totally neglected or else considered as a minor matter quite irrelevant to the course of history. History must, therefore, always be written according to an extraneous standard; the real production of life seems to be primeval history, while the truly historical appears to be separated from ordinary life, something extra-superterrestrial. With this the relation of man to nature is excluded from history and hence the antithesis of nature and history is created. The exponents of this conception of history have consequently only been able to see in history the political actions of princes and States, religious and all sorts of theoretical struggles, and in particular in each historical epoch have had to *share the illusion of that epoch*. For instance, if an epoch imagines itself to be actuated by purely 'political' or 'religious' motives, although 'religion' and 'politics' are only forms of its true motives, the historian accepts this opinion. The 'idea', the 'conception' of the people in question about their real practice, is transformed into the sole determining, active force, which controls and determines their practice. When the crude form in which the division of labour appears with the Indians and Egyptians calls forth the caste-system in their State and religion, the historian believes that the caste-system is the power which has produced this crude social form. While the French and the English at least hold by the political illusion, which is moderately close to reality, the Germans move in the realm of the 'pure spirit', and make religious illusion the driving force of history. The Hegelian philosophy of history is the last consequence, reduced to its 'finest expression', of all this German historiography, for which it is not a question of real, nor even of political, interests, but of pure thoughts. . . . This conception is truly religious: it postulates religious man as the primitive man, the starting-point of history; and in its imagination puts the religious production of fancies in the place of the real production of the means of subsistence and of life itself.

*GI*, pp. 49-52.

## (2) HISTORY AND SOCIAL EVOLUTION*

Why does M. Proudhon talk about God, about universal reason, about the impersonal reason of humanity which never errs, which has always been equal to itself throughout all the ages and of which one need only have the right consciousness in order to know the truth? Why does he resort to feeble Hegelianism to give himself the appearance of a bold thinker?

He himself provides you with the clue to this enigma. M. Proudhon sees in history a series of social developments; he finds progress realized in history; finally he finds that men, as individuals, did not know what they were doing and were mistaken about their own movement, that is to say, their social development seems at the first glance to be distinct, separate and independent of their individual development. He cannot explain these facts, and so the hypothesis of universal reason manifesting itself comes in very handy. Nothing is easier than to invent mystical causes, that is to say, phrases which lack common sense.

But when M. Proudhon admits that he understands nothing about the historical development of humanity—he admits this by using such high-sounding words as: Universal Reason, God, etc.— is he not implicitly and necessarily admitting that he is incapable of understanding *economic development*?

What is society, whatever its form may be? The product of men's reciprocal action. Are men free to choose this or that form of society? By no means. Assume a particular state of development in the productive faculties of man and you will get a particular form of commerce and consumption. Assume particular stages of development in production, commerce and consumption and you will have a corresponding social constitution, a corresponding organization of the family, of orders or of classes, in a word, a corresponding civil society. Assume a partic-

* In this letter Marx criticises Proudhon's *Système des contradictions économiques ou Philosophie de la misère* (1846). His enlarged criticism of this work was published later in book-form under the title *Misère de la philosophie*. (Z.A.J.)

ular civil society and you will get particular political conditions which are only the official expression of civil society. M. Proudhon will never understand this because he thinks he is doing something great by appealing from the state to civil society—that is to say, from the official résumé of society to official society.

It is superfluous to add that men are not free to choose their *productive forces*—which are the basis of all their history—for every productive force is an acquired force, the product of former activity. The productive forces are therefore the result of practical human energy; but this energy is itself conditioned by the circumstances in which men find themselves, by the productive forces already acquired, by the social form which exists before they do, which they do not create, which is the product of the preceding generation. Because of this simple fact that every succeeding generation finds itself in possession of the productive forces acquired by the previous generation, which serve it as the raw material for new production, a coherence arises in human history, a history of humanity takes shape which is all the more a history of humanity as the productive forces of man and therefore his social relations have been more developed. Hence it necessarily follows that the social history of men is never anything but the history of their individual development, whether they are conscious of it or not. Their material relations are the basis of all their relations. These material relations are only the necessary forms in which their material and individual activity is realized.

M. Proudhon mixes up ideas and things. Men never relinquish what they have won, but this does not mean that they never relinquish the social form in which they have acquired certain productive forces. On the contrary, in order that they may not be deprived of the result attained and forfeit the fruits of civilization, they are obliged, from the moment when their mode of carrying on commerce no longer corresponds to the productive forces acquired, to change all their traditional social forms. I am using the word "commerce" here in its widest sense, as we use *Verkehr* in German. For example: the privileges, the institution of guilds and corporations, the regulatory regime of the Middle Ages, were social relations that alone corresponded to the acquired productive forces and to the social condition which had previously existed and from which these institutions had arisen. Under the protection of the regime of corporations and regulations, capital was accumu-

G

lated, overseas trade was developed, colonies were founded. But the fruits of this men would have forfeited if they had tried to retain the forms under whose shelter these fruits had ripened. Hence burst two thunderclaps—the Revolutions of 1648 and 1688. All the old economic forms, the social relations corresponding to them, the political conditions which were the official expression of the old civil society, were destroyed in England. Thus the economic forms in which men produce, consume, and exchange, are *transitory and historical*. With the acquisition of new productive faculties, men change their mode of production and with the mode of production all the economic relations which are merely the necessary relations of this particular mode of production.

This is what M. Proudhon has not understood and still less demonstrated. M. Proudhon, incapable of following the real movement of history, produces a phantasmagoria which presumptuously claims to be dialectical. He does not feel it necessary to speak of the seventeenth, the eighteenth or the nineteenth century, for his history proceeds in the misty realm of imagination and rises far above space and time. In short, it is not history but old Hegelian junk, it is not profane history—a history of man—but sacred history—a history of ideas. From his point of view man is only the instrument of which the idea or the eternal reason makes use in order to unfold itself. The *evolutions* of which M. Proudhon speaks are understood to be evolutions such as are accomplished within the mystic womb of the absolute idea. If you tear the veil from this mystical language, what it comes to is that M. Proudhon is offering you the order in which economic categories arrange themselves inside his own mind. It will not require great exertion on my part to prove to you that it is the order of a very disorderly mind.

M. Proudhon begins his book with a dissertation on *value*, which is his pet subject. I will not enter on an examination of this dissertation today.

The series of economic evolutions of the eternal reason begins with *division of labour*. To M. Proudhon division of labour is a perfectly simple thing. But was not the caste regime also a particular division of labour? Was not the regime of the corporations another division of labour? And is not the division of labour under the system of manufacture, which in England begins in the middle of the seventeenth century and comes to an end in the last part of the eighteenth, also totally different from the division of labour in large-scale, modern industry?

M. Proudhon is so far from the truth that he neglects what even the profane economists attend to. When he talks about division of labour he does not feel it necessary to mention the world *market*. Good. Yet must not the division of labour in the fourteenth and fifteenth centuries, when there were still no colonies, when America did not as yet exist for Europe, and Eastern Asia only existed for her through the medium of Constantinople, have been fundamentally different from what it was in the seventeenth century when colonies were already developed?

And that is not all. Is the whole inner organization of nations, are all their international relations anything else than the expression of a particular division of labour? And must not these change when the division of labour changes?

M. Proudhon has so little understood the problem of the division of labour that he never even mentioned the separation of town and country, which took place in Germany, for instance, from the ninth to the twelfth century. Thus, to M. Proudhon, this separation is an eternal law since he knows neither its origin nor its development. All through his book he speaks as if this creation of a particular mode of production would endure until the end of time. All that M. Proudhon says about the division of labour is only a summary, and moreover a very superficial and incomplete summary, of what Adam Smith and a thousand others have said before him.

The second evolution is *machinery*. The connection between the division of labour and machinery is entirely mystical to M. Proudhon. Each kind of division of labour had its specific instruments of production. Between the middle of the seventeenth and the middle of the eighteenth century, for instance, people did not make everything by hand. They had instruments, and very complicated ones at that, such as looms, ships, levers, etc.

Thus there is nothing more absurd than to derive machinery from division of labour in general.

I may also remark, by the way, that M. Proudhon has understood very little the historical origin of machinery, but has still less understood its development. One can say that up to the year

1825—the period of the first general crisis—the demands of consumption in general increased more rapidly than production, and the development of machinery was a necessary consequence of the needs of the market. Since 1825, the invention and application of machinery has been simply the result of the war between workers and employers. But this is only true of England. As for the European nations, they were driven to adopt machinery owing to English competition both in their home markets and on the world market. Finally, in North America the introduction of machinery was due both to competition with other countries and to lack of hands, that is, to the disproportion between the population of North America and its industrial needs. From these facts you can see what sagacity Monsieur Proudhon develops when he conjures up the spectre of competition as the third evolution, the antithesis to machinery!

Lastly and in general, it is altogether absurd to make *machinery* an economic category alongside with division of labour, competition, credit, etc.

Machinery is no more an economic category than the ox which draws the plough. The application of machinery in the present day is one of the relations of our present economic system, but the way in which machinery is utilized is totally distinct from the machinery itself. Powder is powder whether used to wound a man or to dress his wounds.

M. Proudhon surpasses himself when he allows competition, monopoly, taxes or police, balance of trade, credit and property to develop inside his head in the order in which I have mentioned them. Nearly all credit institutions had been developed in England by the beginning of the eighteenth century, before the invention of machinery. Public credit was only a fresh method of increasing taxation and satisfying the new demands created by the rise of the bourgeoisie to power. Finally, the last category in M. Proudhon's system is constituted by *property*. In the real world, on the other hand, the division of labour and all M. Proudhon's other categories are social relations forming in their entirety what is today known as property; outside these relations bourgeois property is nothing but a metaphysical or juristic illusion. The property of a different epoch, feudal property, develops in a series of entirely different social relations. M. Proudhon, by establishing property as an independent relation, commits more than a mistake in method: he clearly shows that he has not grasped the bond which holds together all forms of *bourgeois* production, that he has not understood the *historical and transitory* character of the forms of production in a particular epoch. M. Proudhon, who does not regard our social institutions as historical products, who can understand neither their origin nor their development, can only produce dogmatic criticism of them.

M. Proudhon is therefore obliged to take refuge in a *fiction* in order to explain development. He imagines that division of labour, credit, machinery, etc., were all invented to serve his fixed idea, the idea of equality. His explanation is sublimely naive. These things were invented in the interests of equality but unfortunately they turned against equality. This constitutes his whole argument. In other words, he makes a gratuitous assumption and then, as the actual development contradicts his fiction at every step, he concludes that there is a contradiction. He conceals from you the fact that the contradiction exists solely between his fixed ideas and the real movement.

Thus, M. Proudhon, mainly because he lacks the historical knowledge, has not perceived that as men develop their productive faculties, that is, as they live, they develop certain relations with one another and that the nature of these relations must necessarily change with the change and growth of the productive faculties. He has not perceived that *economic categories* are only *abstract expressions* of these actual relations and only remain true while these relations exist. He therefore falls into the error of the bourgeois economists, who regard these economic categories as eternal and not as historical laws which are only laws for a particular historical development, for a definite development of the productive forces. Instead, therefore, of regarding the political-economic categories as abstract expressions of the real, transitory, historic social relations, Monsieur Proudhon, thanks to a mystic inversion, sees in the real relations only embodiments of these abstractions. These abstractions themselves are formulas which have been slumbering in the heart of God the Father since the beginning of the world.

Marx's letter to P. V. Annenkov of 28 December 1846,
*SC*, pp. 39–45.

## (3) PRODUCTIVE FORCES, SOCIAL RELATIONS AND SOCIAL IDEAS

M. Proudhon the economist understands very well that men make cloth, linen or silk materials in definite relations of production. But what he has not understood is that these definite social relations are just as much produced by men as linen, flax, etc. Social relations are closely bound up with productive forces. In acquiring new productive forces men change their mode of production; and in changing their mode of production, in changing the way of earning their living, they change all their social relations. The handmill gives you society with the feudal lord; the steam-mill, society with the industrial capitalist.

The same men who establish their social relations in conformity with their material productivity, produce also principles, ideas and categories, in conformity with their social relations.

Thus these ideas, these categories, are as little eternal as the relations they express. They are *historical and transitory products*.

There is a continual movement of growth in productive forces, of destruction in social relations, of formation in ideas; the only immutable thing is the abstraction of movement—*mors immortalis*.*

*PP*, p. 105.

Economists have a singular method of procedure. There are only two kinds of institutions for them, artificial and natural. The institutions of feudalism are artificial institutions, those of the bourgeoisie are natural institutions. In this they resemble the theologians, who likewise establish two kinds of religion. Every religion which is not theirs is an invention of men, while their own is an emanation from God. When the economists say that present-day relations—the relations of bourgeois production—are natural, they imply that these are the relations in which wealth is created and productive forces developed in conformity with the laws of nature. These relations therefore are themselves natural laws

* The phrase 'mors immortalis' (immortal death) comes from Lucretius's *On the Nature of the Universe*, bk. III, 867–9. 'One who no longer is cannot suffer, or differ in any way from one who has never been born, when once this mortal life has been usurped by death immortal' (R. E. Latham's translation). (Z.A.J.)

independent of the influence of time. They are eternal laws which must always govern society. Thus there has been history, but there is no longer any. There has been history, since there were the institutions of feudalism, and in these institutions of feudalism we find quite different relations of production from those of bourgeois society, which the economists try to pass off as natural and as such, eternal.

Feudalism also had its proletariat—serfdom, which contained all the germs of the bourgeoisie. Feudal production also had two antagonistic elements which are likewise designated by the name of the *good side* and the *bad side* of feudalism, irrespective of the fact that it is always the bad side that in the end triumphs over the good side. It is the bad side that produces the movement which makes history, by providing a struggle. If, during the epoch of the domination of feudalism, the economists, enthusiastic over the knightly virtues, the beautiful harmony between rights and duties, the patriarchal life of the towns, the prosperous condition of domestic industry in the countryside, the development of industry organized into corporations, guilds and fraternities, in short, everything that constitutes the good side of feudalism, had set themselves the problem of eliminating everything that cast a shadow on this picture—serfdom, privileges, anarchy—what would have happened? All the elements which called forth the struggle would have been destroyed, and the development of the bourgeoisie nipped in the bud. One would have set oneself the absurd problem of eliminating history.

After the triumph of the bourgeoisie there was no longer any question of the good or the bad side of feudalism. The bourgeoisie took possession of the productive forces it had developed under feudalism. All the old economic forms, the corresponding civil relations, the political state which was the official expression of the old civil society, were smashed.

Thus feudal production, to be judged properly, must be considered as a mode of production founded on antagonism. It must be shown how wealth was produced within this antagonism, how the productive forces were developed at the same time as class antagonisms, how one of the classes, the bad side, the drawback of society, went on growing until the material conditions for its emancipation had attained full maturity. Is not this as good as saying that the mode of production, the relations in which productive forces are developed, are anything but eternal laws, but that they correspond to a definite development of men and of their productive forces, and that a change in men's productive forces necessarily brings about a change in their relations of production? As the main thing is not to be deprived of the fruits of civilization, of the acquired productive forces, the traditional forms in which they were produced must be smashed. From this moment the revolutionary class becomes conservative.

The bourgeoisie begins with a proletariat which is itself a relic of the proletariat of feudal times. In the course of its historical development, the bourgeoisie necessarily develops its antagonistic character, which at first is more or less disguised, existing only in a latent state. As the bourgeoisie develops, there develops in its bosom a new proletariat, a modern proletariat; there develops a struggle between the proletarian class and the bourgeois class, a struggle which, before being felt, perceived, appreciated, understood, avowed and proclaimed aloud by both sides, expresses itself, to start with, merely in partial and momentary conflicts, in subversive acts. On the other hand, if all the members of the modern bourgeoisie have the same interests inasmuch as they form a class as against another class, they have opposite, antagonistic interests inasmuch as they stand face to face with one another. This opposition of interests results from the economic conditions of their bourgeois life. From day to day it thus becomes clearer that the production relations in which the bourgeoisie moves have not a simple, uniform character, but a dual character; that in the selfsame relations in which wealth is produced, poverty is produced also; that in the selfsame relations in which there is a development of the productive forces, there is also a force producing repression; that these relations produce *bourgeois wealth*, i.e., the wealth of the bourgeois class, only by continually annihilating the wealth of the individual members of this class and by producing an evergrowing proletariat.

The more the antagonistic character comes to light, the more the economists, the scientific representatives of bourgeois production, find themselves in conflict with their own theory; and different schools arise.

We have the *fatalist* economists, who in their theory are as indifferent to what they call the drawbacks of bourgeois production as the bourgeois themselves are in practice to the sufferings of the proletarians who help them to acquire wealth. In this fatalist school there are Classics and Romantics. The Classics, like Adam Smith and Ricardo, represent a bourgeoisie which, while still struggling with the relics of feudal society, works only to purge economic relations of feudal taints, to increase the productive forces and to give a new upsurge to industry and commerce. The proletariat that takes part in this struggle and is absorbed in this feverish labour experiences only passing, accidental sufferings, and itself regards them as such. Economists like Adam Smith and Ricardo, who are the historians of this epoch, have no other mission than that of showing how wealth is acquired in bourgeois production relations, of formulating these relations into categories, into laws, and of showing how superior these laws, these categories, are for the production of wealth to the laws and categories of feudal society. Poverty is in their eyes merely the pang which accompanies every childbirth, in nature as in industry.

The Romantics belong to our own age, in which the bourgeoisie is in direct opposition to the proletariat; in which poverty is engendered in as great abundance as wealth. The economists now pose as *blasé* fatalists, who, from their elevated position, cast a proudly disdainful glance at the human machines who manufacture wealth. They copy all the developments given by their predecessors, and the indifference which in the latter was merely naïveté becomes in them coquetry.

Next comes the *humanitarian school*, which sympathizes with the bad side of present-day production relations. It seeks, by way of easing its conscience, to palliate even if slightly the real contrasts; it sincerely deplores the distress of the proletariat, the unbridled competition of the bourgeois among themselves; it counsels the workers to be sober, to work hard and to have few children; it advises the bourgeois to put a reasoned ardour into production. The whole theory of this school rests on interminable distinctions between theory and practice, between principles and results, between idea and application, between form and content, between essence and reality, between right and fact, between the good side and the bad side.

The *philanthropic* school is the humanitarian school carried to perfection. It denies the necessity of antagonism; it wants to turn all men into bourgeois; it wants to realize theory in so far as it is distinguished from practice and contains no antagonism. It goes

G*

without saying that, in theory, it is easy to make an abstraction of the contradictions that are met with at every moment in actual reality. This theory would therefore become idealized reality. The philanthropists, then, want to retain the categories which express bourgeois relations, without the antagonism which constitutes them and is inseparable from them. They think they are seriously fighting bourgeois practice, and they are more bourgeois than the others.

Just as the *economists* are the scientific representatives of the bourgeois class, so the *Socialists* and the *Communists* are the theoreticians of the proletarian class. So long as the proletariat is not yet sufficiently developed to constitute itself as a class, and consequently so long as the struggle itself of the proletariat with the bourgeoisie has not yet assumed a political character, and the productive forces are not yet sufficiently developed in the bosom of the bourgeoisie itself to enable us to catch a glimpse of the material conditions necessary for the emancipation of the proletariat and for the formation of a new society, these theoreticians are merely Utopians who, to meet the wants of the oppressed classes, improvise systems and go in search of a regenerating science. But in the measure that history moves forward, and with it the struggle of the proletariat assumes clearer outlines, they no longer need to seek science in their minds; they have only to take note of what is happening before their eyes and to become its mouthpiece. So long as they look for science and merely make systems, so long as they are at the beginning of the struggle, they see in poverty nothing but poverty, without seeing in it the revolutionary, subversive side, which will overthrow the old society. From this moment, science, which is a product of the historical movement, has associated itself consciously with it, has ceased to be doctrinaire and has become revolutionary.

*PP*, pp. 116–20.

With Storch* himself the *theory of civilization* does not get beyond trivial phrases . . . for example, that the material division of labour is the pre-condition for the division of intellectual

---

* Heinrich Friedrich von Storch (1766–1835) was a Russian economist and historian of German origin. Marx refers to Storch's *Cours d'économie politique* translated by J.-B. Say, Paris, 1823. (Z.A.J.)

labour. How much it *was inevitable* that Storch could not get beyond trivial phrases, how little he had even *formulated* for himself the task, let alone its solution, is apparent from one single circumstance. In order to examine the connection between spiritual production and material production it is above all necessary to grasp the latter itself not as a general category but in *definite historical* form. Thus, for example, different kinds of spiritual production correspond to the capitalist mode of production and to the mode of production of the Middle Ages. If material production itself is not conceived in its *specific historical* form, it is impossible to understand what is specific in the spiritual production corresponding to it and the reciprocal influence of one on the other. Otherwise one cannot get beyond inanities. This because of the talk about 'civilization'.

Further: from the specific form of material production arises in the first place a specific structure of society, in the second place a specific relation of men to nature. Their State and their spiritual outlook is determined by both. Therefore also the kind of their spiritual production.

*Finally*, by spiritual production Storch means also all kinds of professional activities of the ruling class, who carry out social functions as a trade. The existence of these strata, like the function they perform, can only be understood from the specific historical structure of their production relations.

Because Storch does not conceive material production itself *historically*—because he conceives it as production of material goods in general, not as a definite historically developed and specific form of this production—he deprives himself of the basis on which alone can be understood partly the ideological component parts of the ruling class, partly the free spiritual production of this particular social formation. He cannot get beyond meaningless general phrases. Consequently, the relation is not so simple as he presupposes. For instance, capitalist production is hostile to certain branches of spiritual production, for example, art and poetry. If this is left out of account, it opens the way to the illusion of the French in the eighteenth century which has been so beautifully satirised by Lessing.* Because we are further

---

* Marx probably refers to Lessing's *Hamburgische Dramaturgie* in which Lessing ridicules Voltaire. See G. E. Lessing, *Gesammelte Werke*, B. VI, Berlin, 1954, pp. 61 ff. The *Henriade* is a famous epic poem of Voltaire. (Z.A.J.)

ahead than the ancients in mechanics, etc., why shouldn't we be able to make an epic too? And the *Henriade* in place of the *Iliad*!

*TM* 1, pp. 247–8; *TSV* I, pp. 276–7.

## (4) MAN MAKES HISTORY

*History* does *nothing*, it 'possesses *no* immense wealth', it 'wages *no* battles'. It is *man*, real living man, that does all that, that possesses and fights; 'history' is not a person apart, using man as a means for *its own* particular aims; history is *nothing but* the activity of man pursuing his aims.

*HF*, p. 125.

Let us admit with M. Proudhon that real history, history according to the order in time, is the historical sequence in which ideas, categories and principles have manifested themselves.

Each principle has had its own century in which to manifest itself. The principle of authority, for example, had the eleventh century, just as the principle of individualism had the eighteenth century. In logical sequence, it was the century that belonged to the principle, and not the principle that belonged to the century. In other words it was the principle that made the history, and not the history that made the principle. When, consequently, in order to save principles as much as to save history, we ask ourselves why a particular principle was manifested in the eleventh or in the eighteenth century rather than in any other, we are necessarily forced to examine minutely what men were like in the eleventh century, what they were like in the eighteenth, what were their respective needs, their productive forces, their mode of production, the raw materials of their production—in short, what were the relations between man and man which resulted from all these conditions of existence. To get to the bottom of all these questions—what is this but to draw up the real, profane history of men in every century and to present these men as both the authors and the actors of their own drama? But the moment you present men as the actors and authors of their own history, you arrive—by a detour—at the real starting point, because you have abandoned those eternal principles of which you spoke at the outset.

*PP*, pp. 110–11.

## (5) THE LAW OF CIVILIZATION

Things happen in quite a different way from what M. Proudhon imagines. The very moment civilization begins, production begins to be founded on the antagonism of orders, estates, classes, and finally on the antagonism of accumulated labour and actual labour. No antagonism, no progress. This is the law that civilization has followed up to our days. Till now the productive forces have been developed by virtue of this system of class antagonisms. To say now that, because all the needs of all the workers were satisfied, men could devote themselves to the creation of products of a higher order—to more complicated industries—would be to leave class antagonism out of account and turn all historical development upside down.

*PP*, pp. 58–9.

## (6) THE RELATION OF THE FORMS OF PROPERTY TO LAW AND RELIGION

The first form of property, in the ancient world as in the Middle Ages, is tribal property (*Stammeigentum*) . . . In the case of the nations which grew out of the Middle Ages, tribal property evolved through various stages—feudal landed property, corporative movable property, capital invested in manufacture—to modern capital, determined by big industry and universal competition, i.e., pure private property, which has cast off all semblance of a communal institution and has shut out the State from any influence on the development of property. . . .

Civil law develops simultaneously with private property out of the disintegration of the natural community. . . . In civil law the existing property relationships are declared to be the result of the general will. The *jus utendi et abutendi** itself asserts on the one hand the fact that private property has become entirely independent

* The right of using and disposing of what is one's own. (Z.A.J.)

of the community, and on the other the illusion that private property itself is based solely on the private will, the arbitrary disposal of the thing. In practice, the *abuti** has very definite economic limitations for the owner of private property, if he does not wish to see his property and hence his *jus abutendi* pass into other hands, since actually the thing, considered merely with reference to his will, is not a thing at all, but only becomes a thing, true property in intercourse, and independently of the law.

GI, pp. 77–9.

Reduced to their real meaning, these commonplaces [sc. concerning the protection of property by the administration of justice, police, and so forth, Z.A.J.] express more that what their preachers realize, namely, that every form of production creates its own legal relations, forms of government, etc. The crudity and lack of comprehension consist in relating the elements [sc. the form of production and legal relations, Z.A.J.] by a pure act of reflection, as if they were joined accidentally, whereas they are in fact organically interdependent. The bourgeois economists are dimly aware that it is better to carry on production under modern police than it was, e.g., under club law. They forget that club law is also law, and that the right of the stronger continues to exist in other forms even under their 'government of law'.

GKPÖ, pp. 9–10; CPE–I, pp. 273–4 [revised translation].

The religious world is but the reflex of the real world. And for a society based upon the production of commodities, in which the producers in general enter into social relations with one another by treating their products as commodities and values, whereby they reduce their individual private labour to the standard of homogeneous human labour—for such a society, Christianity with its *cultus* of abstract man, more especially in its bourgeois developments, Protestantism, Deism, &c., is the most fitting form of religion. In the ancient Asiatic and other ancient modes of production, we find that the conversion of products

* To consume and use for one's own purpose. (Z.A.J.)

into commodities, and therefore the conversion of men into producers of commodities, holds a subordinate place, which, however,
increases in importance as the primitive communities approach
nearer and nearer to their dissolution. Trading nations, properly
so called, exist in the ancient world only in its interstices, like
the gods of Epicurus in the Intermundia, or like Jews in the pores
of Polish society. Those ancient social organisms of production
are, as compared with bourgeois society, extremely simple and
transparent. But they are founded either on the immature development of man individually, who has not yet severed the um-
bilical cord that unites him with his fellow men in a primitive
tribal community, or upon direct relations of subjection. They can
arise and exist only when the development of the productive
power of labour has not risen beyond a low stage, and when,
therefore, the social relations within the sphere of material life,
between man and man, and between man and Nature, are corre-
spondingly narrow. This narrowness is reflected in the ancient
worship of Nature, and in the other elements of the popular religions. The religious reflex of the real world can, in any case, only
then finally vanish, when the practical relations of every-day life
offer to man none but perfectly intelligible and reasonable relations with regard to his fellow men and to Nature.

$C$ I, p. 79.

## (7) THE PARADOX OF GREEK ART

The case of art shows clearly that certain golden periods of its
development are by no means related to the general development
of society, and therefore of the material base which is, as it were,
the skeleton of its social organization. For instance, consider the
Greeks as compared with the moderns or also with Shakespeare.
As regards certain forms of art, for instance, the epic poem, it is
recognized that they can never be produced in their world epoch-
making classical form as soon as art production as such [art as a
separate form of creation, Z.A.J.] comes into existence. Thus,
within the domain of art itself certain important forms are only
possible at an early stage of its development. If this is the case
with regard to the relation between the various forms of art within

the domain of art itself, it is yet less striking that it also applies to the relation of the whole domain of art to the general development of society. The difficulty lies only in the general comprehension of these contradictions. For no sooner are they specified than they are explained.

Let us take, for instance, the relation of Greek art and then of Shakespeare to the (art of the) present time. It is a known fact that Greek mythology provided not only the armoury of Greek art but also constituted the ground on which it grew. Is the view of nature and social relations, which underlies Greek imagination and thus Greek mythology, possible at the time of automatic machines, railways, steam engines, and electric telegraphs? What happens to Vulcan as against (the steel mills of) Robert & Co; to Jupiter as against a lightning conductor; and to Hermes as against *Crédit Mobilier*?* All mythologies conquer, rule and shape the forces of nature in and through imagination; they disappear, therefore, as soon as the real mastery over the forces of nature is established. What becomes of the Fama** next to Printing House Square?*** Greek art presupposes Greek mythology, that is, nature and the social forms which themselves have already been assimilated in an unconsciously artistic way by the imagination of the people. That is its material. This would not be true to say, however, of any mythology one cares to choose, that is, of any unconsciously accomplished artistic interpretation of nature which by including all that is objective for that very reason includes also society. Egyptian mythology could never be the ground or the womb of Greek art. But in any event it must be a mythology and, therefore, by no means a social development which excludes every mytho-logical attitude, every mythologizing relation to nature; it is this sort of social development which demands from the artist an imagination free from mythology.

Let us consider it from another viewpoint. Is Achilles possible with gunpowder and lead? Or can one at all imagine the *Iliad* together with the printing press or pressing machine? Are not the singing in song and the telling in tale (*Singen und Sagen*) as well as the Muse forced to be silent as the printing press-bar (*Press-*

* *Société générale de crédit mobilier*, a French bank established by brothers Périer which supported railway constructions in many European countries.
** *Die Fama* in German, from Greek *fáma* or *féme*. Marx probably wished to contrast rumour personified with *The Times*.
*** The address of *The Times*.

*engel*) starts working, and do not the conditions necessary for the existence of epic poetry disappear in the same way?

The difficulty does not lie in coming to understand that Greek art and the epic poem are connected with certain forms of social development. The difficulty is that they still afford us artistic pleasure and that in certain respects represent models of perfection and unattainable standards.

A man cannot become a child once again or else he will become childish. But does he not enjoy the naiveté of a child and must he not himself again try to recreate the truth of childhood on a higher level? Does not childhood reveal the specific character of every epoch in its natural state? Why should not the historical childhood of mankind, where it showed itself in its greatest beauty, exert an external attraction as a stage that will never recur? There are ill-bred children and precocious children. Many ancient peoples belong to these categories. The Greeks were normal children. The charm of their art for us does not stand in contradiction to the undeveloped social stage out of which it grew. It is rather a result of that stage and is rather inseparably connected with the fact that the immature social conditions, under which it arose and only could arise, can never return.

*GKPÖ*, pp. 30–1; *CPE–I*, pp. 309–12 [revised translation].

# (B) The Substantive Materialist Conception of History

## 1) FROM THE PREFACE TO *A CONTRIBUTION TO THE CRITIQUE OF POLITICAL ECONOMY*

The first work which I undertook for a solution of the doubts which assailed me was a critical review of the Hegelian philosophy of right, a work the introduction to which appeared in 1844 in the *Deutsch-Französische Jahrbücher*,[1] published in Paris. My investi-

See p. 134.

gation led to the result that legal relations as well as forms of state are to be grasped neither from themselves nor from the so-called general development of the human mind, but rather have their roots in the material conditions of life, the sum total of which Hegel following the example of the Englishmen and Frenchmen of the eighteenth century, combines under the name of 'civil society' that, however, the anatomy of civil society is to be sought in political economy. The investigation of the latter, which I began in Paris I continued in Brussels, whither I had emigrated in consequence of an expulsion order of M. Guizot. The general result at which arrived and which, once won, served as a guiding thread for my studies, can be briefly formulated as follows: in the Social production of their life, men enter into definite relations that are indispensable and independent of their will, relations of production which correspond to a definite stage of development of their material productive forces. The sum total of these relations of production constitutes the economic structure of society, the real foundation, on which rises a legal and political superstructure and to which correspond definite forms of social consciousness. The mode of production of material life conditions the social, political and intellectual life process in general. It is not the consciousness of men that determines their being, but, on the contrary, their social being that determines their consciousness. At a certain stage of their development, the material productive forces of society come in conflict with the existing relations of production, or— what is but a legal expression for the same thing—with the property relations within which they have been at work hitherto From forms of development of the productive forces these relations turn into their fetters. Then begins an epoch of social revolution. With the change of the economic foundation the entire immense superstructure is more or less rapidly transformed. In considering such transformations a distinction should always be made between the material transformation of the economic conditions of production, which can be determined with the precision of natural science, and the legal, political, religious esthetic or philosophic—in short, ideological forms in which men become conscious of this conflict and fight it out. Just as our opinion of an individual is not based on what he thinks of himself, so can we not judge of such a period of transformation by its own consciousness; on the contrary, this consciousness must be

xplained rather from the contradictions of material life, from the
xisting conflict between the social productive forces and the
elations of production. No social order ever perishes before all the
•roductive forces for which there is room in it have developed;
nd new, higher relations of production never appear before the
naterial conditions of their existence have matured in the womb of
he old society itself. Therefore mankind always sets itself only
uch tasks as it can solve; since, looking at the matter more closely,
t will always be found that the task itself arises only when the
naterial conditions for its solution already exist or are at least in
he process of formation. In broad outlines Asiatic, ancient, feudal,
nd modern bourgeois modes of production can be designated
s progressive epochs in the economic formation of society. The
ourgeois relations of production are the last antagonistic form of
he social process of production—antagonistic not in the sense of
ndividual antagonism, but of one arising from the social con-
itions of life of the individuals; at the same time the productive
orces developing in the womb of bourgeois society create the
naterial conditions for the solution of that antagonism. This
ucial formation brings, therefore, the prehistory of human
ociety to a close.

*CPE–P*, pp. 328–9.

## 2) CONFLICT BETWEEN THE PRODUCTIVE FORCES AND THE SOCIAL RELATIONS OF PRODUCTION

"he means of production and of exchange, on whose foundation
he bourgeoisie built itself up, were generated in feudal society.
At a certain stage in the development of these means of production
nd of exchange, the conditions under which feudal society
roduced and exchanged, the feudal organization of agriculture
nd manufacturing industry, in one word, the feudal relations of
roperty became no longer compatible with the already developed
roductive forces; they became so many fetters. They had to be
urst asunder; they were burst asunder.

Into their place stepped free competition, accompanied by a
ocial and political constitution adapted to it, and by the economi-
al and political sway of the bourgeois class.

A similar movement is going on before our own eyes. Modern bourgeois society with its relations of production, of exchange and of property, a society that has conjured up such gigantic means of production and of exchange, is like the sorcerer, who is no longer able to control the powers of the nether world whom he has called up by his spells. For many a decade past the history of industry and commerce is but the history of the revolt of modern productive forces against modern conditions of production, against the property relations that are the conditions for the existence of the bourgeoisie and of its rule. It is enough to mention the commercial crises that by their periodical return put on its trial, each time more threateningly, the existence of the entire bourgeois society. In these crises a great part not only of the existing products, but also of the previously created productive forces, are periodically destroyed. In these crises there breaks out an epidemic that, in all earlier epochs, would have seemed an absurdity—the epidemic of over-production. Society suddenly finds itself put back into a state of momentary barbarism; it appears as if a famine, a universal war of devastation had cut off the supply of every means of subsistence; industry and commerce seem to be destroyed; and why? Because there is too much civilization, too much means of subsistence, too much industry, too much commerce. The productive forces at the disposal of society no longer tend to further the development of the conditions of bourgeois property; on the contrary, they have become too powerful for these conditions, by which they are fettered, and so soon as they overcome these fetters, they bring disorder into the whole of bourgeois society, endanger the existence of bourgeois property. The conditions of bourgeois society are too narrow to comprise the wealth created by them. And how does the bourgeoisie get over these crises? On the one hand by enforced destruction of a mass of productive forces; on the other, by the conquest of new markets, and by the more thorough exploitation of the old ones. That is to say, by paving the way for more extensive and more destructive crises and by diminishing the means whereby crises are prevented.

The weapons with which the bourgeoisie felled feudalism to the ground are now turned against the bourgeoisie itself.

*MCP*, pp. 37–8.

## 3) TECHNOLOGY AND SOCIAL RELATIONS

A critical history of technology would show how little any of the inventions of the eighteenth century are the work of a single individual. Hitherto there is no such book. Darwin has interested us in the history of Nature's Technology, i.e., in the formation of the organs of plants and animals, which organs serve as instruments of production for sustaining life. Does not the history of the productive organs of man, of organs that are the material basis of all social organization, deserve equal attention? And would not such a history be easier to compile, since, as Vico* says, human history differs from natural history in this, that we have made the former, but not the latter? Technology discloses man's mode of dealing with Nature, the process of production by which he sustains his life, and thereby also lays bare the mode of formation of his social relations, and of the mental conceptions that flow from them. Every history of religion even, that fails to take account of this material basis, is uncritical. It is, in reality, much easier to discover by analysis the earthly core of the misty creations of religion, than, conversely, it is to develop from the actual relations of life the corresponding celestialized forms of those relations. The latter method is the only materialistic, and therefore the only scientific one. The weak points in the abstract materialism of natural science, a materialism that excludes history and its process, are at once evident from the abstract and ideological conceptions of its spokesmen, whenever they venture beyond the bounds of their own speciality.

*C* I, p. 372, n. 3.

## 4) GEOGRAPHY, LABOUR PRODUCTIVITY AND SOCIAL RELATIONS

It is only after men have raised themselves above the rank of

* Giambattista Vico (1668–1744), whose book *Scienza nuova* (1725), a work of outstanding merits, passed unnoticed until it was rediscovered by German scholars at the turn of the eighteenth century. Vico made the first modern attempt to formulate the rules of historical method and demanded a historical approach to knowledge. A German translation of *Scienza nuova* had been available since 1822. There is every reason to believe that it exercised a deep influence upon Marx. (Z.A.J.)

animals, when therefore their labour has been to some exten
socialized, that a state of things arises in which the surplus-labou
of the one becomes a condition of existence for the other. At th
dawn of civilization the productiveness acquired by labour i
small, but so too are the wants which develop with and by th
means of satisfying them. Further, at that early period, the portio
of society that lives on the labour of others is infinitely smal
compared with the mass of direct producers. Along with th
progress in the productiveness of labour, that small portion o
society increases both absolutely and relatively.[1] Besides, capita
with its accompanying relations springs up from an economic so
that is the product of a long process of development. The pro
ductiveness of labour that serves as its foundation and starting
point, is a gift, not of Nature, but of a history embracing thousand
of centuries.

Apart from the degree of development, greater or less, in th
form of social production, the productiveness of labour is fettere
by physical conditions. These are all referable to the constitutio
of man himself (race, &c.), and to surrounding Nature. Th
external physical conditions fall into two great economic classes
(1) Natural wealth in means of subsistence, i.e., a fruitful soi
waters teeming with fish, &c., and (2), natural wealth in the in
struments of labour, such as waterfalls, navigable rivers, wood
metal, coal, &c. At the dawn of civilization, it is the first clas
that turns the scale; at a higher stage of development, it is th
second. Compare, for example, England with India, or in ancien
times, Athens and Corinth with the shores of the Black Sea.

The fewer the number of natural wants imperatively callin
for satisfaction, and the greater the natural fertility of the so
and the favourableness of the climate, so much less is the labour
time necessary for the maintenance and reproduction of th
producer. So much greater therefore can be the excess of his labou
for others over his labour for himself. Diodoros* long ago re
marked this in relation to the ancient Egyptians. . . . Just as th

---

[1] 'Among the wild Indians in America, almost everything is the labourer's, 9
parts of a hundred are to be put upon the account of labour. In England
perhaps, the labourer has not 2/3' (*The Advantages of the East India Trade t
England*, London, 1720, p. 73, an anonymous publication).
* Diodoros of Sicily, an ancient historian, who wrote about the middle of th
first century B.C. His main work was *The Historical Library*. Marx quoted it i
*Capital* frequently and extensively. (Z.A.J.)

ndividual labourer can do more surplus-labour in proportion as is necessary labour-time is less, so with regard to the working population. The smaller the part of it which is required for the production of the necessary means of subsistence, so much the greater is the part that can be set to do other work.

Capitalist production once assumed, then, all other circumstances remaining the same, and given the length of the working-day, the quantity of surplus-labour will vary with the physical conditions of labour, especially with the fertility of the soil. But it by no means follows from this that the most fruitful soil is the most fitted for the growth of the capitalist mode of production. This mode is based on the dominion of man over Nature. Where Nature is too lavish, she 'keeps him in hand, like a child in leading-strings'. She does not impose upon him any necessity to develop himself. It is not the tropics with their luxuriant vegetation, but the temperate zone, that is the mother-country of capital. It is not the mere fertility of the soil, but the differentiation of the soil, the variety of its natural products, the changes of the seasons, which form the physical basis for the social division of labour, and which, by changes in the natural surroundings, spur man on to the multiplication of his wants, his capabilities, his means and modes of labour. It is the necessity of bringing a natural force under the control of society, of economizing, of appropriating or subduing it on a large scale by the work of man's hand, that first plays the decisive part in the history of industry. Examples are, the irrigation works in Egypt,[1] Lombardy, Holland, or in India and Persia where irrigation by means of artificial canals, not only supplies the soil with the water indispensable to it, but also carries down to it, in the shape of sediment from the hills, mineral fertilizers. The secret of the flourishing state of industry in Spain and Sicily under the dominion of the Arabs lay in their irrigation works.[2]

Favourable natural conditions alone, give us only the possi-

---

The necessity for predicting the rise and fall of the Nile created Egyptian astronomy, and with it the dominion of the priests, as directors of agriculture. One of the material bases of the power of the State over the small disconnected producing organisms in India, was the regulation of the water supply. The Mahometan rulers of India understood this better than their English successors. It is enough to recall to mind the famine of 1866, which cost the lives of more than a million Hindus in the district of Orissa, in the Bengal presidency.

bility, never the reality, of surplus-labour, nor, consequently of surplus-value and a surplus-product. The result of differenc in the natural conditions of labour is this, that the same quantity of labour satisfies, in different countries, a different mass of re quirements,[3] consequently, that under circumstances in other re spects analogous, the necessary labour-time is different. These conditions affect surplus-labour only as natural limits, i.e., by fixing the points at which labour for others can begin. In pro portion as industry advances, these natural limits recede.

C I, pp. 512–15.

## (5) THE UNIVERSAL SCOPE OF HISTORICAL MATERIALISM

I seize this opportunity of shortly answering an objection taken by a German paper in America to my work *Zur Kritik der politischen Ökonomie* (1859). In the estimation of that paper my view that each special mode of production and the social re lations corresponding to it, in short, that the economic structure o society, is the real basis on which the juridical and political super structure is raised, and to which definite social forms of though correspond; that the mode of production determines the characte of the social, political, and intellectual life generally, all this i very true for our own times, in which material interests preponder ate, but not for the middle ages, in which Catholicism, nor fo Athens and Rome, where politics, reigned supreme. In the firs place it strikes one as an odd thing for any one to suppose tha these well-worn phrases about the middle ages and the ancien

[3] 'There are no two countries which furnish an equal number of the necessaries of life in equal plenty, and with the same quantity of labour. Men's wants increase or diminish with the severity or temperateness of the climate they live in; consequently, the proportion of trade which the inhabitants of different countries are obliged to carry on through necessity cannot be the same, nor is it practicable to ascertain the degree of variation farther than by the degrees of Heat and Cold; from whence one may make this general conclusion, that the quantity of labour required for a certain number of people is greatest in cold climates, and least in hot ones; for in the former men not only want more clothes but the earth more cultivating than in the latter.' (*An Essay on the Governing Causes of the Natural Rate of Interest*, London, 1750, p. 59.) The author of thi epoch-making anonymous work is J. Massie. Hume took his theory of interes from it.

world are unknown to anyone else. This much, however, is clear, that the middle ages could not live on Catholicism, nor the ancient world on politics. On the contrary, it is the mode in which they gained a livelihood that explains why here politics, and there Catholicism, played the chief part. For the rest, it requires but a slight acquaintance with the history of the Roman republic, for example, to be aware that its secret history is the history of its landed property. On the other hand, Don Quixote long ago paid the penalty for wrongly imagining that knight errantry was compatible with all economic forms of society.

C I, p. 82, n. 1.

## 6) HISTORICAL MATERIALISM IS NO MASTER-KEY TO HISTORY

The chapter on primitive accumulation does not pretend to do more than trace the path by which, in Western Europe, the capitalist order of economy emerged from the womb of the feudal order of economy. It therefore describes the historical movement which by divorcing the producers from their means of production converts them into wage workers (proletarians in the modern sense of the word) while it converts those who possess the means of production into capitalists. In that history 'all revolutions are epoch-making that act as levers for the advancement of the capitalist class in course of formation; above all those which, by stripping great masses of men of their traditional means of production and subsistence, suddenly hurl them on the labour market. But the basis of this whole development is the expropriation of the agricultural producer. This has been accomplished in radical fashion only in England . . . but all the countries of Western Europe are going through the same movement', etc. (Capital, French edition, p. 315; cf. C I, p. 716.) At the end of the chapter the historical tendency of production is summed up thus: that it 'itself begets its own negation with the inexorability which governs the metamorphoses of nature'; that it has itself created the elements of new economic order, by giving the greatest impulse at once to the productive forces of social labour and to the integral development of every individual producer; that capitalist property,

resting already, as it actually does, on a collective mode of production, cannot but transform itself into social property. At this
point I have not furnished any proof, for the good reason that this
statement is itself nothing else but a general summary of long ex-
positions previously given in the chapters on capitalist production.

Now what application to Russia could my critic* make of this
historical sketch? Only this: If Russia is tending to become a
capitalist nation after the example of the West-European
countries—and during the last few years she has been taking a lot
of trouble in this direction—she will not succeed without having
first transformed a good part of her peasants into proletarians;
and after that, once taken to the bosom of the capitalist regime,
she will experience its pitiless laws like other profane peoples.
That is all. But that is too little for my critic. He feels he absolutely
must metamorphose my historical sketch of the genesis of
capitalism in Western Europe into an historico-philosophic theory
of the general path every people is fated to tread, whatever the
historical circumstances in which it finds itself, in order that it
may ultimately arrive at the form of economy which ensures,
together with the greatest expansion of the productive powers of
social labour, the most complete development of man. But I beg
his pardon. (He is both honouring and shaming me too much.)
Let us take an example.

In several parts of *Capital* I allude to the fate which overtook
the plebeians of ancient Rome. They were originally free peasants,
each cultivating his own piece of land on his own account. In the
course of Roman history they were expropriated. The same
movement which divorced them from their means of production
and subsistence involved the formation not only of big landed
property but also of big money capital. And so one fine morning
there were to be found on the one hand free men, stripped of
everything except their labour power, and on the other, in order
to exploit this labour, those who held all the acquired wealth in
their possession. What happened? The Roman proletarians became not wage labourers but a *mob* of do-nothings more abject

* N. K. Mikhailovsky (1842–1904), a prominent Russian sociological writer
an early critic of Marxian theories, and a leader of the so-called Liberal
Narodism. Marx refers to Mikhailovsky's article 'Karl Marx before the Tribunal
of Mr Zhukovsky', published in the Russian monthly *Otechestvenniye Zapisk*
(*Notes on the Fatherland*) in 1877. Mikhailovsky was one of the editors of this
magazine.

han the former 'poor whites' in the South of the United States, and alongside of them there developed a mode of production which was not capitalist but based on slavery. Thus events strikingly analogous but taking place in different historical surroundings led to totally different results. By studying each of these forms of evolution separately and then comparing them one can easily find the clue to this phenomenon, but one will never arrive there by using as one's master key a general historico-philosophical theory, the supreme virtue of which consists in being super-historical.*

Marx's letter to the Editors of the *Otechestvenniye Zapiski* (*Notes on the Fatherland*) of November 1877,** *SC*, pp. 378-9.

* In an earlier part of the same letter Marx referred to certain passages in the above quoted article of Mikhailovsky in which he discussed the question of whether 'Russia must begin by destroying the village community in order to pass to the capitalist regime, or whether, on the contrary, she can without experiencing the tortures of this regime appropriate all its fruits by developing the historical conditions specifically her own'. Marx then proceeded to express his own view on the matter. He wrote, 'In order that I might be specially qualified to estimate the economic development in Russia, I learnt Russian and then for many years studied the official publications and others bearing on this subject. I have arrived at this conclusion: If Russia continues to pursue the path she has followed since 1861, she will lose the finest chance ever offered by history to a people and undergo all the fatal vicissitudes of the capitalist regime'. *SC*, pp. 377-8) (Z.A.J.)
** The letter was never sent to its destination and was found by Engels in Marx's papers after the latter's death. It was first published in 1886. (Z.A.J.)

# Part Five

# The Economics and the Sociology
# of Capitalism

# A) The Economic Analysis

## 1) THE PREREQUISITES: THE BUYING AND SELLING OF LABOUR-POWER

By labour-power or capacity for labour is to be understood the aggregate of those mental and physical capabilities existing in a human being, which he exercises whenever he produces a use-value of any description.

But in order that our owner of money may be able to find labour-power offered for sale as a commodity, various conditions must first be fulfilled. The exchange of commodities of itself implies no other relations of dependence than those which result from its own nature. On this assumption, labour-power can appear upon the market as a commodity, only if, and so far as, its possessor, the individual whose labour-power it is, offers it for sale, or sells it, as a commodity. In order that he may be able to do this, he must have it at his disposal, must be the untrammelled owner of his capacity for labour, i.e., of his person. He and the owner of money meet in the market, and deal with each other as on the basis of equal rights, with this difference alone, that one is buyer, the other seller; both, therefore, equal in the eyes of the law. The continuance of this relation demands that the owner of the labour-power should sell it only for a definite period, for if he were to sell it rump and stump, once for all, he would be selling himself, converting himself from a free man into a slave, from an owner of a commodity into a commodity. He must constantly look upon his labour-power as his own property, his own commodity, and this he can only do by placing it at the disposal of the buyer temporarily, for a definite period of time. By this means alone can he avoid renouncing his rights of ownership over it.

The second essential condition to the owner of money findin labour-power in the market as a commodity is this—that th labourer instead of being in the position to sell commodities i which his labour is incorporated, must be obliged to offer for sal as a commodity that very labour-power, which exists only in h living self.

In order that a man may be able to sell commodities other tha labour-power, he must of course have the means of production, a raw material, implements, &c. No boots can be made withou leather. He requires also the means of subsistence. Nobody—no even 'a musician of the future'—can live upon future products, c upon use-values in an unfinished state; and ever since the fir moment of his appearance on the world's stage, man always ha been, and must still be a consumer, both before and while he i producing. In a society where all products assume the form c commodities, these commodities must be sold after they hav been produced; it is only after their sale that they can serve i satisfying the requirements of their producer. The time neces sary for their sale is superadded to that necessary for thei production.

For the conversion of his money into capital, therefore, th owner of money must meet in the market with the free labourer free in the double sense, that as a free man he can dispose of hi labour-power as his own commodity, and that on the other han he has no other commodity for sale, is short of everything neces sary for the realization of his labour-power.

The question why this free labourer confronts him in th market, has no interest for the owner of money, who regard the labour-market as a branch of the general market for com modities. And for the present it interests us just as little. W cling to the fact theoretically, as he does practically. One thing however, is clear—Nature does not produce on the one sid owners of money or commodities, and on the other men possessing nothing but their own labour-power. This relatio has no natural basis, neither is its social basis one that is commo to all historical periods. It is clearly the result of a past historica development, the product of many economic revolutions, o the extinction of a whole series of older forms of social produc tion. . . .

We must now examine more closely this peculiar commodity

labour-power. Like all others it has a value.[1] How is that value determined?

The value of labour-power is determined, as in the case of every other commodity, by the labour-time necessary for the production, and consequently also the reproduction, of this special article. So far as it has value, it represents no more than a definite quantity of the average labour of society incorporated in it. Labour-power exists only as a capacity, or power of the living individual. Its production consequently pre-supposes his existence. Given the individual, the production of labour-power consists in his re-production of himself or his maintenance. For his maintenance he requires a given quantity of the means of subsistence. Therefore the labour-time requisite for the production of labour-power reduces itself to that necessary for the production of those means of subsistence; in other words, the value of labour-power is the value of the means of subsistence necessary for the maintenance of the labourer. Labour-power, however, becomes a reality only by its exercise; it sets itself in action only by working. But thereby a definite quantity of human muscle, nerve, brain, &c., is wasted, and these require to be restored. This increased expenditure demands a larger income.[2] If the owner of labour-power works to-day, tomorrow he must again be able to repeat the same process in the same conditions as regards health and strength. His means of subsistence must therefore be sufficient to maintain him in his normal state as a labouring individual. His natural wants, such as food, clothing, fuel, and housing, vary according to the climatic and other physical conditions of his country. On the other hand, the number and extent of his so-called necessary wants, as also the modes of satisfying them, are themselves the product of historical development, and depend therefore to a great extent on the degree of civilization of a country, more particularly on the conditions under which, and consequently on the habits and degree of comfort in which, the class of free labourers has been formed. In contradistinction, therefore, to the case of other commodities, there enters into the determination of the value of labour-power a

---

[1] 'The value or worth of a man, is as of all other things, his price—that is to say, so much as would be given for the use of his power.' (Th. Hobbes, *Leviathan*, in *Works*, Ed. Sir William Molesworth, London, 1839–44, Vol. iii, p. 76.)
[2] Hence the Roman Villicus, as overlooker of the agricultural slaves, received 'more meagre fare than working slaves, because his work was lighter'. (Th. Mommsen, *Römische Geschichte*, 1856, p. 810.)

H

historical and moral element. Nevertheless, in a given country, at a given period, the average quantity of the means of subsistence necessary for the labourer is practically known.

The owner of labour-power is mortal. If then his appearance in the market is to be continuous, and the continuous conversion of money into capital assumes this, the seller of labour-power must perpetuate himself, 'in the way that every living individual perpetuates himself, by procreation'. The labour-power withdrawn from the market by wear and tear and death, must be continually replaced by, at the very least, an equal amount of fresh labour-power. Hence the sum of the means of subsistence necessary for the production of labour-power must include the means necessary for the labourer's substitutes, i.e., his children, in order that this race of peculiar commodity-owners may perpetuate its appearance in the market.

In order to modify the human organism, so that it may acquire skill and handiness in a given branch of industry, and become labour-power of a special kind, a special education or training is requisite, and this, on its part, costs an equivalent in commodities of a greater or less amount. This amount varies according to the more or less complicated character of the labour-power. The expenses of this education (excessively small in the case of ordinary labour-power), enter *pro tanto* into the total value spent in its production.

The value of labour-power resolves itself into the value of a definite quantity of the means of subsistence. It therefore varies with the value of these means or with the quantity of labour requisite for their production.

C I, pp. 167–72.


## (2) THE ELEMENTARY FACTORS OF THE LABOUR PROCESS

Labour is, in the first place, a process in which both man and Nature participate, and in which man of his own accord starts, regulates, and controls the material reactions between himself and Nature. He opposes himself to Nature as one of her own forces, setting in motion arms and legs, head and hands, the natural forces of his body, in order to appropriate Nature's productions in a form adapted to his own wants. By thus acting on the external world and changing it, he at the same time changes his own nature. He develops his slumbering powers and compels them to act in obedience to his sway. We are not now dealing with those primitive instinctive forms of labour that remind us of the mere animal. An immeasurable interval of time separates the state of things in which a man brings his labour-power to market for sale as a commodity, from that state in which human labour was still in its first instinctive stage. We pre-suppose labour in a form that stamps it as exclusively human. A spider conducts operations that resemble those of a weaver, and a bee puts to shame many an architect in the construction of her cells. But what distinguishes the worst architect from the best of bees is this, that the architect raises his structure in imagination before he erects it in reality. At the end of every labour-process, we get a result that already existed in the imagination of the labourer at its commencement. He not only effects a change of form in the material on which he works, but he also realizes a purpose of his own that gives the law to his *modus operandi*, and to which he must subordinate his will. And this subordination is no mere momentary act. Besides the exertion of the bodily organs, the process demands that, during the whole operation, the workman's will be steadily in consonance with his purpose. This means close attention. The less he is attracted by the nature of the work, and the mode in which it is carried on, and the less, therefore, he enjoys it as something which gives play to his bodily and mental powers, the more close his attention is forced to be.

The elementary factors of the labour-process are (1), the personal activity of man, i.e., work itself, (2) the subject of that work, and (3) its instruments.

The soil (and this, economically speaking, includes water) in the virgin state in which it supplies man with necessaries or the means of subsistence ready to hand, exists independently of him, and is the universal subject of human labour. All those things which labour merely separates from immediate connexion with their environment, are subjects of labour spontaneously provided by Nature. Such are fish which we catch and take from their element, water, timber which we fell in the virgin forest, and ores which we extract from their veins. If, on the other hand, the subject of labour has, so to say, been filtered through previous labour, we call it raw material; such is ore already extracted and ready for washing. All raw material is the subject of labour, but not every subject of labour is raw material; it can only become so, after it has undergone some alteration by means of labour.

An instrument of labour is a thing, or a complex of things, which the labourer interposes between himself and the subject of his labour, and which serves as the conductor of his activity. He makes use of the mechanical, physical, and chemical properties of some substances in order to make other substances subservient to his aims. Leaving out of consideration such ready-made means of subsistence as fruits, in gathering which a man's own limbs serve as the instruments of his labour, the first thing of which the labourer possesses himself is not the subject of labour but its instrument. Thus Nature becomes one of the organs of his activity, one that he annexes to his own bodily organs, adding stature to himself in spite of the Bible. As the earth is his original larder, so too it is his original tool house. It supplies him, for instance, with stones for throwing, grinding, pressing, cutting, &c. The earth itself is an instrument of labour, but when used as such in agriculture implies a whole series of other instruments and a comparatively high development of labour. No sooner does labour undergo the least development, than it requires specially prepared instruments. Thus in the oldest caves we find stone implements and weapons. In the earliest period of human history domesticated animals, i.e., animals which have been bred for the purpose, and have undergone modifications by means of labour, play the chief part as instruments of labour along with specially prepared stones, wood, bones, and shells.[1] The use and fabrication of instruments of labour, although existing in the germ among certain species of animals, is specifically characteristic of the human labour-process, and Franklin therefore defines man as a tool-making animal. Relics of bygone instruments of labour possess the same importance for the investigation of extinct economic forms of society as do fossil bones for the determination of extinct species of animals. It is not the articles made, but how they are made, and by what instruments, that enables us to distinguish different

[1] Turgot in his *Réflexions sur la Formation et la Distribution des Richesses* (1766) brings well into prominence the importance of domesticated animals to early civilization.

economic epochs.[1] Instruments of labour not only supply a standard of the degree of development to which human labour has attained, but they are also indicators of the social conditions under which that labour is carried on. Among the instruments of labour, those of a mechanical nature, which, taken as a whole, we may call the bone and muscles of production, offer much more decided characteristics of a given epoch of production, than those which, like pipes, tubs, baskets, jars, &c., serve only to hold the materials for labour, which latter class we may, in a general way, call the vascular system of production. The latter first begins to play an important part in the chemical industries.

In a wider sense we may include among the instruments of labour, in addition to those things that are used for directly transferring labour to its subject, and which therefore, in one way or another, serve as conductors of activity, all such objects as are necessary for carrying on the labour-process. These do not enter directly into the process, but without them it is either impossible for it to take place at all, or possible only to a partial extent. Once more we find the earth to be a universal instrument of this sort, for it furnishes a *locus standi* to the labourer and a field of employment for his activity. Among instruments that are the result of previous labour and also belong to this class, we find workshops, canals, roads, and so forth.

In the labour-process, therefore, man's activity, with the help of the instruments of labour, effects an alteration, designed from the commencement, in the material worked upon. The process disappears in the product; the latter is a use-value, Nature's material adapted by a change of form to the wants of man. Labour has incorporated itself with its subject: the former is materialized, the latter transformed. That which in the labourer appeared as movement, now appears in the product as a fixed quality without motion. The blacksmith forges and the product is a forging.

If we examine the whole process from the point of view of its

[1] The least important commodities of all for the technological comparison of different epochs of production are articles of luxury, in the strict meaning of the term. However little our written histories up to this time notice the development of material production, which is the basis of all social life, and therefore of all real history, yet prehistoric times have been classified in accordance with the results, not of so-called historical, but of materialistic investigations. These periods have been divided, to correspond with the materials from which their implements and weapons were made, viz. into the stone, the bronze, and the iron ages.

result, the product, it is plain that both the instruments and the subject of labour, are means of production,[1] and that the labour itself is productive labour.[2]

Though a use-value, in the form of a product, issues from the labour-process, yet other use-values, products of previous labour, enter into it as means of production. The same use-value is both the product of a previous process, and a means of production in a later process. Products are therefore not only results, but also essential conditions of labour.

With the exception of the extractive industries, in which the material for labour is provided immediately by Nature, such as mining, hunting, fishing, and agriculture (so far as the latter is confined to breaking up virgin soil), all branches of industry manipulate raw material, objects already filtered through labour, already products of labour. Such is seed in agriculture. Animals and plants, which we are accustomed to consider as products of Nature, are in their present form not only products of, say, last year's labour, but the result of a gradual transformation, continued through many generations, under man's superintendence, and by means of his labour. But in the great majority of cases, instruments of labour show even to the most superficial observer, traces of the labour of past ages.

*C* I, pp. 177–81.

## (3)  LABOUR THEORY OF VALUE*

What is the *value* of a commodity? How is it determined?

At first sight it would seem that the value of a commodity is a thing quite *relative*, and not to be settled without considering one commodity in its relations to all other commodities. In fact, in speaking of the value, the value in exchange of a commodity, we mean the proportional quantities in which it exchanges with all other commodities. But then arises the question: How are the

[1] It appears paradoxical to assert that uncaught fish, for instance, are a means of production in the fishing industry. But hitherto no one has discovered the art of catching fish in waters that contain none.

[2] This method of determining, from the standpoint of the labour-process alone, what is productive labour, is by no means directly applicable to the case of the capitalist process of production.

* Cf. *C* I, pp. 35–70. (Z.A.J.)

proportions in which commodities exchange with each other regulated?

We know from experience that these proportions vary infinitely. Taking one single commodity, wheat, for instance, we shall find that a quarter of wheat exchanges in almost countless variations of proportion with different commodities. Yet, *its value remaining always the same*, whether expressed in silk, gold, or any other commodity, it must be something distinct from, and independent of these *different rates of exchange* with different articles. It must be possible to express, in a very different form, these various equations with various commodities.

Besides, if I say a quarter of wheat exchanges with iron in a certain proportion, or the value of a quarter of wheat is expressed in a certain amount of iron, I say that the value of wheat and its equivalent in iron are equal *to some third thing*, which is neither wheat nor iron, because I suppose them to express the same magnitude in two different shapes. Either of them, the wheat or the iron, must, therefore, independently of the other, be reducible to this third thing which is their common measure. . . .

As the *exchangeable values* of commodities are only *social functions* of those things, and have nothing at all to do with their *natural* qualities, we must first ask, What is the common *social substance* of all commodities? It is *Labour*. To produce a commodity a certain amount of labour must be bestowed upon it, or worked up in it. And I say not only *Labour*, but *Social Labour*. A man who produces an article for his own immediate use, to consume it himself, creates a *product*, but not a *commodity*. As a self-sustaining producer he has nothing to do with society. But to produce a *commodity*, a man must not only produce an article satisfying some *social* want, but his labour itself must form part and parcel of the total sum of labour expended by society. It must be subordinate to the *Division of Labour within Society*. It is nothing without the other divisions of labour, and on its part is required to *integrate* them.

If we consider *commodities as values*, we consider them exclusively under the single aspect of *realized, fixed*, or, if you like, *crystallized social labour*. In this respect they can *differ* only by representing greater or smaller quantities of labour, as, for example, a greater amount of labour may be worked up in a silken handkerchief than in a brick. But how does one measure *quantities of labour?* By the *time the labour lasts*, in measuring the labour by the hour, the day, etc. Of course, to apply this measure, all sorts of labour are reduced to average or simple labour as their unit.

We arrive, therefore, at this conclusion. A commodity has a *value*, because it is a *crystallization of social labour*. The *greatness* of its value, of its *relative* value, depends upon the greater or less amount of that social substance contained in it; that is to say, on the relative mass of labour necessary for its production. The *relative values of commodities* are, therefore, determined by the *respective quantities or amounts of labour, worked up, realized, fixed in them*. The *correlative* quantities of commodities which can be produced in the *same time of labour* are *equal*. Or the value of one commodity is to the value of another commodity as the quantity of labour fixed in the one is to the quantity of labour fixed in the other.

I suspect that many of you will ask, Does there then, indeed, exist such a vast difference, or any whatever, between determining the values of commodities by *wages*, and determining them by the *relative quantities of labour* necessary for their production? You must, however, be aware that the *reward* for labour, and *quantity* of labour, are quite disparate things. Suppose, for example, *equal quantities of labour* to be fixed in one quarter of wheat and one ounce of gold. I resort to the example because it was used by Benjamin Franklin in his first Essay published in 1729, and entitled, *A Modest Enquiry into the Nature and Necessity of a Paper Currency*, where he, one of the first, hit upon the true nature of value. Well. We suppose, then, that one quarter of wheat and one ounce of gold are *equal values* or *equivalents*, because they are *crystallizations of equal amounts of average labour*, of so many days' or so many weeks' labour respectively fixed in them. In thus determining the relative values of gold and corn, do we refer in any way whatever to the *wages* of the agricultural labourer and the miner? Not a bit. We leave it quite *indeterminate how* their day's or week's labour was paid, or even whether wages labour was employed at all. If it was, wages may have been very unequal. The labourer whose labour is realized in the quarter of wheat may receive two bushels only, and the labourer employed in mining may receive one-half of the ounce of gold. Or, supposing their wages to be equal, they may deviate in all possible proportions from the values of the commodities produced by them. They may amount to one-half, one-third, one-fourth, one-fifth, or any other proportional part of the one quarter of corn or the one ounce of gold. Their *wages* can, of course, not *exceed*, not be *more* than the values of the commodities they produced, but they can be *less* in every possible degree. Their *wages* will be *limited* by the *values* of the products, but the *values of their products* will not be limited by the wages. And above all, the values, the relative values of corn and gold, for example, will have been settled without any regard whatever to the value of the labour employed, that is to say, to *wages*. To determine the values of commodities by the *relative quantities of labour fixed in them*, is, therefore, a thing quite different from the tautological method of determining the values of commodities by the value of labour, or by *wages*. This point, however, will be further elucidated in the progress of our enquiry.

In calculating the exchangeable value of a commodity we must add to the quantity of labour *last* employed the quantity of labour *previously* worked up in the raw material of the commodity, and the labour bestowed on the implements, tools, machinery, and buildings, with which such labour is assisted. For example, the value of a certain amount of cotton-yarn is the crystallization of the quantity of labour added to the cotton during the spinning process, the quantity of labour previously realized in the cotton itself, the quantity of labour realized in the coal, oil, and other auxiliary substances used, the quantity of labour fixed in the steam-engine, the spindles, the factory building, and so forth. Instruments of production properly so-called, such as tools, machinery, buildings, serve again and again for a longer or shorter period during repeated processes of production. If they were used up at once, like the raw material, their whole value would at once be transferred to the commodities they assist in producing. But as a spindle, for example, is but gradually used up, an average calculation is made, based upon the average time it lasts, and its average waste of wear and tear during a certain period, say a day. In this way we calculate how much of the value of the spindle is transferred to the yarn daily spun, and how much, therefore, of the total amount of labour realized in a pound of yarn, for example, is due to the quantity of labour previously realized in the spindle. For our present purpose it is not necessary to dwell any longer upon this point.

It might seem that if the value of a commodity is determined by the *quantity of labour bestowed upon its production*, the lazier

H*

a man, or the clumsier a man, the more valuable his commodity, because the greater the time of labour required for finishing the commodity. This, however, would be a sad mistake. You will recollect that I used the word '*Social* labour', and many points are involved in this qualification of '*Social*'. In saying that the value of a commodity is determined by the *quantity of labour* worked up or crystallized in it, we mean *the quantity of labour necessary* for its production in a given state of society, under certain social average conditions of production, with a given social average intensity, and average skill of the labour employed. When, in England, the power-loom came to compete with the hand-loom, only one-half the former time of labour was wanted to convert a given amount of yarn into a yard of cotton or cloth. The poor hand-loom weaver now worked seventeen or eighteen hours daily, instead of the nine or ten hours he had worked before. Still the product of twenty hours of his labour represented now only ten social hours of labour, or ten hours of labour socially necessary for the conversion of a certain amount of yarn into textile stuffs. His product of twenty hours had, therefore, no more value than his former product of ten hours.

If then the quantity of socially necessary labour realized in commodities regulates their exchangeable values, every increase in the quantity of labour wanted for the production of a commodity must augment its value, as every diminution must lower it.

If the respective quantities of labour necessary for the production of the respective commodities remained constant, their relative values also would be constant. But such is not the case. The quantity of labour necessary for the production of a commodity changes continuously with the changes in the productive powers of the labour employed. The greater the productive powers of labour, the more produce is finished in a given time of labour: and the smaller the productive powers of labour, the less produce is finished in the same time. If, for example, in the progress of population it should become necessary to cultivate less fertile soils, the same amount of produce would be only attainable by a greater amount of labour spent, and the value of agricultural produce would consequently rise. On the other hand, if with the modern means of production, a single spinner converts into yarn, during one working day, many thousand times the amount of cotton which he could have spun during the same time with the spinning wheel, it is evident that every single pound of cotton will absorb many thousand times less of spinning labour than it did before, and, consequently, the value added by spinning to every single pound of cotton will be a thousand times less than before. The value of yarn will sink accordingly.

Apart from the different natural energies and acquired working abilities of different peoples, the productive powers of labour must principally depend:

Firstly. Upon the *natural* conditions of labour, such as fertility of soil, mines, and so forth.

Secondly. Upon the progressive improvement of the *Social Powers of Labour*, such as are derived from production on a grand scale, concentration of capital and combination of labour, subdivision of labour, machinery, improved methods, appliance of chemical and other natural agencies, shortening of time and space by means of communication and transport, and every other contrivance by which science presses natural agencies into the service of labour, and by which the social co-operative character of labour is developed. The greater the productive powers of labour, the less labour is bestowed upon a given amount of produce; hence the smaller the value of this produce. The smaller the productive powers of labour, the more labour is bestowed upon the same amount of produce; hence the greater its value. As a general law we may, therefore, set it down that:

*The values of commodities are directly as the times of labour employed in their production, and are inversely as the productive powers of the labour employed.*

*WPP*, pp. 378–82.


# (4) PRODUCTION OF SURPLUS VALUE*

Now suppose that the average amount of the daily necessaries of a labouring man require *six hours of average labour* for their production. Suppose, moreover, six hours of average labour to be also realized in a quantity of gold equal to three shillings. Then three shillings would be the *Price*, or the monetary expression of the *Daily Value* of that man's *Labouring Power*. If he worked daily six hours he would daily produce a value sufficient to buy

* Cf. *C* I, pp. 186–98. (Z.A.J.)

the average amount of his daily necessaries, or to maintain himself as a labouring man.

But our man is a wages labourer. He must, therefore, sell his labouring power to a capitalist. If he sells it at three shillings daily, or eighteen shillings weekly, he sells it at its value. Suppose him to be a spinner. If he works six hours daily he will add to the cotton a value of three shillings daily. This value, daily added by him, would be an exact equivalent for the wages, or the price of his labouring power, received daily. But in that case *no surplus value* or *surplus produce* whatever would go to the capitalist. Here, then, we come to the rub.

In buying the labouring power of the workman, and paying its value, the capitalist, like every other purchaser, has acquired the right to consume or use the commodity bought. You consume or use the labouring power of a man by making him work, as you consume or use a machine by making it run. By paying the daily or weekly value of the labouring power of the workman, the capitalist has, therefore, acquired the right to use or make that labouring power work during the *whole day or week*. The working day or the working week has, of course, certain limits, but those we shall afterwards look more closely at. For the present I want to turn your attention to one decisive point.

The *value* of the labouring power is determined by the quantity of labour necessary to maintain or reproduce it, but the *use* of that labouring power is only limited by the active energies and physical strength of the labourer. The daily or weekly *value* of the labouring power is quite distinct from the daily or weekly exercise of that power, the same as the food a horse wants and the time it can carry the horseman are quite distinct. The quantity of labour by which the *value* of the workman's labouring power is limited forms by no means a limit to the quantity of labour which his labouring power is apt to perform. Take the example of our spinner. We have seen that, to daily reproduce his labouring power, he must daily reproduce a value of three shillings, which he will do by working six hours daily. But this does not disable him from working ten or twelve or more hours a day. But by paying the daily or weekly *value* of the spinner's labouring power, the capitalist has acquired the right of using that labouring power during *the whole day or week*. He will, therefore, make him work say, daily, *twelve* hours. *Over and above* the six hours required to replace his wages, or the value of his labouring power, he will, therefore, have to work *six other hours*, which I shall call hours of *surplus labour*, which surplus labour will realize itself in a *surplus value* and a *surplus produce*. If our spinner, for example, by his daily labour of six hours, added three shillings' value to the cotton, a value forming an exact equivalent to his wages, he will, in twelve hours, add six shillings' worth to the cotton, and produce *a proportional surplus of yarn*. As he has sold his labouring power to the capitalist, the whole value or produce created by him belongs to the capitalist, the owner *pro tem.* (for the time) of his labouring power. By advancing three shillings, the capitalist will, therefore, realize a value of six shillings, because, advancing a value in which six hours of labour are crystallized, he will receive in return a value in which twelve hours of labour are crystallized. By repeating this same process daily, the capitalist will daily advance three shillings and daily pocket six shillings, one-half of which will go to pay wages anew, and the other half of which will form *surplus value*, for which the capitalist pays no equivalent. It is this *sort of exchange between capital and labour* upon which capitalistic production, or the wages system, is founded, and which must constantly result in reproducing the working man as a working man, and the capitalist as a capitalist.

*The rate of surplus value*, all other circumstances remaining the same, will depend on the proportion between that part of the working day necessary to reproduce the value of the labouring power and the *surplus time* or *surplus labour* performed for the capitalist. It will, therefore, depend on the *ratio in which the working day is prolonged over and above that extent*, by working which the working man would only reproduce the value of his labouring power, or replace his wages.

*WPP*, pp. 386–8.

## (5) THE SOCIAL BASIS OF CAPITAL

Capital consists of raw materials, instruments of labour and means of subsistence of all kinds, which are utilized in order to produce new raw materials, new instruments of labour and new means of subsistence. All these component parts of capital are creations of labour, products of labour, *accumulated labour*.

Accumulated labour which serves as a means of new production is capital.

So say the economists.

What is a Negro slave? A man of the black race. The one explanation is as good as the other.

A Negro is a Negro. He only becomes a slave in certain relations. A cotton-spinning jenny is a machine for spinning cotton. It becomes *capital* only in certain relations. Torn from these relationships it is no more capital than gold in itself is *money* or sugar the price of sugar.

In production, men not only act on nature but also on one another. They produce only by cooperating in a certain way and mutually exchanging their activities. In order to produce, they enter into definite connections and relations with one another and only within these social connections and relations does their action on nature, does production, take place.

These social relations into which the producers enter with one another, the conditions under which they exchange their activities and participate in the whole act of production, will naturally vary according to the character of the means of production. With the invention of a new instrument of warfare, firearms, the whole internal organization of the army necessarily changed; the relationships within which individuals can constitute an army and act as an army were transformed and the relations of different armies to one another also changed.

*Thus* the social relations within which individuals produce, *the social relations of production, change, are transformed, with the change and development of the material means of production, the productive forces. The relations of production in their totality constitute what are called the social relations, society, and, specifically a society at a definite stage of historical development*, a society with a peculiar, distinctive character. *Ancient* society, *feudal* society, *bourgeois* society are such totalities of production relations, each of which at the same time denotes a special stage of development in the history of mankind.

*Capital*, also, is a social relation of production. *It is a bourgeois production relation*, a production relation of bourgeois society. Are not the means of subsistence, the instruments of labour, the raw materials of which capital consists, produced and accumulated under given social conditions, in definite social relations? Are they not utilized for new production under given social conditions, in definite social relations? And is it not just this definite social character which turns the products serving for new production into *capital*?

Capital consists not only of means of subsistence, instruments of labour and raw materials, not only of material products; it consists just as much of *exchange values*. All the products of which it consists are *commodities*. Capital is, therefore, not only a sum of material products; it is a sum of commodities, of exchange values, *of social magnitude*. . . .

How, then, does any amount of commodities, of exchange value, become capital?

By maintaining and multiplying itself as an independent social *power*, that is, as the power *of a portion of society*, by means of its *exchange for direct, living labour-power*. The existence of a class which possesses nothing but its capacity to labour is a necessary prerequisite of capital.

It is only the domination of accumulated, past, materialized labour over direct, living labour that turns accumulated labour into capital.

Capital does not consist in accumulated labour serving living labour as a means for new production. It consists in living labour serving accumulated labour as a means for maintaining and multiplying the exchange value of the latter.

What takes place in the exchange between capitalist and wage-worker?

The worker receives means of subsistence in exchange for his labour-power, but the capitalist receives in exchange for his means of subsistence labour, the productive activity of the worker, the creative power whereby the worker not only replaces what he consumes but *gives to the accumulated labour a greater value than it previously possessed*. The worker receives a part of the available means of subsistence from the capitalist. For what purpose do these means of subsistence serve him? For immediate consumption. As soon, however, as I consume the means of subsistence, they are irretrievably lost to me unless I use the time during which I am kept alive by them in order to produce new means of subsistence, in order during consumption to create by my labour new values in place of the values which perish in being consumed. But it is just this noble reproductive power that the worker surrenders to the capitalist in exchange for means of subsistence received. He has, therefore, lost it for himself. . . .

Does a worker in a cotton factory produce merely cotton textiles? No, he produces capital. He produces values which serve afresh to command his labour and by means of it to create new values.

Capital can only increase by exchanging itself for labour-power, by calling wage-labour to life. The labour-power of the wage worker can only be exchanged for capital by increasing capital, by strengthening the power whose slave it is. *Hence, increase of capital is increase of the proletariat, that is, of the working class.*

The interests of the capitalist and those of the worker are, therefore, *one and the same*, assert the bourgeois and their economists. Indeed! The worker perishes if capital does not employ him. Capital perishes if it does not exploit labour-power, and in order to exploit it, it must buy it. The faster capital intended for production, productive capital, increases, the more, therefore, industry prospers, the more the bourgeoisie enriches itself and the better business is, the more workers does the capitalist need; the more dearly does the worker sell himself.

The indispensable condition for a tolerable situation of the worker *is, therefore, the fastest possible growth of productive capital.*

But what is the growth of productive capital? Growth of the power of accumulated labour over living labour. Growth of the domination of the bourgeoisie over the working class. If wage labour produces the wealth of others that rules over it, the power that is hostile to it, capital, then the means of employment, that is, the means of subsistence, flow back to it from this hostile power, on condition that it makes itself afresh into a part of capital, into the lever which hurls capital anew into an accelerated movement of growth.

*To say that the interests of capital and those of the workers are one and the same is only to say that capital and wage labour are two sides of one and the same relation. The one conditions the other, just as usurer and squanderer condition each other.*

As long as the wage worker is a wage worker his lot depends upon capital. That is the much-vaunted community of interests between worker and capitalist.

*WLC*, pp. 83–7.

# 6) THE HISTORICAL ROLE OF THE CAPITALIST

Except as personified capital, the capitalist has no historical value, and no right to that historical existence. . . . But, so far as he is personified capital, it is not values in use and the enjoyment of them, but exchange-value and its augmentation, that spur him into action. Fanatically bent on making value expand itself, he ruthlessly forces the human race to produce for production's sake; he thus forces the development of the productive powers of society, and creates those material conditions, which alone can form the real basis of a higher form of society, a society in which the full and free development of every individual forms the ruling principle. Only as personified capital is the capitalist respectable. As such, he shares with the miser the passion for wealth as wealth. But that which in the miser is a mere idiosyncrasy, is, in the capitalist, the effect of the social mechanism, of which he is but one of the wheels. Moreover, the development of capitalist production makes it constantly necessary to keep increasing the amount of the capital laid out in a given industrial undertaking, and competition makes the immanent laws of capitalist production to be felt by each individual capitalist, as external coercive laws. It compels him to keep constantly extending his capital, in order to preserve it, but extend it he cannot, except by means of progressive accumulation.

So far, therefore, as his actions are a mere function of  capital —endowed as capital is, in his person, with consciousness and a will—his own private consumption is a robbery perpetrated on accumulation, just as in book-keeping by double entry, the private expenditure of the capitalist is placed on the debtor side of his account against his capital. To accumulate is to conquer the world of social wealth, to increase the mass of human beings exploited by him, and thus to extend both the direct and the indirect sway of the capitalist.[1]

*C* I, p. 592.

---

Taking the usurer, that old-fashioned but ever renewed specimen of the capitalist for his text, Luther shows very aptly that the love of power is an element in the desire to get rich.

Accumulate, accumulate! That is Moses and the prophets 'Industry furnishes the material which saving accumulates.' Therefore, save, save, i.e., reconvert the greatest possible portio: of surplus-value, or surplus-product into capital! Accumulatio: for accumulation's sake, production for production's sake: b this formula classical economy expressed the historical missio: of the bourgeoisie, and did not for a single instant deceive itsel over the birth-throes of wealth.[2] But what avails lamentatio: in the face of historical necessity? If to classical economy, th proletarian is but a machine for the production of surplus-value on the other hand, the capitalist is in its eyes only a machine fo the conversion of this surplus-value into additional capita.

*C* I, p. 595.

## (7) THE CAPITALIST'S CONSPICUOUS CONSUMPTION

But original sin is at work everywhere. As capitalist produc tion, accumulation, and wealth, become developed, the capital ist ceases to be the mere incarnation of capital. He has a fellow feeling for his own Adam, and his education gradually enable him to smile at the rage of asceticism as a mere prejudice of th old-fashioned miser. While the capitalist of the classical typ brands individual consumption as a sin against his function, an as 'abstinence' from accumulating, the modernized capitalist : capable of looking upon accumulation as 'abstinence' from pleasur

> Two souls, alas, do dwell within his breast;
> The one is ever parting from the other.[3]

At the historical dawn of capitalist production—and ever capitalist upstart has personally to go through this historic.

[1] A. Smith, *The Wealth of Nations*, bk. III, ch. III.
[2] Even J. B. Say says, 'Les épargnes des riches se font aux dépens des pauvre 'The Roman proletarian lived almost entirely at the expense of society. . . . can almost be said that modern society lives at the expense of the proletarians, ( what it keeps out of the remuneration of labour' (J. C. L. Simonde de Sismonc *Études sur l'économie politique*, t. I, Bruxelles, 1836, p. 24).
[3] See Goethe's *Faust*.

stage—avarice, and desire to get rich, are the ruling passions. But the progress of capitalist production not only creates a world of delights; it lays open, in speculation and the credit system, a thousand sources of sudden enrichment. When a certain stage of development has been reached, a conventional degree of prodigality, which is also an exhibition of wealth, and consequently a source of credit, becomes a business necessity to the 'unfortunate' capitalist. Luxury enters into capital's expenses of representation. Moreover, the capitalist gets rich, not like the miser, in proportion to his personal labour and restricted consumption, but at the same rate as he squeezes out the labour-power of others, and enforces on the labourer abstinence from all life's enjoyments. Although, therefore, the prodigality of the capitalist never possesses the *bona fide* character of the open-handed feudal lord's prodigality, but, on the contrary, has always lurking behind it the most sordid avarice and the most anxious calculation, yet his expenditure grows with his accumulation, without the one necessarily restricting the other. But along with this growth, there is at the same time developed in his breast, a Faustian conflict between the passion for accumulation, and the desire for enjoyment.

                                                                    *C* I, pp. 593–4.

## 8) ACCUMULATION, CONCENTRATION, AND CENTRALIZATION OF CAPITAL

Every individual capital is a larger or smaller concentration of means of production, with a corresponding command over a larger or smaller labour-army. Every accumulation becomes the means of new accumulation. With the increasing mass of wealth which functions as capital, accumulation increases the concentration of that wealth in the hands of individual capitalists, and thereby widens the basis of production on a large scale and of the specific methods of capitalist production. The growth of social capital is effected by the growth of many individual capitals. All other circumstances remaining the same, individual capitals, and with them the concentration of the means of production, increase in such proportion as they form aliquot parts of

the total social capital. At the same time portions of the origina
capitals disengage themselves and function as new independen
capitals. Besides other causes, the division of property, withi
capitalist families, plays a great part in this. With the accumu
lation of capital, therefore, the number of capitalists grows t
a greater or less extent. Two points characterize this kind of con
centration which grows directly out of, or rather is identical with
accumulation. First, the increasing concentration of the socia
means of production in the hands of individual capitalists i
other things remaining equal, limited by the degree of increas
of social wealth. Second, the part of social capital domicile
in each particular sphere of production is divided among man
capitalists who face one another as independent commodity
producers competing with each other. Accumulation and th
concentration accompanying it are, therefore, not only scattere
over many points, but the increase of each functioning capit
is thwarted by the formation of new and the sub-division of ol
capitals. Accumulation, therefore, presents itself on the one han
as increasing concentration of the means of production, and o
the command over labour; on the other, as repulsion of man
individual capitals one from another.

This splitting-up of the total social capital into many indi
vidual capitals or the repulsion of its fractions one from another, i
counteracted by their attraction. This last does not mean tha
simple concentration of the means of production and of the com
mand over labour which is identical with accumulation. I
is concentration of capitals already formed, destruction of thei
individual independence, expropriation of capitalist by capital
ist, transformation of many small into few large capitals. Thi
process differs from the former in this, that it only presuppose
a change in the distribution of capital already to hand, and fun
tioning; its field of action is therefore not limited by the absolut
growth of social wealth, by the absolute limits of accumulatio
Capital grows in one place to a huge mass in a single hand, becaus
it has in another place been lost by many. This is centralizatio
proper, as distinct from accumulation and concentration. . . .

Centralization completes the work of accumulation by enablin
industrial capitalists to extend the scale of their operation
Whether this latter result is the consequence of accumulation o
centralization, whether centralization is accomplished by th

iolent method of annexation—when certain capitals become uch preponderant centres of attraction for others that they shat- er the individual cohesion of the latter and then draw the sep- rate fragments to themselves—or whether the fusion of a num- er of capitals already formed or in process of formation takes lace by the smoother process of organizing joint-stock companies —the economic effect remains the same. Everywhere the increased cale of industrial establishments is the starting-point for a more omprehensive organization of the collective work of many, for a vider development of their material motive forces—in other vords, for the progressive transformation of isolated processes of roduction, carried on by customary methods, into processes of roduction socially combined and scientifically arranged.

*C* I, pp. 624–7.

## 9) THE SO-CALLED PRIMITIVE ACCUMULATION

Ve have seen how money is changed into capital; how through apital surplus-value is made, and from surplus-value more apital. But the accumulation of capital presupposes surplus- alue; surplus-value presupposes capitalist production; capital- tic production presupposes the pre-existence of considerable nasses of capital and of labour power in the hands of producers of ommodities. The whole movement, therefore, seems to turn in a icious circle, out of which we can only get by supposing a rimitive accumulation (previous accumulation of Adam Smith) receding capitalistic accumulation; an accumulation not the result f the capitalist mode of production, but its starting-point.

This primitive accumulation plays in Political Economy about he same part as original sin in theology. Adam bit the apple, and hereupon sin fell on the human race. Its origin is supposed to be xplained when it is told as an anecdote of the past. In times long one by there were two sorts of people; one the diligent, intelligent, nd, above all, frugal élite; the other, lazy rascals, spending their ubstance, and more, in riotous living. The legend of theological riginal sin tells us certainly how man came to be condemned to at his bread in the sweat of his brow; but the history of economic riginal sin reveals to us that there are people to whom this is by no means essential. Never mind! Thus it came to pass that the former sort accumulated wealth, and the latter sort had at last nothing to sell except their own skins. And from this original sin dates the poverty of the great majority that, despite all its labour, has up to now nothing to sell but itself, and the wealth of the few that increases constantly although they have long ceased to work. Such insipid childishness is every day preached to us in the defence of property. M. Thiers,* e.g., had the assurance to repeat it with all the solemnity of a statesman, to the French people, once so *spirituel*. But as soon as the question of property crops up, it becomes a sacred duty to proclaim the intellectual food of the infant as the one thing fit for all ages and for all stages of development. In actual history it is notorious that conquest, enslavement robbery, murder, briefly force, play the great part. In the tender annals of Political Economy, the idyllic reigns from time immemorial. Right and 'labour' were from all time the sole means of enrichment, the present year of course always excepted. As a matter of fact, the methods of primitive accumulation are anything but idyllic.

In themselves money and commodities are no more capital than are the means of production and of subsistence. They want transforming into capital. But this transformation itself can only take place under certain circumstances that centre in this, viz., that two very different kinds of commodity possessors must come face to face and into contact; on the one hand, the owners of money means of production, means of subsistence, who are eager to increase the sum of values they possess, by buying other people's labour-power; on the other hand, free labourers, the sellers of their own labour-power, and therefore the sellers of labour. Free labourers, in the double sense that neither they themselves form part and parcel of the means of production, as in the case of slaves bondsmen, &c., nor do the means of production belong to them as in the case of peasant-proprietors, are, therefore, free from unencumbered by, any means of production of their own. With this polarisation of the market for commodities, the funda

* Adolphe Thiers (1797–1877), a French politician and historian, author of *Histoire de la révolution* (1823–27). He lived in exile during the Second Empire but returned to lead the French Government after the Franco-Prussian war. Marx blamed him personally for the brutal suppression of the Paris Commune and for the massacre of the Communards by the Versailles troops (Z.A.J.)

mental conditions of capitalist production are given. The capitalist system presupposes the complete separation of the labourers from all property in the means by which they can realize their labour. As soon as capitalist production is once on its own legs, it not only maintains this separation, but reproduces it on a continually extending scale. The process, therefore, that clears the way for the capitalist system, can be none other than the process which takes away from the labourer the possession of his means of production; a process that transforms, on the one hand, the social means of subsistence and of production into capital, on the other, the immediate producers into wage-labourers. The so-called primitive accumulation, therefore, is nothing else than the historical process of divorcing the producer from the means of production. It appears as primitive, because it forms the prehistoric stage of capital and of the mode of production corresponding with it.

The economic structure of capitalistic society has grown out of the economic structure of feudal society. The dissolution of the latter set free the elements of the former.

The immediate producer, the labourer, could only dispose of his own person after he had ceased to be attached to the soil and ceased to be the slave, serf, or bondman of another. To become a free seller of labour-power, who carries his commodity wherever he finds a market, he must further have escaped from the regime of the guilds, their rules for apprentices and journeymen, and the impediments of their labour regulations. Hence, the historical movement which changes the producers into wage-workers, appears, on the one hand, as their emancipation from serfdom and from the fetters of the guilds, and this side alone exists for our bourgeois historians. But, on the other hand, these new freedmen became sellers of themselves only after they had been robbed of all their own means of production, and of all the guarantees of existence afforded by the old feudal arrangements. And the history of this, their expropriation, is written in the annals of mankind in letters of blood and fire.

The industrial capitalists, these new potentates, had on their part not only to displace the guild masters of handicrafts, but also the feudal lords, the possessors of the sources of wealth. In this respect their conquest of social power appears as the fruit of a victorious struggle both against feudal lordship and its revolting prerogatives, and against the guilds and the fetters they laid on the

free development of production and the free exploitation of man
by man. The *chevaliers d'industrie*, however, only succeeded in
supplanting the *chevaliers* of the sword by making use of events of
which they themselves were wholly innocent. They have risen by
means as vile as those by which the Roman freedman once on a
time made himself the master of his *patronus*.

The starting-point of the development that gave rise to the
wage-labourer as well as to the capitalist, was the servitude of the
labourer. The advance consisted in a change of form of this
servitude, in the transformation of feudal exploitation into capitalist exploitation. To understand its march, we need not go back very
far. Although we come across the first beginnings of capitalist
production as early as the fourteenth or fifteenth century, sporadi-
cally, in certain towns of the Mediterranean, the capitalistic era
dates from the sixteenth century. Wherever it appears, the
abolition of serfdom has been long effected, and the highest development of the middle ages, the existence of sovereign towns, has been
long on the wane.

In the history of primitive accumulation, all revolutions are
epoch-making that act as levers for the capitalist class in course of
formation; but, above all, those moments when great masses of men
are suddenly and forcibly torn from their means of subsistence,
and hurled as free and 'unattached' proletarians on the labour-
market. The expropriation of the agricultural producer, of the
peasant, from the soil, is the basis of the whole process. The
history of this expropriation, in different countries, assumes
different aspects, and runs through its various phases in different
orders of succession, and at different periods. In England alone,
which we take as our example, has it the classic form.[1]

*C* I, pp. 713–16.

---

[1] In Italy, where capitalistic production developed earliest, the dissolution of
serfdom also took place earlier than elsewhere. The serf was emancipated in
that country before he had acquired any prescriptive right to the soil. His
emancipation at once transformed him into a free proletarian, who, moreover,
found his master ready waiting for him in the towns, for the most part handed
down as legacies from the Roman time. When the revolution of the world-
market, about the end of the fifteenth century, annihilated Northern Italy's
commercial supremacy, a movement in the reverse direction set in. The labourers of the towns were driven *en masse* into the country, and gave an impulse,
never before seen, to the *petite culture*, carried on in the form of gardening.

## 10) THE TRANSFORMATION OF CAPITALIST PRIVATE PROPERTY INTO SOCIALIZED PROPERTY

What does the primitive accumulation of capital, i.e., its historical genesis, resolve itself into? In so far as it is not immediate transformation of slaves and serfs into wage-labourers, and therefore a mere change of form, it only means the expropriation of the immediate producers, i.e., the dissolution of private property based on the labour of its owner. Private property, as the antithesis to social, collective property, exists only where the means of labour and the external conditions of labour belong to private individuals. But according as these private individuals are labourers or not labourers, private property has a different character. The numberless shades, that it at first sight presents, correspond to the intermediate stages lying between these two extremes. The private property of the labourer in his means of production is the foundation of petty industry, whether agricultural, manufacturing, or both; petty industry, again, is an essential condition for the development of social production and of the free individuality of the labourer himself. Of course, this petty mode of production exists also under slavery, serfdom, and other states of dependence. But it flourishes, it lets loose its whole energy, it attains its adequate classical form, only where the labourer is the private owner of his own means of labour set in action by himself: the peasant of the land which he cultivates, the artisan of the tool which he handles as a virtuoso. This mode of production presupposes parcelling of the soil, and scattering of the other means of production. As it excludes the concentration of these means of production, so also it excludes co-operation, division of labour within each separate process of production, the control over, and the productive application of the forces of Nature by society, and the free development of the social productive powers. It is compatible only with a system of production, and a society, moving within narrow and more or less primitive bounds. To perpetuate it would be, as Pecqueur rightly says, 'to decree universal mediocrity'. At a certain stage of development it brings forth the material agencies for its own dissolution. From that moment new forces and new passions spring up in the bosom of society; but the old social organization fetters them and keeps them down. It must be annihilated; it is annihilated. Its annihilation, the transformation of the individualized and scattered means of production into socially concentrated ones, of the pigmy property of the many into the huge property of the few, the expropriation of the great mass of the people from the soil, from the means of subsistence, and from the means of labour, this fearful and painful expropriation of the mass of the people forms the prelude to the history of capital. It comprises a series of forcible methods, of which we have passed in review only those that have been epoch-making as methods of the primitive accumulation of capital. The expropriation of the immediate producers was accomplished with merciless Vandalism, and under the stimulus of passions the most infamous, the most sordid, the pettiest, the most meanly odious. Self-earned private property, that is based, so to say, on the fusing together of the isolated, independent labouring-individual with the conditions of his labour, is supplanted by capitalistic private property, which rests on exploitation of the nominally free labour of others, i.e., on wages-labour.

As soon as this process of transformation has sufficiently decomposed the old society from top to bottom, as soon as the labourers are turned into proletarians, their means of labour into capital, as soon as the capitalist mode of production stands on its own feet, then the further socialization of labour and further transformation of the land and other means of production into socially exploited and, therefore, common means of production, as well as the further expropriation of private proprietors, takes a new form. That which is now to be expropriated is no longer the labourer working for himself, but the capitalist exploiting many labourers. This expropriation is accomplished by the action of the immanent laws of capitalistic production itself, by the centralization of capital. One capitalist always kills many. Hand in hand with this centralization, or this expropriation of many capitalists by few, develop, on an ever-extending scale, the co-operative form of the labour-process, the conscious technical application of science, the methodical cultivation of the soil, the transformation of the instruments of labour into instruments of labour only usable in common, the economizing of all means of production by their use as the means of production of combined, socialized labour, the entanglement of all peoples in the net of the world market, and with this, the international character of the capitalistic régime. Along with the constantly diminishing number of the magnates of capital, who usurp and monopolize all advantages of this process of transformation, grows the mass of misery, oppression, slavery, degradation, exploitation; but with this too grows the revolt of the working-class, a class always increasing in numbers, and disciplined, united, organized by the very mechanism of the process of capitalist production itself. The monopoly of capital becomes a fetter upon the mode of production, which has sprung up and flourished along with, and under it. Centralization of the means of production and socialization of labour at last reach a point where they become incompatible with their capitalist integument. Thus integument is burst asunder. The knell of capitalist private property sounds. The expropriators are expropriated.

The capitalist mode of appropriation, the result of the capitalist mode of production, produces capitalist private property. This is the first negation of individual private property, as founded on the labour of the proprietor. But capitalist production begets, with the inexorability of a law of Nature, its own negation. It is the negation of negation. This does not re-establish private property for the producer, but gives him individual property based on the acquisitions of the capitalist era: i.e., on co-operation and the possession in common of the land and of the means of production.

The transformation of scattered private property, arising from individual labour, into capitalist private property is, naturally, a process, incomparably more protracted, violent, and difficult, than the transformation of capitalistic private property, already practically resting on socialized production, into socialized property. In the former case, we had the expropriation of the mass of the people by a few usurpers; in the latter, we have the expropriation of a few usurpers by the mass of the people.

C I, pp. 761–4.

We have seen that the growing accumulation of capital implies its growing concentration. Thus grows the power of capital, the alienation of the conditions of social production personified in the capitalist from the real producers. Capital comes more and more to the fore as a social power, whose agent is the capitalist. This social power no longer stands in any possible relation to that which the labour of a single individual can create. It becomes an alienated, independent, social power, which stands opposed to society as an object, and as an object that is the capitalist's source of power. The contradiction between the general social power into which capital develops, on the one hand, and the private power of the individual capitalists over these social conditions of production, on the other, becomes ever more irreconcilable, and yet contains the solution of the problem, because it implies at the same time the transformation of the conditions of production into general, common, social, conditions. This transformation stems from the development of the productive forces under capitalist production, and from the ways and means by which this development takes place.

*C* III, p. 259.

## (11) THE REALM OF FREEDOM AND THE REALM OF NECESSITY

The labour-process . . . is human action with a view to the production of use-values, appropriation of natural substances to human requirements; it is the necessary condition for effecting exchange of matter between man and Nature; it is the everlasting Nature-imposed condition of human existence, and therefore is independent of every social phase of that existence, or rather, is common to every such phase. It was, therefore, not necessary to represent our labourer in connexion with other labourers; man and his labour on one side, Nature and its materials on the other, sufficed. As the taste of the porridge does not tell you who grew the oats, no more does this simple process tell you of itself what are the social conditions under which it is taking place, whether under the slave-owner's brutal lash, or the anxious eye of the capitalist, whether Cincinnatus carries it on in tilling his modest farm or a savage in killing wild animals with stones.

*C* I, pp. 183–4.*

* Cf. *C* I, pp. 42–3. (Z.A.J.)

We have seen that the capitalist process of production is a historically determined form of the social process of production in general. The latter is as much a production process of material conditions of human life as a process taking place under specific historical and economic production relations, producing and reproducing these production relations themselves, and thereby also the bearers of this process, their material conditions of existence and their mutual relations, i.e., their particular socio-economic form. For the aggregate of these relations, in which the agents of this production stand with respect to Nature and to one another, and in which they produce, is precisely society, considered from the standpoint of its economic structure. Like all its predecessors, the capitalist process of production proceeds under definite material conditions, which are, however, simultaneously the bearers of definite social relations entered into by individuals in the process of reproducing their life. Those conditions, like these relations, are on the one hand prerequisites, on the other hand results and creations of the capitalist process of production; they are produced and reproduced by it. We saw also that capital— and the capitalist is merely capital personified and functions in the process of production solely as the agent of capital—in its corresponding social process of production, pumps a definite quantity of surplus-labour out of the direct producers, or labourers; capital obtains this surplus-labour without an equivalent, and in essence it always remains forced labour—no matter how much it may seem to result from free contractual agreement. This surplus-labour appears as surplus-value, and this surplus-value exists as a surplus-product. Surplus-labour in general, as labour performed over and above the given requirements, must always remain. In the capitalist as well as in the slave system, etc., it merely assumes an antagonistic form and is supplemented by complete idleness of a stratum of society. A definite quantity of surplus-labour is required as insurance against accidents, and by the necessary and progressive expansion of the process of reproduction in keeping with the development of the needs and the growth of population, which is called accumulation from the viewpoint of the capitalist. It is one of the civilizing aspects of capital that it enforces this surplus-labour in a manner and under conditions which are more advantageous to the development of the productive forces, social relations, and the creation of the elements for a new and higher

form than under the preceding forms of slavery, serfdom, etc.
Thus it gives rise to a stage, on the one hand, in which coercion
and monopolization of social development (including its material
and intellectual advantages) by one portion of society at the expense
of the other are eliminated; on the other hand, it creates the
material means and embryonic conditions, making it possible in a
higher form of society to combine this surplus-labour with a greater
reduction of time devoted to material labour in general. For,
depending on the development of labour productivity, surplus-
labour may be large in a small total working-day, and relatively
small in a large total working-day. If the necessary labour-time $= 3$
and the surplus-labour $= 3$, then the total working-day $= 6$ and
the rate of surplus-labour $= 100\%$. If the necessary labour
$= 9$ and the surplus-labour $= 3$, then the total working-day
$= 12$ and the rate of surplus-labour only $= 33\frac{1}{3}\%$. In that case,
it depends upon the labour productivity how much use-value
shall be produced in a definite time, hence also in a definite surplus
labour-time. The actual wealth of society, and the possibility of
constantly expanding its reproduction process, therefore, do not
depend upon the duration of surplus-labour, but upon its productivity and the more or less copious conditions of production
under which it is performed. In fact, the realm of freedom actually
begins only where labour which is determined by necessity and
mundane considerations ceases; thus in the very nature of things
it lies beyond the sphere of actual material production. Just as the
savage must wrestle with Nature to satisfy his wants, to maintain
and reproduce life, so must civilized man, and he must do so in all
social formations and under all possible modes of production.
With his development this realm of physical necessity expands as a
result of his wants; but, at the same time, the forces of production
which satisfy these wants also increase. Freedom in this field can
only consist in socialized man, the associated producers, rationally
regulating their interchange with Nature, bringing it under their
common control, instead of being ruled by it as by the blind forces
of Nature; and achieving this with the least expenditure of energy
and under conditions most favourable to, and worthy of, their
human nature. But it nonetheless still remains a realm of
necessity. Beyond it begins that development of human energy
which is an end in itself, the true realm of freedom, which,
however, can blossom forth only with this realm of necessity

as its basis. The shortening of the working-day is its basic prerequisite.

*C* III, pp. 798–800.

# (B) *The Sociology of the Process of Production*

## (1) THE ORIGIN OF THE FETISHISM OF COMMODITIES

A commodity is . . . a mysterious thing, simply because in it the social character of men's labour appears to them as an objective character stamped upon the product of that labour; because the relation of the producers to the sum total of their own labour is presented to them as a social relation, existing not between themselves, but between the products of their labour. This is the reason why the products of labour become commodities, social things whose qualities are at the same time perceptible and imperceptible by the senses. In the same way the light from an object is perceived by us not as the subjective excitation of our optic nerve, but as the objective form of something outside the eye itself. But, in the act of seeing, there is at all events, an actual passage of light from one thing to another, from the external object to the eye. There is a physical relation between physical things. But it is different with commodities. There, the existence of the things *quâ* commodities, and the value-relation between the products of labour which stamps them as commodities, have absolutely no connexion with their physical properties and with the material relations arising therefrom. There it is a definite social relation between men, that assumes, in their eyes, the fantastic form of a relation between things. In order, therefore, to find an analogy, we must have recourse to the mist-enveloped regions of the religious world. In that world the productions of the human brain appear as independent beings endowed with life, and entering into relation both with

one another and the human race. So it is in the world of com
modies with the products of men's hands. This I call the Fetishism
which attaches itself to the products of labour, so soon as they are
produced as commodities, and which is therefore inseparable from
the production of commodities.

*C* I, p. 72.


The life-process of society, which is based on the process of
material production, does not strip off its mystical veil until it is
treated as production by freely associated men, and is consciously
regulated by them in accordance with a settled plan. This, however,
demands for society a certain material ground-work or set of
conditions of existence which in their turn are the spontaneous
product of a long and painful process of development.

Political Economy has indeed analysed, however incompletely,
value and its magnitude, and has discovered what lies beneath
these forms. But it has never once asked the question why labour is
represented by the value of its product and labour-time by the
magnitude of that value. These formulae, which bear it stamped
upon them in unmistakable letters that they belong to a state of
society in which the process of production has the mastery over
man, instead of being controlled by him, such formulae appear to
the bourgeois intellect to be as much a self-evident necessity
imposed by Nature as productive labour itself. Hence forms of
social production that preceded the bourgeois form are treated by
the bourgeoisie in much the same way as the Fathers of the Church
treated pre-Christian religions.

*C* I, pp. 80–1.


## (2) DIVISION OF LABOUR IN A SOCIETY AND IN THE WORKSHOP

If we keep labour alone in view, we may designate the separation
of social production into its main divisions or *genera*—viz., agriculture, industries, etc., as division of labour in general, and the
splitting up of these families into species and sub-species, as
division of labour in particular, and the division of labour within
the workshop as division of labour in singular or in detail.

Division of labour in a society, and the corresponding tying down of individuals to a particular calling, develops itself . . . from opposite starting-points. Within a family,[1] and after further development within a tribe, there springs up naturally a division of labour, caused by differences of sex and age, a division that is consequently based on a purely physiological foundation, which division enlarges its materials by the expansion of the community, by the increase of population, and more especially, by the conflicts between different tribes, and the subjugation of one tribe by another. On the other hand, as I have before remarked, the exchange of products springs up at the points where different families, tribes, communities, come in contact; for, in the beginning of civilization, it is not private individuals but families, tribes, etc., that meet on an independent footing. Different communities find different means of production and different means of subsistence in their natural environment. Hence, their modes of production, and of living, and their products are different. It is this spontaneously developed difference which, when different communities come in contact, calls forth the mutual exchange of products and the consequent gradual conversion of those products into commodities. Exchange does not create the differences between the spheres of production, but brings what are already different into relation, and thus converts them into more or less interdependent branches of the collective production of an enlarged society. . . .

The foundation of every division of labour that is well developed, and brought about by the exchange of commodities, is the separation between town and country. It may be said that the whole economic history of society is summed up in the movement of this antithesis. We pass it over, however, for the present.

Just as a certain number of simultaneously employed labourers are the material prerequisites for division of labour in manufacture, so are the number and density of the population, which here correspond to the agglomeration in one workshop, a necessary condition for the division of labour in society. Nevertheless, this

[1] *Note to the third edition.*—Subsequent very searching study of the primitive condition of man, led the author to the conclusion that it was not the family that originally developed into the tribe, but that, on the contrary, the tribe was the primitive and spontaneously developed form of human association, on the basis of blood relationship, and that out of the first incipient loosening of the tribal bonds, the many and various forms of the family were afterwards developed. (F. Engels)

I

density is more or less relative. A relatively thinly populated country, with well developed means of communication, has a denser population than a more numerously populated country, with badly developed means of communication; and in this sense the Northern States of the American Union, for instance, are more thickly populated than India.

Since the production and the circulation of commodities are the general prerequisites of the capitalist mode of production, division of labour in manufacture demands, that division of labour in society at large should previously have attained a certain degree of development. Inversely, the former division reacts upon and develops and multiplies the latter. Simultaneously, with the differentiation of the instruments of labour, the industries that produce these instruments become more and more differentiated. If the manufacturing system seizes upon an industry, which, previously, was carried on in connexion with others, either as a chief or as a subordinate industry, and by one producer, these industries immediately separate their connexion and become independent. If it seizes upon a particular stage in the production of a commodity, the other stages of its production become converted into so many independent industries. It has already been stated, that where the finished article consists merely of a number of parts fitted together, the detail operations may re-establish themselves as genuine and separate handicrafts. In order to carry out more perfectly the division of labour in manufacture, a single branch of production is, according to the varieties of its raw material, or the various forms that one and the same raw material may assume, split up into numerous, and to some extent, entirely new manufactures. Accordingly, in France alone, in the first half of the eighteenth century, over 100 different kinds of silk stuffs were woven, and, in Avignon, it was law that 'every apprentice should devote himself to only one sort of fabrication, and should not learn the preparation of several kinds of stuff at once'. The territorial division of labour, which confines special branches of production to special districts of a country, acquires fresh stimulus from the manufacturing system, which exploits every special advantage. The Colonial system and the opening out of the markets of the world, both of which are included in the general conditions of existence of the manufacturing period, furnish rich material for developing the division of labour in society. It is not the place, here, to go on to show how division of labour seizes upon, not only the economic, but every other sphere of society, and everywhere lays the foundation of that all engrossing system of specializing and sorting men, that development in a man of one single faculty at the expense of all other faculties, which caused A. Ferguson, the master of Adam Smith, to exclaim 'We make a nation of Helots, and have no free citizens.'[1]

But, in spite of the numerous analogies and links connecting them, division of labour in the interior of a society, and that in the interior of a workshop, differ not only in degree, but also in kind. The analogy appears most indisputable where there is an invisible bond uniting the various branches of trade. For instance the cattle-breeder produces hides, the tanner makes the hides into leather, and the shoemaker, the leather into boots. Here the thing produced by each of them is but a step towards the final form, which is the product of all their labours combined. There are, besides, all the various industries that supply the cattle-breeder, the tanner, and the shoemaker with the means of production. Now it is quite possible to imagine, with Adam Smith, that the difference between the above social division of labour, and the division in manufacture, is merely subjective, exists merely for the observer, who, in a manufacture, can see with one glance all the numerous operations being performed on one spot, while in the instance given above, the spreading out of the work over great areas, and the great number of people employed in each branch of labour, obscure the connexion.[2] But what is it that forms the bond between the independent labours of the cattle-breeder, the tanner, and the shoemaker? It is the fact that their respective products are commodities. What, on the other hand, characterises division of labour in manufactures? The fact that the detail labourer produces no commodities.[3] It is only the common product of all the detail labourers that becomes a commodity. Division of labour in society is brought about by the purchase and sale of the products of

[1] A. Ferguson, *History of Civil Society*, Edinburgh, 1767, Part IV, sect. II, p. 285.
[2] A. Smith, *The Wealth of Nations*, bk. I, ch. I.
[3] 'There is no longer anything which we can call the natural reward of individual labour. Each labourer produces only some part of a whole, and each part, having no value or utility in itself, there is nothing on which the labourer can seize, and say: It is my product, this I will keep to myself.' (*Labour Defended against the Claims of Capital*, London, 1825, p. 25.) The author of this admirable work is the Th. Hodgskin I have already cited.

different branches of industry, while the connexion between the detail operations in a workshop is due to the sale of the labour-power of several workmen to one capitalist, who applies it as combined labour-power. The division of labour in the workshop implies concentration of the means of production in the hands of one capitalist; the division of labour in society implies their dispersion among many independent producers of commodities. While within the workshop, the iron law of proportionality subjects definite numbers of workmen to definite functions, in the society outside the workshop, chance and caprice have full play in distributing the producers and their means of production among the various branches of industry. . . .

Division of labour within the workshop implies the undisputed authority of the capitalist over men, that are but parts of a mechanism that belongs to him. The division of labour within the society brings into contact independent commodity-producers, who acknowledge no other authority but that of competition, of the coercion exerted by the pressure of their mutual interests; just as in the animal kingdom, the *bellum omnium contra omnes* more or less preserves the conditions of existence of every species. The same bourgeois mind which praises division of labour in the workshop, life-long annexation of the labourer to a partial operation, and his complete subjection to capital, as being an organization of labour that increases its productiveness—that same bourgeois mind denounces with equal vigour every conscious attempt to socially control and regulate the process of production, as an inroad upon such sacred things as the rights of property, freedom and unrestricted play for the bent of the individual capitalist. It is very characteristic that the enthusiastic apologists of the factory system have nothing more damning to urge against a general organization of the labour of society than that it would turn all society into one immense factory.

*C* I, pp. 351–6.

## (3) DIVISION OF LABOUR IN MANUFACTURE

In manufacture, as well as in simple co-operation, the collective working organism is a form of existence of capital. The mechanism that is made up of numerous individual detail labourers belongs to the capitalist. Hence, the productive power resulting from a combination of labours appears to be the productive power of capital. Manufacture proper not only subjects the previously independent workman to the discipline and command of capital, but, in addition, creates a hierarchic gradation of the workmen themselves.* While simple co-operation leaves the mode of working by the individual for the most part unchanged, manufacture thoroughly revolutionizes it, and seizes labour-power by its very roots. It converts the labourer into a crippled monstrosity, by forcing his detail dexterity at the expense of a world of productive capabilities and instincts; just as in the States of La Plata they butcher a whole beast for the sake of his hide or his tallow. Not only is the detail work distributed to the different individuals, but the individual himself is made the automatic motor of a fractional operation,[1] and the absurd fable of Menenius Agrippa, which makes man a mere fragment of his own body, becomes realized. If, at first, the workman sells his labour-power to capital, because the material means of producing a commodity fail him, now his very labour-power refuses its services unless it has been sold to capital. Its functions can be exercised only in an environment that exists in the workshop of the capitalist after the sale. By nature unfitted to make anything independently, the manufacturing labourer develops productive activity as a mere appendage of the capitalist's workshop. As the chosen people bore in their features the sign manual of Jehovah, so division of labour brands the manufacturing workman as the property of capital.

The knowledge, the judgment, and the will, which, though in ever so small a degree, are practised by the independent peasant or handicraftsman, in the same way as the savage makes the whole art of war consist in the exercise of his personal cunning—these faculties are now required only for the workshop as a whole. Intelligence in production expands in one direction, because it vanishes in many others. What is lost by the detail labourers, is concentrated in the capital that employs them.[2] It is a result of the division of labour in manufactures, that the labourer is brought face to face

---

* For details see C I, pp. 349–50. (Z.A.J.)

[1] Dugald Stewart calls manufacturing labourers 'living automatons . . . employed in the details of the work' (*Lectures on Political Economy*, Collected Works, Edinburgh, 1855, vol. VIII, p. 318).

[2] A. Ferguson, *History of Civil Society*, p. 281: 'The former may have gained what the other has lost.'

with the intellectual potencies of the material process of production, as the property of another, and as a ruling power. This separation begins in simple co-operation, where the capitalist represents to the single workman the oneness and the will of the associated labour. It is developed in manufacture which cuts down the labourer into a detail labourer. It is completed in modern industry, which makes science a productive force distinct from labour and presses it into the service of capital.[1]

In manufacture, in order to make the collective labourer, and through him capital, rich in social productive power, each labourer must be made poor in individual productive powers. 'Ignorance is the mother of industry as well as of superstition. Reflection and fancy are subject to err; but a habit of moving the hand or the foot is independent of either. Manufactures, accordingly, prosper most where the mind is least consulted, and where the workshop may . . . be considered as an engine, the parts of which are men.'[2] As a matter of fact, some few manufacturers in the middle of the eighteenth century preferred, for certain operations that were trade secrets, to employ half-idiotic persons.[3] . . .

Some crippling of body and mind is inseparable even from division of labour in society as a whole. Since, however, manufacture carries this social separation of branches of labour much further and also, by its peculiar division, attacks the individual at the very roots of his life, it is the first to afford the materials for, and to give a start to, industrial pathology.[4]

---

[1] 'The man of knowledge and the productive labourer come to be widely divided from each other, and knowledge, instead of remaining the handmaid of labour in the hand of the labourer to increase his productive powers . . . has almost everywhere arrayed itself against labour . . . systematically deluding and leading them (the labourers) astray in order to render their muscular powers entirely mechanical and obedient.' (W. Thompson, *An Inquiry into the Principles of the Distribution of Wealth*, London, 1824, p. 274.)

[2] A. Ferguson, *History of Civil Society*, p. 280.

[3] J. D. Tuckett, *A History of the Past and Present State of the Labouring Population*, London, 1846.

[4] Ramazzini, professor of practical medicine at Padua, published in 1713 his work *De morbis artificum*, which was translated into French, in 1781, reprinted in 1841 in the *Encyclopédie des Sciences Médicales*, *7-me Dis. Auteurs Classiques*. The period of Modern Mechanical Industry has, of course, very much enlarged his catalogue of labour's diseases. See *Hygiène physique et morale de l'ouvrier dans les grandes villes en général et dans la ville de Lyon en particulier*. Par le Dr A. L. Fonteret, Paris, 1858, and *Die Krankheiten, welche verschiedenen Ständen, Altern und Geschlechtern eigenthümlich sind*. 6 vols, Ulm, 1860, and others. In 1854 the Society of Arts appointed a Commission of Inquiry into

'To subdivide a man is to execute him, if he deserves the sentence, to assassinate him if he does not. . . . The subdivision of labour is the assassination of a people.'[1]

Co-operation based on division of labour, in other words, manufacture, commences as a spontaneous formation. So soon as it attains some consistence and extension, it becomes the recognized methodical and systematic form of capitalist production. History shows how the division of labour peculiar to manufacture, strictly so called, acquires the best adapted form at first by experience, as it were behind the backs of the actors, and then, like the guild handicrafts, strives to hold fast that form when once found, and here and there succeeds in keeping it for centuries. Any alteration in this form, except in trivial matters, is solely owing to a revolution in the instruments of labour. Modern manufacture wherever it arises—I do not here allude to modern industry based on machinery —either finds the *disjecta membra poetae* ready to hand, and only waiting to be collected together, as is the case in the manufacture of clothes in large towns, or it can easily apply to the principle of division, simply by exclusively assigning the various operations of a handicraft (such as book-binding) to particular men. In such cases, a week's experience is enough to determine the proportion between the numbers of the hands necessary for the various functions.

By decomposition of handicrafts, by specialization of the instruments of labour, by the formation of detail labourers, and by grouping and combining the latter into a single mechanism, division of labour in manufacture creates a qualitative gradation, and a quantitative proportion in the social process of production; it consequently creates a definite organization of the labour of society, and thereby develops at the same time new productive forces in the society. In its specific capitalist form—and under the given conditions, it could take no other form than a capitalistic one—manufacture is but a particular method of begetting relative surplus-value, or of augmenting at the expense of the labourer the

industrial pathology. The list of documents collected by this commission is to be seen in the catalogue of the Twickenham Economic Museum. Very important are the official *Reports on Public Health*. See also, Eduard Reich, M.D., *Ueber die Entartung des Menschen*, Erlangen, 1868.

[1] D. Urquhart, *Familiar Words*, London, 1855, p. 119. Hegel held very heretical views on division of labour. In his *Rechtsphilosophie* (*Philosophy of Right*) he says, 'By well educated men we understand, in the first instance, those who can do everything that others do.'

self-expansion of capital—usually called social wealth, 'Wealth of Nations,' etc. It increases the social productive power of labour, not only for the benefit of the capitalist instead of for that of the labourer, but it does this by crippling the individual labourers. It creates new conditions for the lordship of capital over labour. If, therefore, on the one hand, it presents itself historically as a progress and as a necessary phase in the economic development of society, on the other hand, it is a refined and civilized method of exploitation.

*C* I, pp. 360–4.

## (4) DIVISION OF LABOUR IN THE FACTORY

So far as division of labour reappears in the factory, it is primarily a distribution of the workmen among the specialized machines; and of masses of workmen, not however organized into groups, among the various departments of the factory, in each of which they work at a number of similar machines placed together; their co-operation, therefore, is only simple. The organized group, peculiar to manufacture, is replaced by the connexion between the head workman and his few assistants. The essential division is into workmen who are actually employed on the machines (among whom are included a few who look after the engine), and into mere attendants (almost exclusively children) of these workmen. Among the attendants are reckoned more or less all 'Feeders' who supply the machines with the material to be worked. In addition to these two principal classes, there is a numerically unimportant class of persons, whose occupation it is to look after the whole of the machinery and repair it from time to time; such as engineers, mechanics, joiners, etc. This is a superior class of workmen, some of them scientifically educated, others brought up to a trade; it is distinct from the factory operative class, and merely aggregated to it. This division of labour is purely technical.

To work at a machine, the workman should be taught from childhood, in order that he may learn to adapt his own movements to the uniform and unceasing motion of an automaton. When the machinery, as a whole, forms a system of manifold machines, working simultaneously and in concert, the co-operation based upon it requires the distribution of various groups of workmen among the different kinds of machines. But the employment of machinery does away with the necessity of crystallising this distribution after the manner of Manufacture, by the constant annexation of a particular man to a particular function. Since the motion of the whole system does not proceed from the workman, but from the machinery, a change of persons can take place at any time without an interruption of the work. The most striking proof of this is afforded by the *relays system*, put into operation by the manufacturers during their revolt from 1848–1850. Lastly, the quickness with which machine work is learnt by young people does away with the necessity of bringing up for exclusive employment by machinery a special class of operatives. With regard to the work of the mere attendants, it can, to some extent, be replaced in the mill by machines, and owing to its extreme simplicity, it allows of a rapid and constant change of the individuals burdened with this drudgery.

Although then, technically speaking, the old system of division of labour is thrown overboard by machinery, it hangs on in the factory, as a traditional habit handed down from Manufacture, and is afterwards systematically remoulded and established in a more hideous form by capital, as a means of exploiting labour-power. The life-long speciality of handling one and the same tool, now becomes the life-long speciality of serving one and the same machine. Machinery is put to a wrong use, with the object of transforming the workman, from his very childhood, into a part of a detail-machine. In this way, not only are the expenses of his reproduction considerably lessened, but at the same time his helpless dependence upon the factory as a whole, and therefore upon the capitalist, is rendered complete. Here as everywhere else, we must distinguish between the increased productiveness due to the development of the social process of production, and that due to the capitalist exploitation of that process. In handicrafts and manufacture, the workman makes use of a tool, in the factory, the machine makes use of him. There the movements of the instrument of labour proceed from him, here it is the movements of the machine that he must follow. In manufacture the workmen are parts of a living mechanism. In the factory we have a lifeless mechanism independent of the workman, who becomes its mere living appendage. 'The miserable routine of endless drudgery and toil in which

I*

the same mechanical process is gone through over and over again, is like the labour of Sisyphus. The burden of labour, like the rock, keeps ever falling back on the worn-out labourer.'[1] At the same time that factory work exhausts the nervous system to the uttermost it does away with the many-sided play of the muscles, and confiscates every atom of freedom, both in bodily and intellectual activity.[2] The lightening of the labour, even, becomes a sort of torture, since the machine does not free the labourer from work, but deprives the work of all interest. Every kind of capitalist production, in so far as it is not only a labour-process, but also a process of creating surplus-value, has this in common, that it is not the workman that employs the instruments of labour, but the instruments of labour that employ the workman. But it is only in the factory system that this inversion for the first time acquires technical and palpable reality. By means of its conversion into an automaton, the instrument of labour confronts the labourer, during the labour-process, in the shape of capital, of dead labour, that dominates, and pumps dry, living labour-power. The separation of the intellectual powers of production from the manual labour, and the conversion of those powers into the might of capital over labour, is, as we have already shown, finally completed by modern industry erected on the foundation of machinery. The special skill of each individual insignificant factory operative vanishes as an infinitesimal quantity before the science, the gigantic physical forces, and the mass of labour that are embodied in the factory mechanism and, together with that mechanism, constitute the power of the 'master'. This 'master', therefore, in whose brain the machinery and his monopoly of it are inseparably united, whenever he falls out with his 'hands', contemptuously tells them: 'The factory operatives should keep in wholesome remembrance the fact that theirs is really a low species of skilled labour; and that there is none which is more easily acquired, or of its quality more amply remunerated, or which by a short training of the least expert can be more quickly, as well as abundantly, acquired. . . . The master's machinery really plays a far more important part in the business of production than the labour and the skill of the operative, which six months' education can teach,

[1] F. Engels, *Die Lage der arbeitenden Klasse in England*, Leipzig, 1845, p. 217.
[2] F. Engels, l. c., p. 216.

and a common labourer can learn.'[1] The technical subordination of
the workman to the uniform motion of the instrument of labour,
and the peculiar composition of the body of workpeople, consisting
as it does of individuals of both sexes and of all ages, give
rise to a barrack discipline, which is elaborated into a complete
system in the factory, and which fully develops the before mentioned labour of overlooking, thereby dividing the workpeople into
operatives and overlookers, into private soldiers and sergeants of an
industrial army. 'The main difficulty (in the automatic factory) . . .
lay . . . above all in training human beings to renounce their
desultory habits of work, and to identify themselves with the
unvarying regularity of the complex automaton. To devise and
administer a successful code of factory discipline, suited to the
necessities of factory diligence, was the Herculean enterprise, the
noble achievement of Arkwright! Even at the present day, when
the system is perfectly organized and its labour lightened to the
utmost, it is found nearly impossible to convert persons past the
age of puberty, into useful factory hands.[2] The factory code in
which capital formulates, like a private legislator, and at his own
good will, his autocracy over his workpeople, unaccompanied by
that division of responsibility, in other matters so much approved
of by the bourgeoisie, and unaccompanied by the still more
approved representative system, this code is but the capitalistic
caricature of that social regulation of the labour process which
becomes requisite in co-operation on a great scale, and in the
employment in common, of instruments of labour and especially
of machinery. The place of the slave-driver's lash is taken by the
overlooker's book of penalties. All punishments naturally resolve
themselves into fines and deductions from wages, and the law-
giving talent of the factory Lycurgus so arranges matters, that a
violation of his laws is, if possible, more profitable to him than the
keeping of them.

We shall here merely allude to the material conditions under
which factory labour is carried on. Every organ of sense is injured
in an equal degree by artificial elevation of the temperature, by the
dust-laden atmosphere, by the deafening noise, not to mention

[1] *The Master Spinners' and Manufacturers' Defence Fund. Report of the Committee*, Manchester, 1854, p. 17.
[2] A. Ure, *The Philosophy of Manufactures: Or an Exposition of the Scientific,
Moral and Commercial Economy of the Factory System of Great Britain*, 2nd
edition, London, 1835, p. 15.

danger to life and limb among the thickly crowded machinery, which, with the regularity of the seasons, issues its list of the killed and wounded in the industrial battle.[1] Economy of the social means of production, matured and forced as in a hothouse by the factory system, is turned, in the hands of capital, into systematic robbery of what is necessary for the life of the workman while he is at work, robbery of space, light, air, and of protection to his person against the dangerous and unwholesome accompaniments of the productive process, not to mention the robbery of appliances for the comfort of the workman.[2] Is Fourier wrong when he calls factories 'tempered bagnos'?[3]

*C* I, pp. 420-7.

Modern Industry, as we have seen, sweeps away by technical means the manufacturing division of labour, under which each man is bound hand and foot for life to a single detail-operation. At the same time, the capitalist form of that industry reproduces this same division of labour in a still more monstrous shape; in the factory proper, by converting the workman into a living appendage of the machine; and everywhere outside the factory, partly by the sporadic use of machinery and machine workers, partly by re-establishing the division of labour on a fresh basis by the general introduction of the labour of women and children, and of cheap unskilled labour.

The antagonism between the manufacturing division of labour and the methods of Modern Industry makes itself forcibly felt. It manifests itself, amongst other ways, in the frightful fact that a great part of the children employed in modern factories and manufactures, are from their earliest years riveted to the most simple manipulations, and exploited for years, without being taught a single sort of work that would afterwards make

---

[1] The protection afforded by the Factory Acts against dangerous machinery has had a beneficial effect.

[2] In Part I of Book III I shall give an account of a recent campaign by the English manufacturers against the Clauses in the Factory Acts that protect the 'hands' against dangerous machinery.

[3] In those factories that have been longest subject to the Factory Acts, with their compulsory limitation of the hours of labour, and other regulations, many of the older abuses have vanished. The very improvement of the machinery demands to a certain extent 'improved construction of the buildings', and this is an advantage to the workpeople.

them of use, even in the same manufactory or factory. In the English letter-press printing trade for example, there existed formerly a system, corresponding to that in the old manufactures and handicrafts, of advancing the apprentices from easy to more and more difficult work. They went through a course of teaching till they were finished printers. To be able to read and write was for every one of them a requirement of their trade. All this was changed by the printing machine. It employs two sorts of labourers, one grown up, tenters, the other, boys mostly from 11 to 17 years of age whose sole business is either to spread the sheets of paper under the machine, or to take from it the printed sheets. They perform this weary task, in London especially, for 14, 15, and 16 hours at a stretch, during several days in the week, and frequently for 36 hours, with only 2 hours' rest for meals and sleep.[1] A great part of them cannot read, and they are, as a rule, utter savages and very extraordinary creatures . . . As soon as they get too old for such child's work, that is about 17 at the latest, they are discharged from the printing establishments. They become recruits of crime. Several attempts to procure them employment elsewhere were rendered of no avail by their ignorance and brutality, and by their mental and bodily degradation.

As with the division of labour in the interior of the manufacturing workshops, so it is with the division of labour in the interior of society. . . . The principle which it (sc. Modern Industry) pursued, of resolving each process into its constituent movements, without any regard to their possible execution by the hand of man, created the new modern science of technology. The varied, apparently unconnected, and petrified forms of the industrial processes now resolved themselves into so many conscious and systematic applications of natural science to the attainment of given useful effects. Technology also discovered the few main fundamental forms of motion, which, despite the diversity of the instruments used, are necessarily taken by every productive action of the human body; just as the science of mechanics sees in the most complicated machinery nothing but the continual repetition of the simple mechanical powers.

Modern Industry never looks upon and treats the existing form of a process as final. The technical basis of that industry is therefore revolutionary, while all earlier modes of produc-

[1] *Children's Employment Commission*, 5th Report, London, 1866, p. 3, n. 24.

tion were essentially conservative. By means of machinery, chemical processes and other methods, it is continually causing changes not only in the technical basis of production, but also in the functions of the labourer, and in the social combinations of the labour-process. At the same time, it thereby also revolutionizes the division of labour within the society, and incessantly launches masses of capital and of workpeople from one branch of production to another. . . . But if, on the one hand, variation of work at present imposes itself after the manner of an overpowering natural law, and with the blindly destructive action of a natural law that meets with resistance at all points, Modern Industry, on the other hand, through its catastrophes imposes the necessity of recognizing, as a fundamental law of production, variation of work, consequently fitness of the labourer for varied work, consequently the greatest possible development of his varied aptitudes. It becomes a question of life and death for society to adapt the mode of production to the normal functioning of this law. Modern Industry, indeed, compels society, under penalty of death, to replace the detail-worker of to-day, crippled by life-long repetition of one and the same trivial operation, and thus reduced to the mere fragment of a man, by the fully developed individual, fit for a variety of labours, ready to face any change of production, and to whom the different social functions he performs are but so many modes of giving free scope to his own natural and acquired powers.

*CI*, pp. 484–8.

## (5) RELATIVE SURPLUS POPULATION OR INDUSTRIAL RESERVE ARMY

The specifically capitalist mode of production, the development of the productive power of labour corresponding to it, and the change thence resulting in the organic composition of capital, do not merely keep pace with the advance of accumulation, or with the growth of social wealth. They develop at a much quicker rate, because mere accumulation, the absolute increase of the total social capital, is accompanied by the centralization of the individual capitals of which that total is made up; and because the change in the technological composition of the additional capital goes hand in hand with a similar change in the technological composition of the original capital. With the advance of accumulation, therefore, the proportion of constant to variable capital changes. If it was originally say 1:1, it now becomes successively 2:1, 3:1, 4:1, 5:1, 7:1, etc., so that as the capital increases, instead of $\frac{1}{2}$ of its total value, only $\frac{1}{3}$, $\frac{1}{4}$, $\frac{1}{5}$, $\frac{1}{6}$, $\frac{1}{8}$, etc., is transformed into labour power, and, on the other hand, $\frac{2}{3}$, $\frac{3}{4}$, $\frac{4}{5}$, $\frac{5}{6}$, $\frac{7}{8}$, into means of production. Since the demand for labour is determined not by the amount of capital as a whole, but by its variable constituent alone, that demand falls progressively with the increase of the total capital, instead of, as previously assumed, rising in proportion to it. It falls relatively to the magnitude of the total capital, and at an accelerated rate, as this magnitude increases. With the growth of the total capital, its variable constituent or the labour incorporated in it, also does increase, but in a constantly diminishing proportion. The intermediate pauses are shortened, in which accumulation works as simple extension of production, on a given technical basis. It is not merely that an accelerated accumulation of total capital, accelerated in a constantly growing progression, is needed to absorb an additional number of labourers, or even, on account of the constant metamorphosis of old capital, to keep employed those already functioning. In its turn, this increasing accumulation and centralization becomes a source of new changes in the composition of capital, of a more accelerated diminution of its variable, as compared with its constant constituent. This accelerated relative diminution of the variable constituent, that goes along with the accelerated increase of the total capital, and moves more rapidly than this increase, takes the inverse form, at the other pole, of an apparently absolute increase of the labouring population, an increase always moving more rapidly than that of the variable capital or the means of employment. But in fact, it is capitalistic accumulation itself that constantly produces, and produces in the direct ratio of its own energy and extent, a relatively redundant population of labourers, i.e., a population of greater extent than suffices for the average needs of the self-expansion of capital, and therefore a surplus-population. . . .

But if a surplus labouring population is a necessary product of accumulation or of the development of wealth on a capitalist basis, this surplus-population becomes, conversely, the lever of capitalistic accumulation, nay, a condition of existence of the capitalist mode of production. It forms a disposable industrial reserve army, that belongs to capital quite as absolutely as if the latter had bred it at its own cost. Independently of the limits of the actual increase of population, it creates, for the changing needs of the self-expansion of capital, a mass of human material always ready for exploitation. With accumulation, and the development of the productiveness of labour that accompanies it, the power of sudden expansion of capital grows also. . . . The mass of social wealth, overflowing with the advance of accumulation, and transformable into additional capital, thrusts itself frantically into old branches of production, whose market suddenly expands, or into newly formed branches, such as railways, etc., the need for which grows out of the development of the old ones. In all such cases, there must be the possibility of throwing great masses of men suddenly on the decisive points without injury to the scale of production in other spheres. Overpopulation supplies these masses.

*C* I, pp. 629–32.

## (6) CAPITALISM IN THE SPHERE OF IMMATERIAL PRODUCTION*

A writer is a productive labourer not in so far as he produces ideas, but in so far as he enriches the publisher who publishes his works, or if he is a wage-labourer for a capitalist.

*TM*, T.1, p. 121; *TSV* I, pp. 153–4.

It follows from what has been said that the designation of labour as *productive labour* has absolutely nothing to do with the *determinate content* of the labour, its special utility, or the particular use-value in which it manifests itself.

* In *Theories of Surplus-Value* Marx discussed in detail the distinction between productive and unproductive labour which he found in the works of classical economists. In the capitalist sense, productive labour is that which reproduces the value of its own labour power and in addition produces surplus value for the capitalist. In his criticism Marx pointed out that this concept of productive labour disregards the usefulness of labour other than that involved in the production of capital; that it cannot be consistently applied; and that it debases the worth of labour, in particular, in the artistic and scientific field. (Z.A.J.)

*The same* kind of labour may be *productive* or *unproductive*. For example, Milton who wrote *Paradise Lost* for five pounds was an *unproductive labourer*. On the other hand, the writer who turns out stuff for his publisher in factory style, is a *productive labourer*. Milton produced *Paradise Lost* for the same reason that a silk worm produces silk. It was an activity of *his* nature. Later, he sold the product for five pounds. But the literary proletarian of Leipzig, who fabricates books (for example, Compedia of Economics) under the direction of his publisher, is a *productive labourer*; for his product is from the outset subsumed under capital, and comes into being only for the purpose of increasing that capital. A singer who sings her song for her own account is an *unproductive labourer*. But the same singer commissioned by an entrepreneur to sing in order to make money for him is a *productive labourer*; for she produces capital.

*TM*, T.1, pp. 364–5; *TSV* I, p. 389.

In a social order dominated by capitalist production even the non-capitalist producer is gripped by capitalist conceptions. Balzac, who is generally remarkable for his profound grasp of reality, aptly describes in his last novel, *Les Paysans*, how a petty peasant performs many small tasks gratuitously for his usurer, whose goodwill he is eager to retain, and how he fancies that he does not give the latter something for nothing because his own labour does not cost him any cash outlay. As for the usurer, he thus fells two dogs with one stone. He saves the cash outlay for wages and enmeshes the peasant, who is gradually ruined by depriving his own field of labour, deeper and deeper in the spider-web of usury.

*C* III, p. 39.

Only bourgeois narrow-mindedness, which regards the capitalist forms of production as absolute forms—hence the eternal, natural forms of production—can confuse the question of what is *productive labour* from the standpoint of capital with the question of what labour is productive in general, or what is productive labour in general; and consequently fancy itself very wise in giving the answer that all labour which produces anything at all, which has any kind of result, is by that very fact productive labour.

TM, T.1, p. 356; TSV I, pp. 380–1.

## (7) THE SOCIAL FUNCTION OF PRODUCTION

Among the ancients we discover no single enquiry as to which form of landed property, etc., is the most productive, which create maximum wealth. Wealth does not appear as the aim of production although Cato may well investigate the most profitable cultivation of fields, or Brutus may even lend money at the most favourabl rate of interest. The enquiry is always about what kind of propert creates the best citizens. Wealth as an end in itself appears onl among a few trading peoples—monopolists of the carrying trade— who live in the pores of the ancient world like the Jews in medieva society. Wealth is on the one hand a thing, realized in things, i material products as against man as a subject. On the other hand in its capacity as value, it is the mere right to command othe people's labour, not for the purpose of dominion, but of privat enjoyment, etc. In all its forms it appears in the form of object whether of things or of relationships by means of things, which li outside of, and as it were accidentally beside, the individual.

Thus the ancient conception, in which man always appears (i however narrowly national, religious or political a definition as the aim of production, seems very much more exalted than th modern world, in which production is the aim of man and wealt the aim of production. In fact, however, when the narrow bour geois form has been peeled away, what is wealth, if not th universality of needs, capacities, enjoyments, productive power etc., of individuals, produced in universal exchange? What, if nc the full development of human control over the forces of nature— those of his own nature as well as those of so-called 'nature' What, if not the absolute elaboration of his creative disposition without any preconditions other than antecedent historical evolv tion which makes the totality of this evolution—i.e., the evolutio of all human powers as such, unmeasured by any *previously establ lished* yardstick—an end in itself? What is this, if not a situatio where man does not reproduce himself in any determined forn but produces his totality? Where he does not seek to remai something formed by the past, but is in the absolute movement of becoming? In bourgeois political economy—and in the epoch of production to which it corresponds—this complete elaboration of what lies within man appears as the total alienation, and the destruction of all fixed, one-sided purposes as the sacrifice of the end in itself to a wholly external compulsion. Hence in one way the childlike world of the ancients appears to be superior; and this is so, in so far as we seek for closed shape, form and established limitation. The ancients provide a narrow satisfaction, whereas the modern world leaves us unsatisfied, or, where it appears to be satisfied with itself, is *vulgar* and *mean*.

*GKPÖ*, pp. 387–8; *PEF*, pp. 84–5.

## (8) THE SOCIAL COST OF ECONOMIC PROGRESS*

I cannot part with the subject of India without some concluding remarks.

The profound hypocrisy and inherent barbarism of bourgeois civilization lies unveiled before our eyes, turning from its home, where it assumes respectable forms, to the colonies, where it goes naked. They are the defenders of property, but did any revolutionary party ever originate agrarian revolutions like those in Bengal, in Madras, and in Bombay? Did they not, in India, to borrow an expression of that great robber, Lord Clive himself, resort to atrocious extortion, when simple corruption could not keep pace with their rapacity? While they prated in Europe about the inviolable sanctity of the national debt, did they not confiscate in India the dividends of the *rayahs*, who had invested their private savings in the Company's own funds? While they combated the French Revolution under the pretext of defending 'our holy religion,' did they not forbid, at the same time, Christianity to be propagated in India, and did they not, in order to make money out of the pilgrims streaming to the temples of Orissa and Bengal, take up the trade in the murder and prostitution perpetrated in the temple of Juggernaut? These are the men of 'Property, Order, Family, and Religion'.

The devastating effects of English industry, when contemplated

* Cf. 'Forced Emigration', *The People's Paper*, 16 April, 1853. (Z.A.J.)

with regard to India, a country as vast as Europe, and containing 150 millions of acres, are palpable and confounding. But we must not forget that they are only the organic results of the whole system of production as it is now constituted. That production rests on the supreme rule of capital. The centralization of capital is essential to the existence of capital as an independent power. The destructive influence of that centralization upon the markets of the world does but reveal, in the most gigantic dimensions, the inherent organic laws of political economy now at work in every civilized town. The bourgeois period of history has to create the material basis of the new world—on the one hand the universal intercourse founded upon the mutual dependency of mankind, and the means of that intercourse; on the other hand the development of the productive powers of man and the transformation of material production into a scientific domination of natural agencies. Bourgeois industry and commerce create these material conditions of a new world in the same way as geological revolutions have created the surface of the earth. When a great social revolution shall have mastered the results of the bourgeois epoch, the market of the world and the modern powers of production, and subjected them to the common control of the most advanced peoples, then only will human progress cease to resemble that hideous pagan idol, who would not drink the nectar but from the skulls of the slain.

*FRBRI*, pp. 323–4

# Part Six
# The Sociology of Politics

# *A)* *The State*

## 1) THE CONCEPT OF CIVIL SOCIETY

Civil society embraces the whole material intercourse of individuals within a definite stage of the development of productive forces. It embraces the whole commercial and industrial life of a given stage and, in so far, transcends the State and the nation, though, on the other hand again, it must assert itself in its foreign relations as nationality, and inwardly must organise itself as State. The word 'civil society' (*bürgerliche Gesellschaft*)[1] emerged in the eighteenth century, when property relationships had already extricated themselves from the ancient and medieval communal society. Civil society as such only develops with the bourgeoisie; the social organization evolving directly out of production and commerce, which in all ages forms the basis of the State and of the rest of the idealistic superstructure, has, however, always been designated by the same name.

*GI*, p. 48.

Society, as it appears to the economist, is *civil* society, in which each individual is a totality of needs and only exists for another person, as the other exists for him, in so far as each becomes a means for the other. The economist (like politics in its *rights of man*) reduces everything to man, i.e., to the individual, whom he deprives of all characteristics in order to classify him as a capitalist or a worker.

*EPM*, p. 181.

'*Bürgerliche Gesellschaft*' can mean either 'bourgeois society' or 'civil society'.

## (2) CIVIL SOCIETY AND THE STATE

The *State* will *never* look for the cause of *social defects* in 'the
State and *social order* (*die Einrichtung der Gesellschaft*)'. . . .
Where there are political parties, the members of each one
discover the source of *every* evil in the fact that not they but their
opponents are at *the helm* of the State. Even radical and revolutionary politicians do not search for the source of evil in *the very*
*nature* of the State but in a particular *form of the State* which they
wish to replace by *another* form.

From a *political* point of view, the *State* and the *social order* are
not two different things. The State is the order of society. In so
far as the State concedes the existence of *social* abuses, it derives
them either from *natural laws* which no human power can control,
or from *private life* which is independent of the State, or from the
*shortcomings of the administration* which is dependent on it. Thus,
in England poverty is said to result from the *natural law* which
states that the population always exceeds the means of subsistence. From another point of view, England explains *pauperism*
by the *moral corruption of the poor*, just as the King of Prussia
explains it by the *unchristian dispositions of the rich* and the Convention by the *suspect counter-revolutionary views* of the *property*
*owners*. Consequently, England punishes the poor, the King of
Prussia reproves the rich, and the Convention beheads property
owners.

Finally, *all* States look for the cause of social evil in the *unin-*
*tentional* or *wilful failings* of the *administration*. Therefore, they
see *disciplinary punishment* of the administration as the remedy for
their own defects. Why? Precisely because the *administration* is the
*organizing* activity of the State.

*CMN*, pp. 400–1.


The more powerful the State and the more *political* the country,
the less it is inclined to look for the cause of social defects and to
grasp their *general* source in the *principle of the State*, that is, in
the *existing structure of society*, of which the State is the active,
conscious and official expression. *Political* mind (*der politische*

*Verstand*) is precisely *political* mind because it thinks *within* the confines of politics. The more incisive and vigorous political mind is, the less it is able to comprehend social defects. The *classical* period of political mind is the *French Revolution*. Far from discovering the source of social defects in the principle of the State, the heroes of the French Revolution discover more readily the source of all political abuses in social shortcomings. For instance, *Robespierre* sees in great poverty and great riches only an obstacle to *pure democracy*. Consequently, he wishes to establish a general *Spartan* frugality of life. The will is the principle of politics. The more one-sided that is really, the more perfect is political mind, the more it believes in the *omnipotence* of the will, the blinder it is to natural and mental limitations of the will, and thus the more incapable it is of discovering the source of social defects.

*CMN*, p. 402.

It is so wrong to think that social misery produces *political* mind (*der politische Verstand*) that it is right to think conversely that social prosperity produces *political* mind. . . . The more developed and universal the *political mind* of a nation is, the more the *proletariat*—at least in the beginnings of the movement—wastes its strength on foolish and useless rebellions which are drowned in blood. Since the proletariat thinks in political categories, it sees the cause of all abuses in the *will* and all the means of remedy in *force* and *overthrow* of a *particular* form of the State. The proof lies in the first insurrections of the *French* proletariat.* The workers of Lyon believed that they had pursued only political ends and that they had been only soldiers of the Republic, while in fact they were soldiers of socialism. Thus their political thinking concealed from them the sources of social misery, thus distorted their understanding of their true ends, and for the same reason their *political mind* deceived their *social instinct*.

*CMN*, pp. 406-7.

Marx refers to the insurrections of the workers of Lyon in 1831 and 1834. Z.A.J.)

The members of the civil society are not *atoms*. The *specific property* of the atom is that it has *no* properties and is therefore not connected with beings outside it by any relations determined by its own *natural necessity*. The atom *has no needs*, it is *self-sufficient*; the world outside it is absolute *vacuum*, i.e., it is contentless, senseless, meaningless, just because the atom has *all its fullness* in itself. The egotistic individual in civil society may in his non-sensuous imagination and lifeless abstraction inflate himself to the size of an *atom*, i.e., to an unrelated, self-sufficient, wantless, *absolutely full*, blessed being. Unblessed *sensuous reality* does not bother about his imagination; each of his senses compels him to believe in the existence of the world and the individuals outside him and even his *profane* stomach reminds him every day that the world *outside* him is *not empty*, but is what really fills. Every activity and property of his being, every one of his vital urges becomes a *need, a necessity*, which his *self-seeking* transforms into seeking for other things and human beings outside him. But as the need of one individual has no self-understood sense for the other egotistic individual capable of satisfying that need and therefore no direct connection with its satisfaction, each individual has to create that connection; it thus becomes the intermediary between the need of another and the object of that need. Therefore, it is natural necessity, *essential human properties*, however alienated they may seem to be, and *interest* that hold the members of civil society together: *civil*, not *political* life is their *real* tie. It is therefore not the *State* that holds the *atoms* of civil society together, but the fact that they are atoms only in *imagination*, in the *heaven* of their fancy, but in *reality* beings tremendously different from atoms, in other words, not *divine egoists*, but *egotistic human beings*. Only *political superstition* today imagines that social life must be held together by the State whereas in reality the State is held together by civil life.

*HF*, pp. 162–3.

In actual history, those theoreticians who regarded *power* as the basis of right were in direct contradiction to those who looked on *will* as the basis of right. . . . If power is taken as the basis of right, as Hobbes, etc. do, then right, law, etc. are merely

he symptom, the expression of *other* relations upon which State
ower rests. The material life of individuals, which by no means
epends merely on their 'will', their mode of production and form
f intercourse, which mutually determine each other—this is the
eal basis of the State and remains so at all the stages at which
ivision of labour and private property are still necessary, quite
ndependently of the *will* of individuals. These actual relations are
n no way created by the State power; on the contrary they are the
ower creating it. The individuals who rule in these conditions,
esides having to constitute their power in the form of the *State*,
ave to give their will, which is determined by these definite
onditions, a universal expression as the will of the State, as
aw—an expression whose content is always determined by the
elations of this class, as the civil and criminal law demonstrates
n the clearest possible way. Just as the weight of their bodies does
ot depend on their idealistic will or on their arbitrary decision, so
lso the fact that they enforce their own will in the form of law,
nd at the same time make it independent of the personal arbi-
rariness of each individual among them, does not depend on
heir idealistic will. Their personal rule must at the same time
e constituted as average rule. Their personal power is based
n conditions of life which as they develop are common to many
ndividuals, and the continuance of which they, as ruling in-
lividuals, have to maintain against others and, at the same time,
naintain that they hold good for all. The expression of this will,
vhich is determined by their common interests, is law. . . . The
ame applies to the classes which are ruled, whose will plays just as
mall a part in determining the existence of law and the State.
'or example, so long as the productive forces are still insufficiently
leveloped to make competition superfluous, and therefore would
;ive rise to competition over and over again, for so long the classes
vhich are ruled would be wanting the impossible if they had the
will' to abolish competition and with it the State and the law.
ncidentally, too, it is only in the imagination of the ideologist
hat this 'will' arises before conditions have developed far enough
o make its production possible. After conditions have developed
ufficiently to produce it, the ideologist is able to imagine this will
s being purely arbitrary and therefore as conceivable at all times
nd under all circumstances.

*GI*, pp. 357–8.

The specific economic form, in which unpaid surplus-labour is pumped out of direct producers, determines the relationship of rulers and ruled, as it grows directly out of production itself and, in turn, reacts upon it as a determining element. Upon this, however, is founded the entire formation of the economic community which grows up out of the production relations themselves, thereby simultaneously its specific political form. It is always the direct relationship of the owners of the conditions of production to the direct producers—a relation always naturally corresponding to a definite stage in the development of the methods of labour and thereby, its social productivity—which reveals the innermost secret, the hidden basis of the entire social structure, and with it the political form of the relation of sovereignty and dependence, in short, the corresponding specific form of the State. This does not prevent the same economic basis—the same from the standpoint of its main conditions—due to innumerable different empirical circumstances, natural environment, racial relations, external historical influences, etc., from showing infinite variations and gradations in appearance, which can be ascertained only by analysis of the empirically given circumstances.

*C* III, p. 772.

## (3) THE BOURGEOISIE AND THE STATE

'Power rules also property'.

In any case, property is a kind of power. For instance, capital is called by the economists 'the power over the labour of others'.

We are faced, therefore, with two kinds of power, the power of property, that is, of property owners on the one hand, and political power, the might of the State, on the other. 'Power rules also property' means that property does not control political power; rather it is property that is harassed by political power, e.g., by means of arbitrary taxation, confiscations, privileges, disturbing interference of the bureaucracy in industry, commerce, and so forth.

In other words, the bourgeoisie is not as yet politically constituted as a class, and the might of the State is not as yet its wn might. Herr Heinzen's* assertion becomes meaningless, however, with respect to those countries where the bourgeoisie has already conquered political power and where political authority is but the domination of the bourgeois class over the whole society, and not of a particular bourgeois over his workers. Of course, the propertyless are not affected by political authority as far as it is concerned directly with property.

*MCCM*, pp. 337–8.

By the mere fact that it is a *class* and no longer an *estate*, the bourgeoisie is forced to organize itself no longer locally, but nationally, and to give a general form to its mean average interest. Through the emancipation of private property from the community, the State has become a separate entity, beside and outside civil society; but it is nothing more than the form of organization which the bourgeois necessarily adopt both for internal and external purposes, for the mutual guarantee of their property and interests. The independence of the State is only found nowadays in those countries where the estates have not yet completely developed into classes, where the estates, done away with in more advanced countries, still have a part to play, and where there exists a mixture; countries, that is to say, in which no one section of the population can achieve dominance over the others. This is the case particularly in Germany. The most perfect example of the modern State is North America. The modern French, English and American writers all express the opinion that the State exists only for the sake of private property, so that this fact has penetrated into the consciousness of the normal man.

Since the State is the form in which the individuals of a ruling class assert their common interests, and in which the whole civil society of an epoch is epitomized, it follows that the State mediates in the formation of all common institutions and that the institutions receive a political form. Hence the illusion that law is based on the will, and indeed on the will divorced from its real basis—on *free* will. Similarly, justice is in its turn reduced to the actual laws.

*GI*, p. 78.

* See p. 145 n.

Each step in the development of the bourgeoisie was accom
panied by a corresponding political advance of that class. A
oppressed class under the sway of the feudal nobility, an armed an
self-governing association in the mediaeval commune; her
independent urban republic (as in Italy and Germany), ther
taxable 'third estate' of the monarchy (as in France), afterwards, i
the period of manufacture proper, serving either the semi-feuda
or the absolute monarchy as a counterpoise against the nobilit
and, in fact, corner stone of the great monarchies in general, th
bourgeoisie has at last, since the establishment of Modern Industr
and of the world market, conquered for itself, in the moder
representative State, exclusive political sway. The executive of th
modern State is but a committee for managing the commo
affairs of the whole bourgeoisie.

*MCP*, pp. 34–5.

The centralized State power, with its ubiquitous organs o
standing army, police, bureaucracy, clergy, and judicature—
organs wrought after the plan of a systematic and hierarchi
division of labour—originates from the days of absolute monarchy
serving nascent middle-class society as a mighty weapon in it
struggles against feudalism. Still, its development remaine
clogged by all manner of mediaeval rubbish, seignorial rights, loca
privileges, municipal and guild monopolies and provincial con
stitutions. The gigantic broom of the French Revolution of th
eighteenth century swept away all these relics of bygone times
thus clearing simultaneously the social soil of its last hindrances t
the superstructure of the modern State edifice raised under th
First Empire, itself the offspring of the coalition wars of old semi
feudal Europe against modern France. During the subsequen
*régimes* the Government, placed under parliamentary control—
that is, under the direct control of the propertied classes—becam
not only a hotbed of huge national debts and crushing taxes; wit
its irresistible allurements of place, pelf, and patronage, it becam
not only the bone of contention between the rival factions an
adventurers of the ruling classes; but its political character change
simultaneously with the economic changes of society. At the sam
pace at which the progress of modern industry developed

widened, intensified, the class antagonism between capital and labour, the State power assumed more and more the character of the national power of capital over labour, of public force organized for social enslavement, of an engine of class despotism. After every revolution marking a progressive phase in the class struggle, the purely repressive character of the State power stands out in bolder and bolder relief. . . .*

The restraints by which their own divisions** had under former *régimes* still checked the State power, were removed by their union; and in view of the threatening upheaval of the proletariat, they now used that State power mercilessly and ostentatiously as the national war-engine of capital against labour. In their uninterrupted crusade against the producing masses they were, however, bound not only to invest the executive with continually increased powers of repression, but at the same time to divest their own parliamentary stronghold—the National Assembly—one by one, of all its own means of defence against the Executive. The Executive, in the person of Louis Bonaparte, turned them out. The natural offspring of the 'Party-of-Order' Republic was the Second Empire.

*CWF*, pp. 468–9.


## 4) THE WORKING CLASS AND THE STATE

We have seen above that the first step in the revolution by the working class is to raise the proletariat to the position of ruling class, to win the battle of democracy.

The proletariat will use its political supremacy to wrest, by degrees, all capital from the bourgeoisie, to centralize all instruments of production in the hands of the State, i.e., of the proletariat organized as the ruling class; and to increase the total of productive forces as rapidly as possible.

Of course, in the beginning, this cannot be effected except by means of despotic inroads on the rights of property, and on the conditions of bourgeois production; by means of measures, therefore, which appear economically insufficient and untenable, but

---

* Cf. *EBLB*, p. 301. (Z.A.J.)
** Marx refers to the divisions of the ruling bourgeoisie into different factions and groups of interests. (Z.A.J.)

which, in the course of the movement, outstrip themselve
necessitate further inroads upon the old social order, and a
unavoidable as a means of entirely revolutionizing the mode
production.

*MCP*, p. 50.

We now come to the *Chartists*, the politically active portion
the British *working class*. The six points of the Charter which the
contend for contain nothing but the demand of *Universal Suffrag*
and of the conditions without which Universal Suffrage would b
illusory for the working class; such as the ballot, payment
members, annual general elections. But Universal Suffrage is th
equivalent of political power for the working class of Englan
where the proletariat forms the large majority of the population
where, in a long, though underground civil war, it has gained
clear consciousness of its position as a class, and where even th
rural districts know no longer any peasants, but only landlord
industrial capitalists (farmers) and hired labourers. The carryin
of Universal Suffrage in England would, therefore, be a far mo
socialistic measure than anything which has been honoured wit
that name on the Continent.

Its inevitable result, here, is *the political supremacy of the workin
class*.

*CH, NYDT*, 25 August 1852.

If you look at the last chapter of my *Eighteenth Brumaire*,* yo
will find that I declare that the next attempt of the French Revolu
tion will be no longer, as before, to transfer the bureaucratic
military machine from one hand to another, but *to smash* i
and this is the preliminary condition for every real people'
revolution on the Continent.

Marx's letter to L. Kugelmann of 12 April 1871.
*SC*, p. 318.

The Paris Commune was, of course, to serve as a model to all th
great industrial centres of France. The communal *régime* onc
* See *EBLB*, p. 301 and *CWF*, p. 468 (Z.A.J.)

established in Paris and the secondary centres, the old centralized Government would in the provinces, too, have to give way to the self-government of the producers. . . . The few but important functions which still would remain for a central government were not to be suppressed, as has been intentionally mis-stated, but were to be discharged by Communal, and therefore strictly responsible agents. The unity of the nation was not to be broken, but, on the contrary, to be organized by the Communal Constitution, and to become a reality by the destruction of the State power which claimed to be the embodiment of that unity independent of, and superior to, the nation itself, from which it was but a parasitic excrescence. While the merely repressive organs of the old governmental power were to be amputated, its legitimate functions were to be wrested from an authority usurping pre-eminence over society itself, and restored to the responsible agents of society. Instead of deciding once in three or six years which member of the ruling class was to misrepresent the people in Parliament, Universal Suffrage was to serve the people, constituted in Communes. . . . Nothing could be more foreign to the spirit of the Commune than to supersede Universal Suffrage by hierarchic investiture.

*CWF*, 471–2.

However much the state of things may have altered during the last twenty-five years, the general principles laid down in this *Manifesto* are, on the whole, as correct today as ever. Here and there some detail might be improved. The practical application of the principles will depend, as the *Manifesto* itself states, everywhere and at all times, on the historical conditions for the time being existing, and, for that reason, no special stress is laid on the revolutionary measures proposed at the end of Section II. That passage would, in many respects, be very differently worded today. In view of the gigantic strides of Modern Industry in the last twenty-five years, and of the accompanying improved and extended party organization of the working class, in view of the practical experience gained, first in the February Revolution, and then, still more, in the Paris Commune, where the proletariat for the first time held political power for two whole months, this programme has in some detail become antiquated. One thing espec-

K

ially was proved by the Commune, viz., that 'the working class
cannot simply lay hold of the ready-made state machinery, and
wield it for its own purposes'.*

*MCP–P*, pp. 21–2.

## (5) THE STATE IN COMMUNIST SOCIETY

The different states of the different civilized countries, in spite
of their manifold diversity of form, all have this in common, that
they are based on modern bourgeois society, only one more or less
capitalistically developed. They have, therefore, also certain
essential features in common. In this sense it is possible to
speak of the 'present-day State,' in contrast with the future, in
which its present root, bourgeois society, will have died off.

The question then arises: what transformation will the State
undergo in communist society? In other words, what social
functions will remain in existence there that are analogous to
present functions of the State? This question can only be answered
scientifically, and one does not get a flea-hop nearer to the problem
by a thousandfold combination of the word people with the word
State.

Between capitalist and communist society lies the period of
the revolutionary transformation of the one into the other. There
corresponds to this also a political transition period in which the
state can be nothing but *the revolutionary dictatorship of the proletariat.*

*CGP*, p. 30.

# (B)  The Nature of Revolution

## (1) PHILOSOPHICAL AND REAL LIBERATION

We shall, of course, not take the trouble to enlighten our wise
philosophers** by explaining to them that the 'liberation' of

* *CWF*, p. 468.
** That is, the Young Hegelians, in particular, Bruno Bauer and Max Stirner.
(Z.A.J.)

nan' is not advanced a single step by reducing philosophy, 
neology, substance and all the trash to self-consciousness and by 
berating man from the domination of these phrases, which have 
ever held him in thrall. Nor will we explain to them that it is only 
ossible to achieve real liberation in the real world and by employ-
ng real means, that slavery cannot be abolished without the 
team-engine and the mule and spinning-jenny, serfdom cannot 
e abolished without improved agriculture, and that, in general, 
eople cannot be liberated as long as they are unable to obtain 
ood and drink, housing and clothing in adequate quality and 
uantity. 'Liberation' is a historical and not a mental act, and it is 
rought about by historical conditions, the [development] of 
ndustry, commerce, [agri]culture, the [conditions of inter-
ourse]¹ [. . .].

*GI*, pp. 55–6.

## 2) COMMUNIST CONSCIOUSNESS, CLASS POLARIZATION AND THE REVOLUTION

Finally, from the conception of history we have sketched we 
obtain these further conclusions: (1) In the development of 
productive forces there comes a stage when productive forces and 
means of intercourse are brought into being, which, under the 
existing relationships, only cause mischief, and are no longer 
productive but destructive forces (machinery and money); and 
connected with this a class is called forth, which has to bear all the 
burdens of society without enjoying its advantages, which, ousted 
from society, is forced into the most decided antagonism to all other 
classes; a class which forms the majority of all members of 
society, and from which emanates the consciousness of the 
necessity of a fundamental revolution, the communist con-
ciousness, which may, of course, arise among the other classes 
oo through the contemplation of the situation of this class. (2) 
The conditions under which definite productive forces can be 
pplied, are the conditions of the rule of a definite class of society, 
whose social power, deriving from its property, has its *practical-
dealistic* expression in each case in the form of the State; and,

¹ The following lines cannot be deciphered for the sheet of paper is badly 
damaged. (Editor of the English Translation)

therefore, every revolutionary struggle is directed against a class which till then has been in power.[1] (3) In all revolutions up till now the mode of activity always remained unscathed and it was only a question of a different distribution of this activity, a new distribution of labour to other persons, whilst the communist revolution is directed against the preceding *mode* of activity, does away with *labour*, and abolishes the rule of all classes with the classes themselves, because it is carried through by the class which no longer counts as a class in society, is not recognized as a class, and is in itself the expression of the dissolution of all classes, nationalities, etc., within present society; and (4) Both for the production on a mass scale of this communist consciousness, and for the success of the cause itself, the alteration of men on a mass scale is necessary, an alteration which can only take place in a practical movement, a *revolution*; this revolution is necessary, therefore, not only because the *ruling* class cannot be overthrown in any other way, but also because the class *overthrowing it* can only in a revolution succeed in ridding itself of all the muck of ages and become fitted to found society anew.

*GI* pp. 85–6.

What is the basis of a partial, merely political revolution? Simply this: a *section of civil society* emancipates itself and attains universal domination; a determinate class undertakes from its *particular situation*, a general emancipation of society. This class emancipates society as a whole, but only on condition that the whole of society is in the same situation as this class; for example, that it possesses or can easily acquire money or culture.

No class in civil society can play this part unless it can arouse, in itself and in the masses, a moment of enthusiasm in which it associates and mingles with society at large, identifies itself with it, and is felt and recognized as the *general representative* of this society. Its aims and interests must genuinely be the aims and interests of society itself, of which it becomes in reality the social head and heart. It is only in the name of general interests that a particular class can claim general supremacy. In order to attain this

---

[1] Marginal note by Marx: The people are interested in maintaining the present state of production.

liberating position, and the political direction of all spheres of society, revolutionary energy and consciousness of its own power do not suffice. For a *popular revolution* and the *emancipation of a particular class* of civil society to coincide, for *one* class to represent the whole of society, another class must concentrate in itself all the evils of society, a particular class must embody and represent a general obstacle and limitation. A particular social sphere must be regarded as the *notorious crime* of the whole society, so that emancipation from this sphere appears as a general emancipation. For *one* class to be the liberating class *par excellence*, it is necessary that another class should be openly the oppressing class. The negative significance of the French nobility and clergy produced the positive significance of the bourgeoisie, the class which stood next to them and opposed them.

*CHPR*, pp. 55–6.

As soon as it has risen up, a class in which the revolutionary interests of society are concentrated finds the content and the material for its revolutionary activity directly in its own situation: foes to be laid low, measures dictated by the needs of the struggle to be taken; the consequences of its own deeds drive it on. It makes no theoretical enquiries into its own task. The French working class had not attained this level; it was still incapable of accomplishing its own revolution.*

The development of the industrial proletariat is, in general, conditioned by the development of the industrial bourgeoisie. Only under its rule does the proletariat gain that extensive national existence which can raise its revolution to a national one, and does it itself create the modern means of production, which become just so many means of its revolutionary emancipation. Only its rule tears up the material roots of feudal society and levels the ground on which alone a proletarian revolution is possible. French industry is more developed and the French bourgeoisie more revolutionary than that of the rest of the Continent. But was not the February Revolution levelled directly against the finance aristocracy? This fact proved that the industrial bourgeoisie did not rule France. The industrial bourgeoisie can rule only where modern industry

* Marx refers to the class consciousness of the French workers at the time of the February Revolution (1848) and the June Insurrection (1848). (Z.A.J.)

shapes all property relations to suit itself, and industry can wi
this power only where it has conquered the world market, fo
national market only through a more or less modified system c
industry, to a great extent, maintains its command even of th
national market only through a more or less modified system o
prohibitive duties. While, therefore, the French proletariat, at th
moment of a revolution, possesses in Paris actual power an
influence which spur it on to a drive beyond its means, in the rest o
France it is crowded into separate, scattered industrial centres
being almost lost in the superior numbers of peasants and pett
bourgeois. The struggle against capital in its developed, moder
form, in its decisive aspect, the struggle of the industrial wageworke
against the industrial bourgeois, is in France a partial phenom
enon, which after the February days could so much the less suppl
the national content of the revolution, since the struggle agains
capital's secondary modes of exploitation, that of the peasan
against usury and mortgages or of the petty bourgeois against th
wholesale dealer, banker and manufacturer, in a word, agains
bankruptcy, was still hidden in the general uprising against th
finance aristocracy. Nothing is more understandable, then, tha
that the Paris proletariat sought to secure the advancement of it
own interests *side by side* with those of the bourgeoisie, instead o
enforcing them as the revolutionary interests of society itself, tha
it let the *red* flag be lowered to the *tricolour*. The French worker
could not take a step forward, could not touch a hair of the bour
geois order, until the course of the revolution had aroused the mas
of the nation, peasants and petty bourgeois, standing between th
proletariat and the bourgeoisie, against this order, against the rul
of capital, and had forced it to attach itself to the proletarians a
their protagonists. The workers could buy this victory only
through the tremendous defeat in June.

*CSF*, pp. 136–7.


## (3) SOCIAL AND POLITICAL REVOLUTION

'The Prussian'* concludes his contribution fittingly with the
following statement

* The pseudonym of Arnold Ruge. (Z.A.J.)

A *social revolution without a political soul* (that is, without an integrating body of ideas which apply to the whole society) is impossible. . . .

A *'social'* revolution with a *political soul* is either a compound nonsensical expression, if 'The Prussian' understands by 'social' revolution a 'social' revolution as *distinct* from a political revolution and nevertheless bestows upon the social revolution a political, instead of a social, soul. Or *'a social revolution with a political soul'* is but a *paraphrase* of what otherwise is called a *'political revolution'* or *' revolution pure and simple'*. Every revolution breaks up the *old society*, and to that extent it is *social*. Every revolution overthrows the *old authority*, and to that extent it is *political*. . . .

But while a *social revolution* with a *political soul* is either a paraphrase or a meaningless expression, a *political revolution* with a *social soul* is a meaningful phrase. The *revolution in general*—the *overthrow* of the existing power and the *breaking up* of the old social relations—is a *political act*. *Socialism* cannot be put into effect without a *revolution*. It requires this *political* act to the extent that it needs the *overthrow* and the *break up* of the existing order. However, when the *organizing activity* of socialism begins and when its *own aims*, its *soul*, comes to the fore, socialism abandons its *political* cloak.

*CMN*, pp. 408-9.

## (4) CLASS ANALYSIS OF THE REVOLUTIONS
### OF 1648, 1789, AND 1848

The *Prussian March Revolution** must not be confused with the *English* Revolution of 1648 or the French of 1789.

In 1648 the bourgeoisie was allied with the modern nobility against the monarchy, against the feudal nobility and against the established church.

In 1789 the bourgeoisie was allied with the people against the monarchy, the nobility and the established church.

The Revolution of 1789 had as its prototype (at least in Europe) only the Revolution of 1648, and the Revolution of 1648 only the insurrection of the Netherlanders against Spain. Not only in time

* In 1848. (Z.A.J.)

but also in content both revolutions were a century beyond their prototypes.

In both revolutions the bourgeoisie was the class that *really* formed the van of the movement. The *proletariat* and *the strata of the burghers which did not belong to the bourgeoisie* either had as yet no interest separate from those of the bourgeoisie or they did not yet constitute independently developed classes or subdivisions of classes. Hence where they came out in opposition to the bour-geoisie, as for instance in France in 1793 till 1794, they fought only for the realization of the interests of the bourgeoisie, even if not in *the fashion* of the bourgeoisie. The *whole French terrorism* was nothing but a *plebeian manner* of settling accounts with the *enemies of the bourgeoisie*, with absolutism, feudalism and philistinism.

The Revolutions of 1648 and 1789 were not *English* and *French* revolutions; they were revolutions of a *European* pattern. They were not the victory of a *definite* class of society over the *old political order*; they were the *proclamation of political order for the new European society*. The bourgeoisie was victorious in these revolutions but the *victory of the bourgeoisie* was at that time the *victory of a new order of society*, the victory of bourgeois property over feudal prop-erty, of nationality over provincialism, of competition over the guild, of partition over primogeniture, of the owner of the land over the domination of the owner by the land, of enlightenment over superstition, of the family over the family name, of industry over heroic laziness, of civil law over medieval privilege. The Revolution of 1648 was the victory of the seventeenth century over the six-teenth century, the Revolution of 1789 the victory of the eight-eenth century over the seventeenth century. These revolutions expressed still more the needs of the world of that day than of the sectors of the world in which they occurred, of England and France.

In the *March Revolution in Prussia* there was nothing of the kind. The February Revolution had *abolished* the constitutional mon-archy in reality and the rule of the bourgeoisie in the mind. The March Revolution in Prussia was to *establish* the constitutional monarchy in the mind and the rule of the bourgeoisie in reality. Far from being a *European revolution* it was but the stunted after-effect of a European revolution in a backward country. Instead of being ahead of its age it trailed more than half a century behind it. It was *secondary* from the outset, but it is a known fact that

:condary diseases are more difficult to cure and at the same time
·aste the body more than original disease. It was not a question
f the establishment of a new society but of the rebirth in Berlin
f the society that had passed away in Paris. The March Revolu-
on in Prussia was not even *national, German*; it was *provincial-
'russian* from its inception. The Vienna, Cassel, Munich and every
ther sort of provincial uprising swept on alongside of it and con-
:sted its lead.

While 1648 and 1789 had taken infinite pride in being the acme
f creation, it was the ambition of the Berlin of 1848 to form an
nachronism. Their light was like the light of the stars which
:aches us who dwell on earth only after the bodies which radiated
: have been extinct for a hundred-thousand years. The March
:evolution in Prussia was, in miniature—as it was everything in
niniature—just such a star for Europe. Its light was the light of the
orpse of a society that had long ago become putrefied.

The German bourgeoisie had developed so slothfully, cravenly
nd slowly that at the moment when it menacingly faced feudalism
nd absolutism it saw itself menacingly faced by the proletariat and
ll factions of the burghers whose interests and ideas were akin to
hose of the proletariat. And it saw inimically arrayed not only a
lass *behind* it but all of Europe *before* it. The Prussian bourgeoisie
vas not, as the French of 1789 had been, the class which represent-
d the *whole* of modern society *vis-à-vis* the representatives of the
ld society, the monarchy and the nobility. It had sunk to the level
·f a sort of *social estate*, as distinctly opposed to the crown as to the
ieople, eager to be in the opposition to both, irresolute against each
·f its opponents, taken severally, because it always saw both of
hem before or behind it; inclined from the very beginning to
ietray the people and compromise with the crowned represen-
ative of the old society because it itself already belonged to the old
ociety; representing not the interests of a new society against an
ild but renewed interests within a superannuated society; at the
teering wheel of the revolution not because the people stood
iehind it but because the people prodded it on before it; in the van
iot because it represented the initiative of a new but only the
·ancour of an old social epoch; a stratum of the old state that had
iot cropped out but been upheaved to the surface of the new state
iy an earthquake.

*BCR*, pp. 63–5.

K*

## (5) BOURGEOIS AND PROLETARIAN
## REVOLUTIONS

The contemporary *bourgeois* property relations are 'maintained by the might of the State which the bourgeoisie has organize for the protection of its property relations. Therefore, th proletarians must overthrow the political power wherever thi power is already in the hands of the bourgeoisie. They themselve must become a power and, to begin with, a revolutionar power. . . .

Although the bourgeoisie 'maintains' politically, that is, throug its State power, 'the injustice in property relations', the bourgeoisi does not *create* it. 'The injustice in property relations', whic is conditioned by the contemporary division of labour, the forms c exchange, competition, concentration, and so forth, does not resul by any means from the political domination of the bourgeois clas On the contrary, the political domination of the bourgeois clas results from those modern relations of production which th bourgeois economists have declared to be necessary and etern laws. If the proletariat should, therefore, overthrow the politic authority of the bourgeoisie, its victory will be only temporary only an instant in time in the interest of the *bourgeois revolut* itself, as in 1794. This will happen as long as in the course o history, in its 'movement', the material conditions, which necessi tate the abolition of the bourgeois mode of production and, thus the final overthrow of the bourgeois political authority, are not a yet created. The reign of terror in France was bound, therefore, t serve only the purpose of magically sprinting away with its power ful blows the remnants of feudalism from French soil. Th timidly considerate bourgeoisie would not have accomplished thi work for decades. Thus, the bloody deed of the people merel paved the way for the bourgeoisie. Similarly, the overthrow of th absolute monarchy would have been only temporary, if the econ omic conditions for the domination of the bourgeoisie had not a yet reached maturity. Men do not build a new world for them selves out of the 'blessings of this world' (*Erdengütern*), as crud superstitions would have it, but out of the historical achieve ments of their crumbling world. In the course of their developmen they themselves must first *produce* the *material conditions* of a new

ociety, and no effort of intellect or will can liberate them from this
ate.

*MCCM*, pp. 338–9.

Why should the German workers prefer the brutal oppression of
n absolute (monarchic) government, with its semi-feudal en-
ourage, to the *direct domination of the bourgeoisie*? The workers
now very well that the bourgeoisie not only has to make them
vider political concessions than the absolute monarchy but also
hat it creates, in the interest of its commerce and industry, and
gainst its own will, the conditions for the unification of the work-
ng class. And the unification of the workers is the first require-
nent of their victory. The workers know that the abolition of the
*ourgeois* relations of property cannot be brought about by preserv-
ng the *feudal* property relations. They know that their own
evolutionary movement can only be precipitated by the revolu-
ionary movement of the bourgeoisie against the feudal estates and
bsolute monarchy. They know that their own struggle against the
ourgeoisie can only begin on the day when the bourgeoisie is
ictorious over feudalism. For all that they do not share Herr
Heinzen's bourgeois illusions. They can and must treat the
*ourgeois revolution* as a condition for the *workers' revolution*,
lthough they cannot for a single moment regard the former as
heir *ultimate goal*.

*MCCM*, p. 352.

The Paris proletariat was *forced* into the June insurrection by
he bourgeoisie. This sufficed to mark its doom. Its immediate,
vowed needs did not drive it to engage in a fight for the forcible
verthrow of the bourgeoisie, nor was it equal to this task. The
*Moniteur** had to inform it officially that the time was past when
he republic saw any occasion to bow and scrape to its illusions, and
nly its defeat convinced it of the truth that the slightest improve-
nent in its position remains a *Utopia within* the bourgeois republic,
a Utopia that becomes a crime as soon as it wants to become a
reality. In place of its demands, exuberant in form, but petty and

---

* *Moniteur Universel* was the official organ of the French Government. (Z.A.J.)

even bourgeois still in content, the concession of which it wanted t
wring from the February republic, there appeared the bold sloga
of revolutionary struggle: *Overthrow of the bourgeoisie! Dic
tatorship of the working class*!

By making its burial place the birthplace of the *bourgeo*
*republic*, the proletariat compelled the latter to come out forthwith i
its pure form as the State whose admitted object it is to perpetuat
the rule of capital, the slavery of labour. Having constantly before it
eyes the scarred, irreconcilable, invincible enemy—invincibl
because its existence is the condition of its own life—bourgeoi
rule, freed from all fetters, was bound to turn immediately int
*bourgeois terrorism*. With the proletariat removed for the tim
being from the stage and bourgeois dictatorship recognize
officially, the middle strata of bourgeois society, the petty bour
geoisie and the peasant class, had to adhere more and more closel
to the proletariat as their position became more unbearable an
their antagonism to the bourgeoisie more acute. Just as earlie
they had to find the cause of their distress in its upsurge, so now i
its defeat.

*CSF*, p. 149.

The June struggle in Paris, the fall of Vienna, the tragicomedy c
Berlin's November 1848,* the desperate exertions of Poland, Ital
and Hungary, the starving of Ireland into submission—these wer
the chief factors which characterized the European class struggl
between bourgeoisie and working class and by means of which w
proved that every revolutionary upheaval, however remote from
the class struggle its goal may appear to be, must fail until th
revolutionary working class is victorious, that every social reforn
remains a Utopia until the proletarian revolution and the feudalisti
counter-revolution measure swords in a *world war*.

*WLC*, p. 74.

* Marx refers to three events which occurred in 1848, the rising of Parisia
workers in June, which was precipitated by the closing down of the so-calle
national workshops; the recapture of Vienna by the Imperial troops under th
command of Windischgrätz on the last day of October and the subsequent régim
of suppression; and the dissolution of the Prussian National Assembly i
November without any opposition from the population of Berlin. (Z.A.J.)

The social revolution of the nineteenth century cannot draw its poetry from the past, but only from the future. It cannot begin with itself before it has stripped off all superstition in regard to the past. Earlier revolutions required recollections of past world history in order to drug themselves concerning their own content. In order to arrive at its own content, the revolution of the nineteenth century must let the dead bury their dead. There the phrase went beyond the content; here the content goes beyond the phrase. . . .

Bourgeois revolutions, like those of the eighteenth century, storm swiftly from success to success; their dramatic effects outdo each other; men and things seem set in sparkling brilliants; ecstasy is the everyday spirit; but they are short-lived; soon they have attained their zenith, and a long crapulent depression lays hold of society before it learns soberly to assimilate the results of its storm-and-stress period. On the other hand, proletarian revolutions, like those of the nineteenth century, criticize themselves constantly, interrupt themselves continually in their own course, come back to the apparently accomplished in order to begin it afresh, deride with unmerciful thoroughness the inadequacies, weaknesses and paltrinesses of their first attempts, seem to throw down their adversary only in order that he may draw new strength from the earth and rise again, more gigantic, before them, recoil ever and anon from the indefinite prodigiousness of their own aims, until a situation has been created which makes all turning back impossible, and the conditions themselves cry out,

*Hic Rhodus, hic salta!*[1]
*Here is the rose, here dance!*


## (6) THE FAILURE OF REVOLUTIONS IN TIMES OF PROSPERITY

With this general prosperity, in which the productive forces of bourgeois society develop as luxuriantly as is at all possible within bourgeois relationships, there can be no talk of a real revolution.

---

[1] 'Here is Rhodes, leap here!' is a phrase taken from one of Aesop's fables. It implies 'Show right here by action what you claim to be able to do'. (Editor of the English Translation).                      *EBLB*, pp. 227–8.

Such a revolution is only possible in the periods when *both* these *factors*, the *modern* productive *forces* and the *bourgeois productive forms* come *in collision* with each other. The various quarrels in which the representatives of the individual factions of the Continental party of Order* now indulge and mutually compromise themselves, far from providing the occasion for new revolutions are, on the contrary, possible only because the basis of the relationships is momentarily so secure and, what the reaction does not know, so *bourgeois*. From it all attempts of the reaction to hold up bourgeois development will rebound just as certainly as all moral indignation and all enthusiastic proclamations of the democrats. *A new revolution is possible only in consequence of a new crisis. It is, however, just as certain as this crisis.*

*CSF*, p. 210.

## (7) THE SOCIAL REVOLUTION OF THE NINETEENTH CENTURY

The so-called Revolutions of 1848 were but poor incidents—small fractures and fissures in the dry crust of European society. However, they denounced the abyss. Beneath the apparently solid surface, they betrayed oceans of liquid matter, only needing expansion to rend into fragments continents of hard rock. Noisily and confusedly they proclaimed the emancipation of the Proletarian, i.e., the secret of the nineteenth century, and of the revolution of that century. That social revolution, it is true, was no novelty invented in 1848. Steam, electricity, and the self-acting mule were revolutionists of a rather more dangerous character than even citizens Barbès, Raspail and Blanqui.** But, although the

---

* The Party of Order, led by Thiers, was a coalition of conservative republicans, royalists and men of property who, after the June Insurrection of 1848, became the strongest political force in France. (Z.A.J.)

** Armand Barbès participated in many plots against Louis-Philippe and was one of the leaders of the extreme revolutionary groups during the 1848 revolution.

Louis Auguste Blanqui (1801–1881) was the greatest revolutionary leader of the nineteenth century whose whole life was an uninterrupted series of plots and imprisonments.

François Vincent Raspail (1794–1878) like Blanqui spent much of his life in prison or in exile because of his activities against the Bourbon and Orléans monarchies and, later, against the Second Empire.

atmosphere in which we live weighs upon every one with a 20,000 lb. force, do you feel it? No more than European society before 1848 felt the revolutionary atmosphere enveloping and pressing it from all sides. There is one great fact, characteristic of this our nineteenth century, a fact which no party dares deny. On the one hand, there have started into life industrial and scientific forces, which no epoch of the former human history had ever suspected. On the other hand, there exist symptoms of decay, far surpassing the horrors recorded of the latter times of the Roman Empire. In our days everything seems pregnant with its contrary. Machinery, gifted with the wonderful power of shortening and fructifying human labour, we behold starving and overworking it. The new-fangled sources of wealth, by some strange weird spell, are turned into sources of want. The victories of art seem bought by the loss of character. At the same pace that mankind masters nature, man seems to become enslaved to other men or to his own infamy. Even the pure light of science seems unable to shine but on the dark background of ignorance. All our invention and progress seem to result in endowing material forces with intellectual life, and in stultifying human life into a material force. This antagonism between modern industry and science on the one hand, modern misery and dissolution on the other hand; this antagonism between the productive powers, and the social relations of our epoch is a fact, palpable, overwhelming, and not to be controverted. Some parties may wail over it; others may wish to get rid of modern arts, in order to get rid of modern conflicts. Or they may imagine that so signal a progress in industry wants to be completed by as signal a regress in politics. On our part, we do not mistake the shape of the shrewd spirit that continues to mark all these contradictions. We know that to work well the new-fangled forces of society, they only want to be mastered by new-fangled men—and such are the working men. They are as much the invention of modern times as machinery itself. In the signs that bewilder the middle class, the aristocracy and the poor prophets of regression, we do recognize our brave friend, Robin Goodfellow, the old mole that can work in the earth so fast, that worthy pioneer—the Revolution. The English working men are the first-born sons of modern industry. They will then, certainly, not be the last in aiding the social revolution produced by that industry, a revolution, which means the emancipation of their own class all over the world, which is as

292 KARL MARX: ECONOMY, CLASS AND SOCIAL REVOLUTION

universal as capital-rule and wages-slavery. I know the heroic struggles the English working class have gone through since the middle of the last century—struggles less glorious, because they are shrouded in obscurity, and burked by the middle-class historian. To revenge the misdeeds of the ruling class, there existed in the middle ages, in Germany, a secret tribunal, called the '*Vehmgericht.*' If a red cross was seen marked on a house, people knew that its owner was doomed by the '*Vehm.*' All the houses of Europe are now marked with the mysterious red cross. History is the judge—its executioner, the proletarian.

*SAPP*, pp. 325–6.

## (8) REVOLUTION BY FORCE AND BY PEACEFUL MEANS

The prophet* paints the transition from present social isolation to communal life in truly idyllic colours . . . . He transforms the real social movement which already, in all civilized countries, proclaims the approach of a terrible social upheaval into a process of *comfortable* and *peaceful conversion*, a *quiet life* which will permit the owners and rulers of the world to slumber on *in complete peace of mind*.

*GI*, pp. 594–5.

The Communists disdain to conceal their views and aims. They openly declare that their ends can be attained only by the forcible overthrow of all existing social conditions. Let the ruling classes tremble at a Communist revolution.

*MCP*, p. 61.

When, in the course of development, class distinctions have disappeared, and all production has been concentrated in the hands of a vast association of the whole nation, the public power will lose its political character. Political power, properly so called, is merely

---

* Georg Kuhlmann, author of the book, *Die neue Welt oder das Reich des Geistes auf Erden.* Verkündigung, Genf, 1845. (Z.A.J.)

the organized power of one class for oppressing another. If the proletariat during its contest with the bourgeoisie is compelled, by the force of circumstances, to organize itself as a class, if, by means of a revolution, it makes itself the ruling class, and, as such, sweeps away by force the old conditions of production, then it will, along with these conditions, have swept away the conditions for the existence of class antagonisms and of classes generally, and will thereby have abolished its own supremacy as a class.

In place of the old bourgeois society, with its classes and class antagonisms, we shall have an association, in which the free development of each is the condition for the free development of all.

*MCP*, p. 51.

'The power of the capitalist over all the wealth of the country is a complete change in the right of property, and by what law, or series of laws, was it effected?' The author[1] should have remembered that revolutions are not made by laws. . . .

The different momenta of primitive accumulation distribute themselves now, more or less in chronological order, particularly over Spain, Portugal, Holland, France, and England. In England at the end of the seventeenth century, they arrive at a systematical combination, embracing the colonies, the national debt, the modern mode of taxation, and the protectionist system. These methods depend in part on brute force, e.g., the colonial system. But they all employ the power of the State, the concentrated and organized force of society, to hasten, hothouse fashion, the process of transformation of the feudal mode of production into the capitalist mode, and to shorten the transition. Force is the midwife of every old society pregnant with a new one. It is itself an economic power.

*C* I, pp. 750–1.

One day, the worker must seize political supremacy, in order to found the new organization of labour. He must overthrow the old political system and its dependent institutions or forfeit the

[1] (T. Hodgskin), *The Natural and Artificial Rights of Property Contrasted*, London, 1832, p. 99.

opportunity of ever seeing his kingdom established on earth; the early Christians paid this forfeit for ignoring the political system and deeming it unworthy of their consideration.

But we have not asserted that the means to this end should be the same everywhere.

We know that one has to take into account the institutions, customs and traditions of various countries, and we do not deny that there are certain countries, such as America and England, to which if I were better acquainted with your institutions, I would also add Holland, where the workers can attain their goal by peaceful means. While this may be true, we must also recognize that in most countries on the Continent force must be the lever of our revolutions. It is to force that we must one day resort in order to establish the dominion of labour.

Report of Marx's speech at a meeting in Amsterdam on 8 September, 1872, *La Liberté*, 15 September, 1872.

# (C) *The Working Class Movement*

## (1) COMMUNISM

Communism differs from all previous movements in that it overturns the basis of all earlier relations of production and intercourse, and for the first time consciously treats all natural premises as the creatures of hitherto existing men, strips them of their natural character and subjugates them to the power of the united individuals. Its organization is, therefore, essentially economic, the material production of the conditions of this unity; it turns existing conditions into conditions of unity. The reality, which communism is creating, is precisely the true basis for rendering it impossible that anything should exist independently of individuals, in so far as reality is only a product of the preceding intercourse of individuals themselves.

*GI*, pp. 86–7.

In history up to the present it is certainly an empirical fact that separate individuals have, with the broadening of their activity into world-historical activity, become more and more enslaved under a power alien to them . . . a power which has become more and more enormous and, in the last instance, turns out to be the *world market*. But it is just as empirically established that, by the overthrow of the existing state of society by the communist revolution . . . and the abolition of private property which is identical with it, this power, which so baffles the German theoreticians, will be dissolved; and that then the liberation of each single individual will be accomplished in the measure in which history becomes transformed into world history. From the above it is clear that the real intellectual wealth of the individual depends entirely on the wealth of his real connexions. Only then will the separate individuals be liberated from the various national and local barriers, be brought into practical connexion with the material and intellectual production of the whole world and be put in a position to acquire the capacity to enjoy this all-sided production of the whole earth (the creations of man). *All-round dependence*, this natural form of the *world-historical* co-operation of individuals, will be transformed by this communist revolution into the control and conscious mastery of these powers, which, born of the action of men on one another, have till now overawed and governed men as powers completely alien to them.

*GI*, pp. 48–9.

Only in community [with others] has each individual the means of cultivating his gifts in all directions; only in the community, therefore, is personal freedom possible. In the previous substitutes for the community, in the State, etc., personal freedom has existed only for the individuals who developed within the relationships of the ruling class, and only in so far as they were individuals of this class. The illusory community, in which individuals have up till now combined, always took on an independent existence in relation to them, and was at the same time, since it was the combination of one class over against another, not only a completely illusory community, but a new fetter as well. In the real community the individuals obtain their freedom in and through their association.

*GI*, pp. 91–2.

## (2) THE SHORT- AND LONG-RANGE AIMS OF THE COMMUNISTS\*

The proletariat goes through various stages of development. With its birth begins its struggle with the bourgeoisie. At first the contest is carried on by individual labourers, then by the work-people of a factory, then by the operatives of one trade, in one locality, against the individual bourgeois who directly exploits them. They direct their attacks not against the bourgeois conditions of production, but against the instruments of production them-selves; they destroy imported wares that compete with their labour, they smash to pieces machinery, they set factories ablaze, they seek to restore by force the vanished status of the workman of the Middle Ages. . . .

But with the development of industry the proletariat not only increases in number; it becomes concentrated in greater masses, its strength grows, and it feels that strength more. The various interests and conditions of life within the ranks of the proletariat are more and more equalized, in proportion as machinery obliterates all distinctions of labour, and nearly everywhere re-duces wages to the same low level. The growing competition among the bourgeois, and the resulting commercial crises, make the wages of the workers ever more fluctuating. The unceasing improvement of machinery, ever more rapidly developing, makes their livelihood more and more precarious; the collisions between individual workmen and individual bourgeois take more and more the character of collisions between two classes. Thereupon the workers begin to form combinations (Trades' Unions) against the bourgeois; they club together in order to keep up the rate of wages; they found permanent associations in order to make provision beforehand for these occasional revolts. Here and there the contest breaks out into riots.

---

\* 'The Communists fight for the attainment of the immediate aims, for the enforcement of the momentary interests of the working class; but in the move-ment of the present, they also represent and take care of the future of that movement' (*MCP*, p. 60). (Z.A.J.)

Now and then the workers are victorious, but only for a time. The real fruit of their battles lies, not in the immediate result, but in the ever-expanding union of the workers. This union is helped on by the improved means of communication that are created by modern industry and that place the workers of different localities in contact with one another. It was just this contact that was needed to centralize the numerous local struggles, all of the same character, into one national struggle between classes. But every class struggle is a political struggle. And that union, to attain which the burghers of the Middle Ages, with their miserable highways, required centuries, the modern proletarians, thanks to railways, achieve in a few years.

This organization of the proletarians into a class, and consequently into a political party, is continually being upset again by the competition between the workers themselves. But it ever rises up again, stronger, firmer, mightier. It compels legislative recognition of particular interests of the workers, by taking advantage of the divisions among the bourgeoisie itself. Thus the ten-hours' bill in England was carried.

Altogether collisions between the classes of the old society further, in many ways, the course of development of the proletariat. The bourgeoisie finds itself involved in a constant battle. At first with the aristocracy; later on, with those portions of the bourgeoisie itself, whose interests have become antagonistic to the progress of industry; at all times, with the bourgeoisie of foreign countries. In all these battles it sees itself compelled to appeal to the proletariat, to ask for its help, and thus, to drag it into the political arena. The bourgeoisie itself, therefore, supplies the proletariat with its own elements of political and general education, in other words, it furnishes the proletariat with weapons for fighting the bourgeoisie.

*MCP*, pp. 40–1.

In all countries of Europe it has now become a truth demonstrable to every unprejudiced mind, and only denied by those whose interest it is to hedge other people in a fool's paradise, that no improvement of machinery, no appliance of science to production, no contrivances of communication, no new colonies, no emigration, no opening of markets, no free trade, nor all these things put together, will do away with the miseries of the industrious masses; but that, on the present false base, every fresh development of the productive powers of labour must tend to deepen social contrasts and point social antagonisms. Death by starvation rose almost to the rank of an institution during this intoxicating epoch of economic progress,* in the metropolis of the British Empire. That epoch is marked in the annals of the world by the quickened return, the widening compass, and the deadlier effects of the social pest called a commercial and industrial crisis. . . . .

At the same time, the experience of the period from 1848 to 1864 has proved beyond doubt that, however excellent in principle, and however useful in practice, co-operative labour, if kept within the narrow circle of the casual efforts of private workmen, will never be able to arrest the growth in geometrical progression of monopoly, to free the masses, nor even to perceptibly lighten the burden of their miseries. . . . . To save the industrious masses, co-operative labour ought to be developed to national dimension, and, consequently, to be fostered by national means. Yet, the lords of land and the lords of capital will always use their political priviledges for the defence and perpetuation of their economic monopolies. So far from promoting, they will continue to lay every possible impediment in the way of the emancipation of labour. . . . . To conquer political power has therefore become the great duty of the working classes. They seem to have comprehended this, for in England, Germany, Italy, and France there have taken place simultaneous revivals, and simultaneous efforts are being made at the political reorganization of the working men's party.

*IAWMIA*, pp. 346–8.

The political movement of the working class has as its ultimate object, of course, the conquest of political power for this class, and this naturally requires a previous organization of the working class developed up to a certain point and arising precisely from its economic struggles.

On the other hand, however, every movement in which the working class comes out as a *class* against the ruling classes and

* That is, in the years 1848–64. (Z.A.J.)

ries to coerce them by pressure from without is a political movement. For instance, the attempt in a particular factory or even in a
particular trade to force a shorter working day out of individual
capitalists by strikes, etc., is a purely economic movement. On the
other hand the movement to force through an eight-hour, etc.,
*law*, is a *political* movement. And in this way, out of the separate
economic movements of the workers there grows up everywhere a
*political* movement, that is to say, a movement of the *class*, with
the object of enforcing its interests in a general form, in a form
possessing general, socially coercive force. While these movements presuppose a certain degree of previous organization, they
are in turn equally a means of developing this organization.

Where the working class is not yet far enough advanced in its
organization to undertake a decisive campaign against the collective
power, i.e., the political power of the ruling classes, it must at any
rate be trained for this by continual agitation against this power
and by a hostile attitude toward the policies of the ruling classes.
Otherwise it remains a plaything in their hands, as the September
revolution in France showed, and as is also proved to a certain
extent by the game that Messrs. Gladstone & Co. have been
successfully engaged in in England up to the present time.

Marx's letter to F. Bolte of 23 November 1871.

*SC*. pp. 328-9.

The immediate aim of the Communists is the same as that of
all the other proletarian parties: formation of the proletariat into
a class, overthrow of the bourgeois supremacy, conquest of
political power by the proletariat.

The theoretical conclusions of the Communists are in no way
based on ideas or principles that have been invented, or discovered,
by this or that would-be universal reformer.

They merely express, in general terms, actual relations spring-
ing from an existing class struggle, from a historical movement
going on under our very eyes. The abolition of existing property-
relations is not at all a distinctive feature of Communism.

All property relations in the past have continually been subject
to historical change consequent upon the change in historical
conditions.

The French Revolution, for example, abolished feudal property in favour of bourgeois property.

The distinguishing feature of Communism is not the abolition of property generally, but the abolition of bourgeois property. But modern bourgeois private property is the final and most complete expression of the system of producing and appropriating products that is based on class antagonism, on the exploitation of the many by the few.

In this sense, the theory of the Communists may be summed up in the single sentence: Abolition of private property.

*MCP*, pp. 44–5.

If one imagines the antithesis of communism to the world of private property in its crudest form, i.e., in the most abstract form in which the real conditions of that antithesis are ignored, then one is faced with the antithesis of property and lack of property. The abolition of this antithesis can be viewed as the abolition of either the one side or the other; either property can be abolished in which case universal lack of property or destitution results, or else the lack of property may be abolished, which means the establishment of true property. In reality, the actual property owners stand on one side and the propertyless communist proletarians on the other. This opposition becomes keener day by day and is rapidly driving to a crisis. If, then, the theoretical representatives of the proletariat wish their literary activity to have any practical effect, they must first and foremost insist that all phrases be swept aside which tend to dim the realization of the sharpness of this opposition, all phrases tending to conceal this opposition and giving the bourgeois a chance to approach the communists for safety's sake on the strength of their philanthropic enthusiasms. All these bad qualities are, however, to be found in the catchwords of the true socialists and particularly in 'true property'. Of course, we realize that the communist movement cannot be destroyed by a few German phrasemongers. But in a country like Germany—where philosophic phrases have for centuries exerted a certain power, and where, moreover, communist consciousness is anyhow less keen and determined because class contradictions do not exist in as acute a form as in other

nations—it is, nevertheless, necessary to resist all phrases which
obscure and dilute still further the realization that communism is
totally opposed to the existing world order.

*GI*, pp. 516–7.

The multiplicity of interpretations to which the Commune has
been subjected, and the multiplicity of interests which construed
it in their favour, show that it was a thoroughly expansive
political form, while all previous forms of government had been
emphatically repressive. Its true secret was this. It was essentially
a working-class government, the produce of the struggle of the
producing against the appropriating class, the political form at
last discovered under which to work out the economic emancipation of labour.

Except on this last condition, the Communal Constitution
would have been an impossibility and a delusion. The political
rule of the producer cannot coexist with the perpetuation of his
social slavery. The Commune was therefore to serve as a lever for
uprooting the economic foundations upon which rests the existence
of classes, and therefore of class rule. With labour emancipated,
every man becomes a working man and productive labour ceases
to be a class attribute. . . .

The working class did not expect miracles from the Commune.
They have no ready-made Utopias to introduce *par décret du
peuple*. They know that in order to work out their own emancipation, and along with it that higher form to which present society is
irresistibly tending by its own economic agencies, they will have
to pass through long struggles, through a series of historic processes, transforming circumstances and men. They have no
ideals to realize, but to set free the elements of the new society
with which old collapsing bourgeois society itself is pregnant.

*CWF*, pp. 473–5.

The doctrinaire and necessarily fantastic anticipation of the
programme of action for a revolution of the future only diverts one
from the struggle of the present. The dream that the end of the
world was near inspired the early Christians in their struggle with

the Roman Empire and gave them confidence in victory
Scientific insight into the inevitable disintegration of the dominant
order of society continually proceeding before our eyes and the
ever-growing fury into which the masses are lashed by the old
ghostly governments, while at the same time the positive develop
ment of the means of production advances with gigantic strides—
all this is a sufficient guarantee that the moment a real proletarian
revolution breaks out the conditions (though these are certain no
to be idyllic) of its immediately next *modus operandi* will be i
existence.

Marx's letter to F. Domela-Nieuwenhuis of 22 February 1881.
*SC*, pp. 410–1.

## (3) THE RELATION OF THE WORKERS' MOVE-MENT TO THE BOURGEOIS DEMOCRATS*

The petty-bourgeois democratic party in Germany is very power
ful; it comprises not only the majority of the bourgeois in
habitants of the towns, the small people in industry and trade an
the guild masters; it numbers among the followers also the
peasants and the rural proletariat, in so far as the latter has no
yet found a support in the independent urban proletariat.

The relation of the revolutionary workers' party to the petty
bourgeois democrats is this: it marches together with them against
the faction which it aims at overthrowing, it opposes them i
everything whereby they seek to consolidate their position in their
own interests.

Far from desiring to revolutionize all society for the revolutionar
proletarians, the democratic petty bourgeois strive for a chang
in social conditions by means of which existing society will b
made as tolerable and comfortable as possible for them. Henc
they demand above all diminution of state expenditure by
curtailment of the bureaucracy and shifting the chief taxes on t
the big landowners and bourgeois. Further, they demand th
abolition of the pressure of big capital on small, through publi

---

* Marx attached a considerable importance to this matter because in 1850 h
believed, for a short time, that another revolution on the Continent was immine
and that 'the bourgeois revolution in Germany will be but the prelude to a
immediately following proletarian revolution' (*MCP*, p. 61). (Z.A.J.)

credit institutions and laws against usury, by which means it will be possible for them and the peasants to obtain advances, on favourable conditions, from the State instead of from the capitalists; they also demand the establishment of bourgeois property relations in the countryside by the complete abolition of feudalism. To accomplish all this they need a democratic state structure, either constitutional or republican, that will give them and their allies, the peasants, a majority; also a democratic communal structure that will give them direct control over communal property and over a series of functions now performed by the bureaucrats. . . .

But these demands can in no wise suffice for the party of the proletariat. While the democratic petty bourgeois wish to bring the revolution to a conclusion as quickly as possible, and with the achievement, at most, of the above demands, it is our interest and our task to make the revolution permanent, until all more or less possessing classes have been forced out of their position of dominance, until the proletariat has conquered state power, and the association of proletarians, not only in one country but in all the dominant countries of the world, has advanced so far that competition among the proletarians of these countries has ceased and that at least the decisive productive forces are concentrated in the hands of the proletarians. For us the issue cannot be the alteration of private property but only its annihilation, not the smoothing over of class antagonisms but the abolition of classes, not the improvement of existing society but the foundation of a new one.

*ACL*, pp. 101–2.


# (4) THE TWO PHASES OF COMMUNIST SOCIETY

But one of the most vital principles of communism, a principle which distinguishes it from all reactionary socialism, is its empiric view, based on a knowledge of man's nature, that differences of *brain* and of intellectual capacity do not imply any differences whatsoever in the nature of the *stomach* and of physical *needs*; therefore the false tenet, based upon the existing circumstances, '*to each according* to his abilities', must be changed, in so far as it relates to enjoyment in its narrower sense, into the tenet, '*to each*

*according to his need*'; in other words, a *different form* of activity, o
labour, does not justify *inequality*, confers no *privileges* in respec
of possession and enjoyment.

*GI*, p. 593.

What we have to deal with here is a communist society, not as i
has *developed* on its own foundations, but, on the contrary, just a
it *emerges* from capitalist society; which is thus in every respect
economically, morally and intellectually, still stamped with the
birthmarks of the old society from whose womb it emerges
Accordingly, the individual producer receives back from society—
after the deductions have been made—exactly what he gives to it
What he has given to it is his individual quantum of labour. Fo
example, the social working day consists of the sum of the
individual hours of work; the individual labour time of the
individual producer is the part of the social working day con
tributed by him, his share in it. He receives a certificate from
society that he has furnished such and such an amount of labou
(after deducting his labour for the common funds), and with thi
certificate he draws from the social stock of means of consumptio
as much as costs the same amount of labour. The same amount o
labour which he has given to society in one form he receives bac
in another.

Here obviously the same principle prevails as that which regu
lates the exchange of commodities, as far as this is exchange o
equal values. Content and form are changed, because under the
altered circumstances no one can give anything except his labour
and because, on the other hand, nothing can pass to the ownershi
of individuals except individual means of consumption. But, a
far as the distribution of the latter among the individual producer
is concerned, the same principle prevails as in the exchange of com
modity-equivalents: a given amount of labour in one form i
exchanged for an equal amount of labour in another form.

Hence, *equal right* here is still in principle—*bourgeois right*
although principle and practice are no longer at loggerheads, whil
the exchange of equivalents in commodity exchange only exist
*on the average* and not in the individual case.

In spite of this advance, this *equal right* is still constantl
stigmatized by a bourgeois limitation. The right of the producers i

*proportional* to the labour they supply; the equality consists in the fact that measurement is made with an *equal standard*, labour.

But one man is superior to another physically or mentally and so supplies more labour in the same time, or can labour for a longer time; and labour, to serve as a measure, must be defined by its duration or intensity, otherwise it ceases to be a standard of measurement. This *equal* right is an unequal right for unequal labour. It recognizes no class differences, because everyone is only a worker like everyone else; but it tacitly recognizes unequal individual endowment and thus productive capacity as natural privileges. *It is, therefore, a right of inequality, in its content, like every right*. Right by its very nature can consist only in the application of an equal standard; but unequal individuals (and they would not be different individuals if they were not unequal) are measurable only by an equal standard in so far as they are brought under an equal point of view, are taken from one *definite* side only, for instance, in the present case, are regarded *only as workers*, and nothing more is seen in them, everything else being ignored. Further, one worker is married, another not; one has more children than another, and so on and so forth. Thus, with an equal performance of labour, and hence an equal share in the social consumption fund, one will in fact receive more than another, one will be richer than another, and so on. To avoid all these defects, right instead of being equal would have to be unequal.

But these defects are inevitable in the first phase of communist society as it is when it has just emerged after prolonged birth pangs from capitalist society. Right can never be higher than the economic structure of society and its cultural development conditioned thereby.

In a higher phase of communist society, after the enslaving subordination of the individual to the division of labour, and therewith also the antithesis between mental and physical labour, has vanished; after labour has become not only a means of life but life's prime want; after the productive forces have also increased with the all-round development of the individual, and all the springs of co-operative wealth flow more abundantly—only then can the narrow horizon of bourgeois right be crossed in its entirety and society inscribe on its banners: From each according to his ability, to each according to his needs!

*CGP*, pp. 21–3.

# Notes to Introductory Essay

1 *EPM*, pp. 160–2.
2 *HF*, p. 173.
3 L. Feuerbach, *The Essence of Christianity*, Harper Torchbooks, New York, 1957, p. 87.
4 Naturalism is thus the contrary of supernaturalism which asserts precisely that mind transcends nature.
5 *The Essence of Christianity*, p. 82
6 J. S. Mill, *A System of Logic*, bk. VI, ch. VII, § 1; H. Spencer, *The Study of Sociology*, ch. III; *The Principles of Sociology*, vol. I, ch. II, § 6 and 13, pp. 8–9, 14 of the 1904 edition. Spencer claimed that the characteristics of human individuals and the external conditions under which they live are the two primary causal factors of social phenomena. He conceded that the latter factor may modify society and that society, once it is formed, may influence individuals. But the power which the external conditions or society exert is not effective unless it changes first the individuals who alone are the determining cause of social phenomena. As Spencer explained it further on, the Science of Sociology starts with 'social units' (human individuals) as possessed of certain original and acquired characteristics and gives an account of 'all the phenomena that result from their combined action' (*The Principles of Sociology*, vol. I, ch. XXVII, § 210, p. 426).
7 As far as philosophical criticism is concerned, Ferguson (*An Essay on the History of Civil Society*, pt. III, sec. II, p. 121 ff. of the 1966 edition) and Hegel (*Philosophy of Right*, Oxford, 1962, pp. 122 ff.) should be mentioned in view of the fact that Marx knew these philosophers intimately. Many of Hegel's ideas can be found in Kant's *Idee zu einer allgemeinen Geschichte in weltbürgerlicher Absicht* (1784). See I. Kant, *Kleinere Schriften zur Geschichtsphilosophie, Ethik und Politik*, hrgn. von K. Vorländer, Philosophische Bibliothek, Verlag von Felix Meiner, pp. 5 ff. This short work was translated into French and was highly appreciated by Comte and the Saint-Simonists. See Comte's letter to Gustave d'Eichthal of 10 December 1824 in É. Littré, *Auguste Comte et la philosophie positive*, Paris, 1864, pp. 153 ff.; *Doctrine de Saint-Simon: Exposition*, Première année, 1829, Paris, 1924, p. 207,

note 93. For the impact of new scientific ideas, see J. W. Burrow, *Evolution and Society: A Study in Victorian Social Theory*, Cambridge, 1966, pp. 108 ff.

8   This idea, too, is not Marx's exclusive property. It was formulated roughly at the same time by Comte (*Système de politique positive*, in *Oeuvres de Saint-Simon et d'Enfantin*, Paris 1865–78, XXXVIIIᵉ vol., pp. 93–4, 108–12; *Cours de philosophie positive*, Paris, 1908, vol. IV, pp. 294–317) and J. S. Mill (*A System of Logic*, bk. VI, ch. X, § 2–4). Comte's influence on Marx is now well established.

9   *EPM*, pp. 157, 162.

10   É. Durkheim, *Montesquieu and Rousseau: Forerunners of Sociology*, The University of Michigan Press, 1960, p. 57.

11   Also the three 'moments' of reflection, designated as 'Thesis', 'Antithesis' and 'Synthesis', are first to be found in Fichte, although only Hegel developed this procedure by making each conception become its opposite and, from the contradiction of the two, making the higher synthesis emerge, and so forth, indefinitely.

12   *Grundlagen der gesamten Wissenschaftslehre* (1794). From the point of view here considered, the first and second parts of *Wissenschaftslehre* are particularly important.

13   G. W. F. Hegel, *The Philosophy of History*, Dover Publications, New York, 1956, p. 55.

14   L. Feuerbach, *The Essence of Christianity*, XXXVIII, pp. 14, 46, 63, 226, 248.

15   Marx, *TF* IV; *KHS*, *MEW* B. 1, p. 294.

16   Marx, *KHS*, *MEW* B. 1, pp. 203 5.

17   The idea that 'work is the first attribute, the essential characteristic of man' is basic to Proudhon's anarchic socialism. See *Système des contradictions économiques ou Philosophie de la misère* (1846), *Oeuvres Complètes de P. -J. Proudhon*, Paris, 1923 ff., vol. II, p. 361. There is no reason to suppose that Proudhon owed his idea about work to Marx, although Marx's later conceptions of man as *homo faber*, a tool making animal, may have been influenced by Proudhon.

18   Tocqueville made a similar comment. 'A theory of manufacture more powerful than manners and laws binds him (the workman) to a craft, and frequently to a spot, which he cannot leave: it assigns to him a certain place in society beyond which he cannot go: in the midst of universal movement it has rendered him stationary' (*Democracy in America*, pt. II, ch. XXVIII). While for Marx division of labour had an 'enslaving effect', in the case of Tocqueville division of labour restricts or bars entirely vertical mobility.

19   E. Fromm, *The Fear of Freedom* (1942) and *The Sane Society* (1956); C. Wright Mills, *White Collar* (1951). According to Mills, alienation appears in all varieties of social structure, because each of them 'makes

for the ascendancy of the cheerful robot', Mills's term for the 'alienated man' (*The Sociological Imagination*, New York, 1959, p. 171).

20 L. Feuer, 'What Is Alienation? The Career of a Concept', *New Politics*, 1962, p. 129.

21 R. A. Nisbet, *The Sociological Tradition*, London, 1967, pp. 264 ff.

22 See his *Critique de la raison dialectique*, Tome I, Paris, 1960, pp. 60–63.

23 See, e.g., A. Schaff, *Marksizm a jednostka ludzka*, Warszawa, 1965, or K. Kosik, 'Man and Philosophy' and P. Vranicki, 'Socialism and the Problem of Alienation' in E. Fromm (Ed.), *Socialist Humanism*, London, 1967, pp. 148–156, 277–290.

24 See J. -Y. Calvez, *La Pensée de Karl Marx*, Paris, 1956, and O. Schatz and E. F. Winter, 'Alienation, Marxism and Humanism', in E. Fromm (Ed.), *Socialist Humanism*, pp. 291–308.

25 For the general distinction see R. Dahrendorf, *Class and Class Conflict in an Industrial Society*, London, 1959, pp. 157 ff. Kant and the Saint-Simonists are never mentioned in this context, although Kant influenced Comte and the Saint-Simonists and the latter influenced Marx. See I. Kant, *Idee zu einer allgemeinen Geschichte in weltbürgerlicher Absicht*, pp. 8–10; *Doctrine de Saint-Simon: Exposition*, Première année, p. 225.

26 *MCP*, p. 33; cf. Marx's letter to the Chartist Congress held in Manchester in March, 1854, *The People's Paper* of 18 March, 1854.

27 *An Essay on the History of Civil Society*, pt. IV, sec. II, pp. 184 ff., of the 1966 edition. Marx recognized the fact that division of labour in the workshop which is the distinguishing principle of the capitalist mode of production, produces a 'hierarchy of labour-powers, to which there corresponds a scale of wages'. He found the idea of the hierarchic gradation of labourers according to their natural and acquired capabilities in Andrew Ure's *The Philosophy of Manufactures*. But Marx attached no importance whatsoever to stratification based on the size of wage or an occupational status. He considered the dichotomic division of labour into skilled and unskilled, unknown to the handicrafts, a much more significant development than the emergence of new forms of stratification (*C* I, pp. 349–50, 367). This was a more significant development because it showed clearly that the basic tendency of modern industry is to substitute a more simple, subordinate occupation for the more complex and superior function. Modern industry does not diversify the occupational stratification but simplifies it more and more. See *WLC*, pp. 95–6.

28 *The Rules of Sociological Method*, Glencoe, New York, 1958, pp. 2, 101–4.

29 K. R. Popper, *The Logic of Scientific Discovery*, London, 1959, pp. 62–4.

30 For the distinction of the three ways in which the universality of scientific laws can be construed and the discussion of the universality in respect to spatio-temporal scope see H. Mehlberg *The Reach of Science*, University of Toronto Press, pp. 158 ff.

31 V. I. Lenin, 'A Great Beginning', *Collected Works*, Moscow, 1960 ff., vol. XXIX, p. 421.

32 The closest approximation to Lenin's definitional statement is Engels's footnote to the English edition of the *Manifesto of the Communist Party* of 1888 in which Engels defines the bourgeoisie and the proletariat in terms of their relation to the means of production. See Marx–Engels, *SW* vol. I, p. 33, footnote *a*.

33 I have in mind such works as R. Aron, 'Social Structure and Ruling Class' in L. A. Coser (Ed.), *Political Sociology: Selected Essays*, Harper Torchbooks, 1966, pp. 51 ff.; *Main Currents in Sociological Thought*, London, 1965, vol. I, pp. 161 ff.; S. Össowski, *Class Structure in the Social Consciousness*, New York, 1963, ch. V; T. B. Bottomore, *Classes in Modern Society*, London, 1965, pp. 17 ff.

34 The three criteria are not of the same kind, for the first two are 'objective' (non-psychological) and the third is 'subjective' (psychological).

35 R. Aron, *Main Currents in Sociological Thought*, vol. I, p. 161. The above passage is usually understood to refer to the three 'orders' of Adam Smith (*The Wealth of Nations*, bk. I, ch. VI) but it is more likely that Marx speaks of the 'three classes of the community' mentioned in a similar context by D. Ricardo in *The Principles of Political Economy and Taxation*, Everyman's Library, p. 1.

36 This would explain the fact, to which T. B. Bottomore draws attention, that while income differences produce some social separation of groups, they do not give rise, by themselves, to economic inequalities. 'Distinctions based upon property ownership and inheritance are more strongly felt, and are more divisive in their effects, than those which arise from differences in earned income' (*Classes in Modern Society*, p. 57).

37 A. Ferguson, *An Essay on the History of Civil Society*, pt. II, sec. III, p. 98 of the 1966 edition.

38 de Tocqueville and J. S. Mill were in no doubt about the fact of social vertical mobility and its importance in modern times, although Tocqueville was not certain whether social mobility did not affect only the 'elements of which the class of the rich is composed', leaving the poor 'fixed' (*Democracy in America*, pt. II, ch. XXVIII). But J. S. Mill did not make any qualification and regarded the chances of vertical social mobility as the peculiar characteristic which chiefly distinguishes modern life from that of times past. See *The Subjection of Women*, ch. I, The World's Classics, Oxford University Press, vol. CLXX, p. 445. Marx

assumed the possibility that isolated individuals can change class membership, *MCP*, pp. 41–2; *EBLB* p. 232; *C* III, p. 587, but did not recognize vertical mobility between generations as a significant social phenomenon.

39   *Leviathan*, pt. I, ch. X.

40   *The Wealth of Nations*, bk. I, ch. V.

41   C. Wright Mills, *The Power Elite*, A Galaxy Book, 1959, p. 277; R. Dahrendorf, *Class and Class Conflict in an Industrial Society*, pp. 23, 141.

42   Marx, *GI*, pp. 68–9; G. Sorel, *Reflections on Violence*, Glencoe, 1950; G. Simmel, *Conflict*, Glencoe, 1955, pp. 17 ff. *Conflict* is a translation of chapter IV of *Soziologie*.

43   A. de Tocqueville, *The Recollections*, London, 1948, pp. 12–3; T. Carlyle, *Past and Present*, Everyman's Library, p. 203; F. Engels, *The Condition of the Working Class in England*, Oxford, 1958, p. 26. Cf. A. Briggs, 'The Language of "Class" in Early Nineteenth-Century England', in A. Briggs and J. Saville (Eds.), *Essays in Labour History*, Papermac, pp. 61–9.

44   Marx, *SAPP*, p. 325.

45   N. Bukharin, *Historical Materialism: A System of Sociology*, London, 1928, p. 278.

46   Marx, *PP*, pp. 165–6.

47   This little book, as distinguished as other historical contributions of Marx, is now recognized as the work of Engels, written on behalf of Marx. But the circumstances in which this collection of essays was produced strongly suggest that Engels could have used at least some materials prepared by Marx.

48   R. Aron, 'Social Structure and the Ruling Class', p. 53.

49   For a detailed study of Saint-Simon's and the Saint-Simonist ideas see E. Halévy, *The Era of Tyrannies: Essays on Socialism and War*, London, 1967, pp. 17 ff.; É. Durkheim, *Socialism and Saint-Simon*, London, 1959, chs. VII–VIII. Spencer used the terms 'militant' and 'industrial' to differentiate the two types of society. See *The Principles of Sociology*, vol. II, chs. XVII and XVIII.

50   *L'Industrie*, *Oeuvres de Saint-Simon et d'Enfantin*, XVIIIᵉ vol., p. 188.

51   *L'Organisateur*, *Oeuvres de Saint-Simon et d'Enfantin*, XXᵉ vol., pp. 120–1, 150; *Doctrine de Saint-Simon: Exposition*, Première année, p. 225. This is the first formulation of Engels's famous statement to the effect that once the State takes possession of the means of production 'in the name of the society', State interference in social relations becomes superfluous and the 'government of persons is replaced by the administration of things, and by the conduct of processes of production' (*Anti-Dühring*, Moscow, 1959, p. 387). Also some other phrases, later

made famous by Marx, for instance, 'the exploitation of man by man' or 'from each according to his ability, to each according to his needs', were either paraphrased or taken as they stood from the sayings of the *Doctrine de Saint-Simon*. See pp. 162, 244, 248.

52 Saint-Simon recognized the existence of social classes and in their conflict and struggle saw the key to the understanding of the historical process (he used the terms '*la lutte*' and '*le conflit*', and only his disciples —Bazard and Enfantin in particular—used '*l'antagonisme*' in preference to the other two). But Saint-Simon was a confused thinker and a careless writer and his list of classes, and even their names, changed from one publication to another. For Saint-Simon's concept of social class see F. E. Manuel, *The New World of Henri St Simon*, Notre Dame, 1963, ch. XXI.

53 For details and evidence see Z. A. Jordan, *The Evolution of Dialectical Materialism*, London, 1967, pp. 122-4.

54 Marx described one species of Asiatic societies, based on second-hand sources, in *C* I, pp. 357-8. In the light of a bulky manuscript of Marx, published under the title *Grundrisse der Kritik der politischen Ökonomie* in 1953, it is now believed that Marx did not consider the list of historical epochs as necessarily following each other in the indicated order. For details see E. Hobsbawm's Introduction to *PEF*.

55 *C* I, p. 371.

56 K. A. Wittfogel, *Oriental Despotism: A Comparative Study of Total Power*, Yale University Press, 1957.

57 *L'Organisateur, Oeuvres de Saint-Simon et d'Enfantin*, XXᵉ vol., pp. 89-100; *Mémoire sur la science de l'homme, Oeuvres de Saint-Simon et d'Enfantin*, XLᵉ vol., p. 191.

58 *C* I, pp. 363-4.

59 *C* I, p. 383.

60 *C* I, p. 386.

61 *C* I, pp. 339-50.

62 *CPE-P*, p. 329.

63 *C* I, p. 364.

64 H. B. Acton, *What Marx Really Said*, London, 1967, pp. 54 ff.

65 *L'Industrie, Oeuvres de Saint-Simon et d'Enfantin*, XIXᵉ vol., pp. 23, 39; *Mémoire sur la science de l'homme. Oeuvres de Saint-Simon et d'Enfantin*, XLᵉ vol., p. 18.

66 G. Gurvitch, *La vocation actuelle de la sociologie*, Paris, 1963, vol. II, p. 229.

67 *MCP*, p. 49.

68 See H. B. Acton, *The Illusion of the Epoch*, London, 1955, pp. 159 ff., for a critical analysis of these concepts which are not always mutually exclusive but overlap each other. R. Aron makes the same criticism in *Main Currents in Sociological Thought*, vol. I, pp. 158 ff.

69   V. Pareto, *The Mind and Society: A Treatise on General Sociology*, New York, Dover Publications, 1963, § 829, p. 492.

70   Engels's letter to J. Bloch of 21–22 September, 1890.

71   For a more detailed account of Engels's view see Jordan, *The Evolution of Dialectical Materialism*, pp. 325–29.

72   *GI*, p. 41.

73   F. Engels, 'Karl Marx', *SW* II, p. 149.

74   J. S. Mill, *The Principles of Political Economy*, Preliminary Remarks and bk. II, ch. I. However, Mill argued that the distribution of wealth is not subject to natural laws but follows rules which society can make and change as it wishes. This was an important insight of far-reaching consequences that remained unnoticed or was rejected as entirely unjustifiable. Marx criticized it sharply and repeatedly. See *CPE-I*, pp. 283 ff.; *GKPÖ*, p. 717.

75   Halévy, *The Era of Tyrannies*, pp. 55–6.

76   The drafts of a letter to V. I. Zasulich, *SA* III, pp. 195 ff.

77   For the criticism of this view from the standpoint of the utility school see L. Robbins, *An Essay on the Nature and Significance of Economic Science*, London, 1949, pp. 80 ff. In my opinion, this argument misses the relevant logical point in the adversary's proposition.

78   F. Engels, 'Speech at the Graveside of Karl Marx', *SW* II, p. 153.

79   In the Marxian terminology an article produced for immediate consumption has a use value only and is called 'product'. 'Commodity' is synonymous with 'article produced for exchange'. An article is a commodity if and only if it has an exchange value.

80   Marx, *WPP*, p. 379.

81   Marx, *CPE*, p. 64

82   Marx, *GKPÖ*, p. 498.

83   J. M. Keynes described *Capital* as 'an obsolete economic text-book' which was 'not only scientifically erroneous but without interest or application for the modern world' (*Essays in Persuasion*, London, 1933, p. 300). Yet it can be reasonably suggested that Keynes derived a profound inspiration not only from Malthus's concept of effective demand (an influence which is widely recognized) but also from Marx's theory of economic crises. Since for Marx the purpose of capitalist production was the accumulation and transformation of surplus value into capital, capitalist production involved a conflict between consumption and production. Although Marx believed that economic crises could not be explained simply by underconsumption, he regarded it as one of their necessary conditions and thought that it supported the belief concerning the self-destruction of capitalism. Speaking generally, Keynes's strategy consisted in the prevention of crises by the elimination of this particular necessary condition, that is, of underconsumption, thus preserving the capitalist system and making it function smoothly. For a more detailed

examination of the underconsumption aspect of crises in *Capital* see
R. Roll, *A History of Economic Thought*, London, 1961, pp. 285–7.
For an incisive analysis of Marx's theory of economic crises see M.
Dobb, *Political Economy and Capitalism: Some Essays in Economic
Tradition*, London, 1937, ch. IV.

84 For details see F. M. Gottheil, *Marx's Economic Predictions*,
Evanston, 1966, Part II, pp. 93 ff.

85 By 'organic composition of capital' Marx understands the proportion between its constant and variable part.

86 P. M. Sweezy (Ed.), *Karl Marx and the Close of His System* by
Eugen von Böhm-Bawerk and *Böhm-Bawerk's Criticism of Marx* by
Rudolf Hilferding, New York, 1966. The parts of *Capital* to which
reference is made above are *C* I, pp. 306–7 and C III, pp. 152 ff.
Professor J. Robinson's comment comes from *An Essay on Marxian
Economics*, London, 1957, p. 22.

87 V. Pareto, *The Mind and Society*, § 1859, 2021, 2313[10], pp. 1294,
1412, 1666.

88 P. Bigo, *Marxisme et humanisme*, Paris, 1961, pp. 34–7.

89 H. Spencer, *The Principles of Sociology*, vol. II, § 441, p. 245 of
the 1904 edition.

90 B. Mandeville, *The Fable of the Bees*, Ed. by F. B. Kaye, Oxford,
1924, vol. II, p. 142.

91 A. Ferguson, *An Essay on the History of Civil Society*, Pt. IV, sec.
I; A. Smith, *The Wealth of Nations*, bk. I, chs. I and II. According to
Adam Smith, the division of labour arises from the human propensity to
exchange one thing for another which in turn can be reduced to man's
'need of the co-operation and assistance of great multitudes'. The concept of division of labour (the work being 'divided and subdivided into a
great variety of different labours') was used earlier by Mandeville in
*The Fable of the Bees*. In *Capital* (I, p. 354, f. 2) Marx noted certain
striking similarities between Mandeville and Adam Smith which are
now commonly recognized. See *The Wealth of Nations*, bk. I, ch. I and
*The Fable of the Bees*, vol. I, pp. 169–70, 356–8. As Marx pointed out, the
concept of the division of labour should be traced back to Sir William
Petty's *Essay Concerning the Multiplication of Mankind* (1682). See
Sir William Petty, *Several Essays in Political Arithmetick*, London, 1699,
p. 35, and Marx, *CPE*, p. 57, f. 1.

92 *The Division of Labour in Society*, Glencoe, 1960, pp. 60–2. For
Comte see *Cours de philosophie positive*, vol. IV, pp. 314–15. Compared with Marx, Comte is vague and indulges in trivial generalities.
Perhaps it is worth noting that Spencer went further than any other
social scientist, since he suggested that the social division of labour
should be deduced from the 'physiological division of labour'. See *The
Principles of Sociology*, vol. I, § 217, p. 440 of the 1904 edition.

L*

93   *C* I, pp. 350–1. The failure to distinguish between the various meanings of the term sometimes leads to serious misinterpretations of Marx's views on division of labour. This happens, for instance, in R. Tucker, *Philosophy and Myth in Karl Marx*, Cambridge, 1961, pp. 184 ff. For Max Weber's view on the matter see *The Theory of Social and Economic Organization*, Edinburgh, 1947, pp. 201 ff. Apart from the social and technical division, Weber has also an economic division of labour but the latter appears to be concerned with the organization of production in autonomous units.

94   *C* I, pp. 350–1, 359; *GI*, pp. 42–3.

95   Marx regarded castes as some kind of guilds which, like guilds, are bound to disappear in an industrial society because they are destroyed by division of labour in the workshop. In his view, castes and guilds result from the tendency, characteristic among 'earlier societies', to make trades hereditary. They reflect the social division of labour, which, unlike division of labour in the workshop, is common to all economic formations, and arises from the 'action of the same natural law that regulates the differentiation of plants and animals into species and varieties, except that, when a certain degree of development has been reached, the heredity of castes and the exclusiveness of guilds are ordained as a law of society' (*C* I, pp. 339–40).

96   *GI*, p. 32.

97   *C* I, pp. 351–2; cf. *PP*, p. 138

98   *The Division of Labour in Society*, p. 175.

99   *C* I, pp. 357–8.

100   *C* I, p. 352; *PP*, p. 122; *GI*, pp. 32–3, 43, 64–5, 81. The emergence of the Marxian class of priests and ideologists has a curious parallel in Comte's 'speculative class' which came into being at the theological stage and became the vanguard of intellectual and moral progress. See *Cours de philosophie positive*, vol. IV, pp. 359–61.

101   *C* I, pp. 336–42, 359.

102   *C* I, pp. 352–3; *GI*, p. 42; *The Division of Labour in Society*, p. 257. In *The Rules of Sociological Method*, pp. 114–15, Durkheim suggests, as Marx did, that in defining physical density the means of communication should be taken into account. Marx acknowledged that this idea occurred to him when he read James Mill's *Elements of Political Economy* and Thomas Hodgskin's *Popular Political Economy*.

103   *GI*, pp. 32–3; p. 39; *C* I, pp. 355–6.

104   *WLC*, p. 93.

105   See below pp. 247–50; *WLC*, pp. 92–6. In his evaluation of the sociological and psychological effects of job specialization Marx followed closely not only Ferguson, whom he admired and praised, but also Adam Smith and Proudhon, whom he held in low esteem or sharply criticized. It was Adam Smith, for instance, who wrote the words sounding as if

they came from the pen of Marx, 'The man whose whole life is spent in performing a few simple operations . . . becomes as stupid and ignorant as it is possible for a human creature to become' (*The Wealth of Nations*, bk. V, ch. I, pt. III, art. II).

106   See G. Friedmann, *The Anatomy of Work*, London, 1961.

107   See, for instance, S. M. Lipset, *The Political Man*, London, 1960, pp. 24 ff.; T. B. Bottomore, *Elites and Society*, Penguin Books, p. 133.

108   *GI*, pp. 44–5, 69, 83–4, 315–16, 431–2, 482–3.

109   For reasons given above, Marx regarded division of labour in the factory as more damaging to the welfare and interests of the workers than anything that had gone before and as a process carried beyond what was necessary for productiveness and efficiency.

110   Marx's letter to the Chartist Congress held in Manchester in March 1854, *The People's Paper* of 18 March 1854.

111   See below p. 5 4; cf. *CPE*, pp. 33–4.

112   Marx, *GKPÖ*, p. 599.

113   Contrary to what is often said, Marx attached considerable importance to the struggle of British workers for shorter hours of work. See *C* I, ch. X, pp. 298–302 in particular. He regarded the organized action of the workers as essential, because the legislation of 1847 and 1850 (the Ten-Hour Act) was an outcome of the political struggle between the landed and industrial bourgeoisie; it was not prompted by their desire to improve the lot of the workers. See 'Parliamentary Debates—The Clergy and the Struggle for the Ten-Hour Day— Starvation', *New York Daily Tribune* of 15 March, 1853

114   *EPM*, p. 125.

115   *C* I, 487–8.

116   *GKPÖ*, p. 599.

117   *The Division of Labour in Society*, pp. 41–6, 406–9. The alternatives formulated by Durkheim can be found in Hegel, *Philosophy of Right*, pp. 128 ff. Marx must have known them too, for he seems to refer to this particular part of *Philosophy of Right* in *Capital* (I, p. 363, f 3). If I understand Hegel right, and one can never be sure about it, Hegel, like Durkheim, considered division of labour to be a solidary force.

118   R. Bendix and S. M. Lipset, 'The Field of Political Sociology', in L. A. Coser (Ed.), *Political Sociology: Selected Essays*, New York, 1967, p. 26.

119   M. Weber, 'Politics as a Vocation', in H. H. Gerth and C. Wright Mills (Eds.), *From Max Weber: Essays in Sociology*, London, 1957, p. 78.

120   Cf. É. Durkheim, *Socialism and Saint-Simon*, p. 147–9.

121   *C* I, p. 316; III, p. 797.

122   G. Mosca, *The Ruling Class*, New York, 1939, p. 439; K. R.

Popper, *The Open Society and Its Enemies*, Harper Torchbooks, 1962, vol. II, ch. XVII.

123  *MCP*, p. 51.

124  See M. Weber, *The Theory of Social and Economic Organization*, pp. 139–44; H. H. Gerth and C. Wright Mills (Eds.), *From Max Weber*, Part II. The whole of Weber's sociology of power (*Wirtschaft and Gesellschaft*, ch. 9) is now available in a new English translation. See *Economy and Society*, edited by G. Roth and C. Wittich, New York, 1968, vol. II, pp. 901-940.

125  J. Locke, *Of Civil Government*, bk. II, § 3; cf. bk. II, § 94; A. Smith, *The Wealth of Nations*, bk. V, ch. I, pt. II.

126  L. von Stein, *Der Begriff der Gesellschaft und die soziale Geschichte der Französischen Revolution bis zum Jahre 1830*. Nachdruck der Ausgabe von 1921. Hildesheim, B. 1, pp. 49–52.

127  H. Spencer, *The Principles of Sociology*, vol. II, ch. XIV; F. Engels, 'On Authority', *SW* I, pp. 575–8; *The Origin of the Family, Private Property and the State*, *SW* II, pp. 288 ff.; K. Marx, *The German Ideology*, pp. 45–6; J. Plamenatz, *Man and Society*, London, 1963, vol. II, p. 364. The doctrine of the disappearance of the State is really Engels's contribution and there is practically nothing in Marx's writings to attribute it to Marx.

128  For a detailed discussion of these points see T. B. Bottomore, *Classes in Modern Society*, pp. 22 ff.

129  L. Gumplowicz, *Grundriss der Soziologie*, Innsbruck, 1926, pp. 92–3. Cf. M. Weber, *The Theory of Social and Economic Organization*, p. 147. Gumplowicz may have been influenced by Spencer who argued that 'ownership is established by force' or, as he said elsewhere, by 'an external or internal aggression', but wished it to be understood historically rather than sociologically (*The Principles of Sociology*, vol. II, ch. XV). Marx had no doubts whatsoever that production presupposed some form of property relations and that the latter could not exist without the safeguards of a legal order, that is, ultimately, without the support of force. He maintained, however, that 'every form of production creates its own legal relations' and denied that a system of production is established by a legal order. The distinction between law and the system of production (property) is made for analytical purposes, for actually they 'constitute an organic union' (*CPE-I*, p. 273).

130  S. Ossowski, *Class Structure in the Social Consciousness*, p. 184.

131  R. Aron, 'Social Class, Political Class, Ruling Class' in R. Bendix and S. M. Lipset (Eds.), *Class, Status and Power*, Second Edition, London, 1967, p. 208.

132  G. Mosca, *The Ruling Class*, pp. 50 ff.; V. Pareto, *The Mind and Society*, § 2026–59, pp. 1421 ff. Neither Mosca nor Pareto concealed their hostility to Marxian political sociology, and Mosca's theory of

*lites* has a 'specifically anti-Marxist bent' (J. H. Meisel, *The Myth of the Ruling Class: Gaetano Mosca and the Elite*, Ann Arbor Paperbacks, 1962, p. 10).

33   See R. Aron's 'Social Class, Political Class, Ruling Class'. In an earlier publication, 'Social Structure and the Ruling Class' (pp. 87 ff.) Aron argues for a synthesis of the two theories, first suggested by Michels.

34   See T. B. Bottomore, *Elites and Society*, chs. VI and VII.

35   R. Michels, *Political Parties: A Sociological Study of the Oligarhical Tendencies of Modern Democracy*, Collier Books Edition, New York, 1962, p. 354.

36   *The Mind and Society*, § 2056, p. 1431.

37   Those who are familiar with the works of Max Weber, Bertrand Russell and, more recently, R. Dahrendorf, would be well aware of these ideas which, however, have to be mentioned.

38   The distinction between theoretical sociology and sociological theory comes from H. L. Zetterberg, *On Theory and Verification in Sociology*, 3rd Edition. The Bedminster Press, 1965, p. 22.

39   The anti-naturalistic trend, which claims precisely that knowledge of the social and physical world is basically different, was represented in Germany by such thinkers as Wilhelm Dilthey, Wilhelm Windelband, Heinrich Rickert and Max Weber; through their direct and indirect influence it has gained a considerable following in contemporary sociology.

40   The concept of theoretical orientation, as it is presented here, is taken from R. K. Merton, *Social Theory and Social Structure*, revised edition. Glencoe, 1957, pp. 87-9. A. Inkeles (*What Is Sociology? An Introduction to the Discipline and Profession*. Prentice–Hall, 1965, pp. 28–30) substitutes the term 'model' for Merton's 'orientation' and uses it in so many senses, which are sometimes incompatible, that his concept of model is practically useless.

41   M. Weber, *The Methodology of the Social Sciences*, translated and edited by E. A. Shils and H. A. Finch. Glencoe, 1949, p. 26. The whole paragraph, in which this statement occurs, deserves a close study, since it reveals the deep impact of the conflict-orientation on one of the most outstanding sociological minds in our century.

42   Contrary to what is frequently claimed, the Marxian concept of progress has little in common with the optimistic faith in progress of the French Enlightenment or of the Victorian era, including the Spencerian idea of cosmic evolution, a process which was held to be both necessary and beneficial. Marx was fully aware of the enormous social cost of economic progress, but he considered that this was a necessary condition of the all-round qualitative improvement in the life of man which could be termed 'progress' in general. See, e.g., *FRBRI*.

143   As in the case of alienation, Marx neither introduced the concep
nor coined the term 'ideology'. Much of what has been said about th
Marxian concept of ideology is based on the pronouncements of Marx
interpreters and followers who were anxious to ascribe to him the
own views. For a competent and comprehensive analysis of the concep
see G. Lichtheim, 'The Concept of Ideology', *History and Theor*
vol. IV, 1965, pp. 164–95.

144   Apart from the extensive use of statistical evidence in *Capital*, se
Marx's article 'Capital Punishment—Mr Cobden's Pamphlets-
Regulations of the Bank of England' in *NYDT* of 18 February, 185
The questionnaire was published in French under the title 'Enquê
Ouvrière' in *La Revue Socialiste* of 20 April, 1880. An English tran
lation of it is available in T. B. Bottomore and M. Rubel (Eds.), *Ka
Marx: Selected Writings in Sociology and Social Philosophy*, 2nd Editio
London, 1961, pp. 210–18.

# Further Reading

Acton, H. B. *The Illusion of the Epoch: Marxism-Leninism as a Philosophical Creed.* London, 1955.
*What Marx Really Said.* London, 1967.

Aron, R. *Main Currents in Sociological Thought*, vol. I. London, 1965.

Berlin, Sir Isaiah *Karl Marx.* Home University Library, 3rd Edition, 1962.

Bottomore, T. B. 'Marx's Sociology and Social Philosophy' in T. B. Bottomore and M. Rubel (Eds.), *Karl Marx: Selected Writings in Sociology and Social Philosophy*, 2nd edition. London, 1961.
'The Influence of Marx's Sociological Thought' in T. B. Bottomore and M. Rubel (Eds.), *Karl Marx: Selected Writings in Sociology and Social Philosophy*, 2nd Edition. London, 1961.

Dahrendorf, R. *Class and Class Conflict in Industrial Society.* London, 1959, Part One.

Gottheil, F. M. *Marx's Economic Predictions.* Evanston, 1966.

Hook, S. *From Hegel to Marx: Studies in the Development of Karl Marx.* Ann Arbor Paperback, 1962.

Jordan, Z. A. *The Evolution of Dialectical Materialism: A Philosophical and Sociological Analysis.* London, 1967, ch. II.

Korsch, K. *Karl Marx.* New York, 1963 (reprint).

Labriola, A. *Essays on the Materialistic Conception of History.* New York, 1966 (reprint).

Lange, O. *Political Economy*, vol. I. Pergamon Press, 1963.

Laski, H. J. *Communist Manifesto: Socialist Landmark. A New Appreciation Written for the Labour Party.* London, 1948 or any later impression.

Michels, R. *First Lectures in Political Sociology*, Harper Torchbooks. New York, 1965.

Ossowski, S. *Class Structure in the Social Consciousness*. London, 1963, ch. V.

Plamenatz, J. *German Marxism and Russian Communism*. London, 1955, Part I.
*Man and Society*, vol. II. London, 1963, chs. V–VI.

Popper, Sir Karl. *The Open Society and Its Enemies*, 4th Edition. London, 1962, chs. XIII-XXII.

Robinson, J. *An Essay on Marxian Economics*, 2nd Edition. London, 1962.

Seligman, E. R. A. *The Economic Interpretation of History*, 2nd Edition. Columbia Paperback Edition, 1961.

Venable, V. *Human Nature: The Marxian View*, Meridian Books. New York, 1966.

# Index